GERMAN
Phrase book

Carol Stanley and Philippa Goodrich

BBC Books

BBC Books publishes courses on the following languages:

ARABIC	ITALIAN
CHINESE	JAPANESE
FRENCH	PORTUGUESE
GERMAN	RUSSIAN
GREEK	SPANISH
HINDI URDU	TURKISH

For further information write to:
BBC Books
Language Enquiry Service
Room A3116
Woodlands
80 Wood Lane
London W12 0TT

Consultant: Dorothee Hübsch-Wiggington

Cover designed by Peter Bridgewater and Annie Moss

Published by BBC Books
A Division of BBC Worldwide Ltd
Woodlands, 80 Wood Lane, London W12 0TT

ISBN 0 563 39990 2

First published 1991
This edition published 1995
© Carol Stanley and Philippa Goodrich 1991
Reprinted 1991, 1992, 1993 (twice), 1997

Set in Times Roman by Ace Filmsetting Ltd, Frome
Text printed by Redwood Books, Trowbridge, Wiltshire
Cover printed by Belmont Press

CONTENTS

HOW TO USE THIS BOOK

Communicating in a foreign language doesn't have to be difficult – you can convey a lot with just a few words (plus a few gestures and a bit of mime). Just remember: keep it simple. Don't try to come out with long, grammatically perfect sentences when one or two words will get your meaning across.

Inside the front and back cover of this book is a list of all-purpose phrases. Some will help you to make contact – greetings, 'please' and 'thank you', 'yes' and 'no'. Some are to get people to help you understand what they're saying to you. And some are questions like 'do you have . . . ?' and 'where is . . . ?', to which you can add words from the Dictionary at the back of the book.

The book is divided into sections for different situations, such as Road travel, Shopping, Health and so on. In each section you'll find
● Words and phrases that you'll see on signs or in print
● Useful tips and information
● Phrases you are likely to want to say
● Things that people may say to you

Many of the phrases can be adapted by simply using another word from the Dictionary. For instance, take the question **Ist der Flughafen weit?** (Is the airport far away?) – if you want to know if the *station* is far away, just substitute **der Bahnhof** (the station) for **der Flughafen** to give **Ist der Bahnhof weit?** You can use the blank bits of pages to make a note of words that are particularly useful to you.

All the phrases have a simple pronunciation guide underneath based on English sounds – this is explained in Pronunciation (page 7).

If you want some guidance on how the German language works, see Basic grammar (page 178).

There's a handy reference section (starts page 189) which contains lists of days and months, countries and nationalities, general signs and notices that you'll see, conversion tables, national holidays and useful addresses. Numbers appear on pages 211–12.

The 5000-word Dictionary (page 213) comes in two sections – German–English and English–German.

At the end of the book (page 285) is an Emergencies section (which we hope you *won't* have to use).

Wherever possible, work out in advance what you want to say – if you're going shopping, for instance, write out a shopping list in German. If you're buying travel tickets, work out how to say where you want to go, how many tickets you want, single or return, etc.

Above all – don't be shy! It'll be appreciated if you try to say a few words, even if it's only 'good morning' and 'goodbye' – and in fact those are the very sorts of phrases that are worth learning as you'll hear them and need to use them all the time.

The authors would welcome any suggestions or comments about this book, but in the meantime: Have a good trip! – **Gute Reise!**

PRONUNCIATION

You don't need perfect pronunciation to be able to communicate – it's enough to get the sounds approximately right and stress words in the correct place. If you want to hear real German voices and to practise trying to sound like them, then listen to the cassette.

German pronunciation is very regular – you can tell how a word is pronounced from the way it's written, once you know what each letter (or group of letters) represents. Long words in German are often a combination of several shorter words, so it may help with pronunciation to split the long word into its individual parts. A pronunciation guide is given with the phrases in this book – the system is based on English sounds, as described below.

Many German consonants are pronounced in a similar way to English.

The final 'e' on a word is always pronounced.

For the German alphabet, see page 10.

Stress

In this book, a stressed syllable is shown in the pronunciation guide by bold type:
problaym, *kilomayter*.

Vowels

	Approx. English equivalent	Shown in book as	Example	
a	a in 'cat'	a	danke	*danke*
or	a in 'car'	aa	abend	*aabent*
ai and ay	i in 'pile'	iy	Kaiser	*kiyzer*
au	ow in 'cow'	ow	Raucher	*rowker*
ä	e in 'let'	e	Geschäft	*gesheft*
or	ay in 'pay'	ay	spät	*shpayt*
äu	oy in 'boy'	oy	Kohlensäure	*kohlenzoyre*
e	e in 'let'	e	essen	*essen*
or	ay in 'pay'	ay	gehen	*gayen*
ei and ey	i in 'pile'	iy	Bein	*biyn*
eu	oy in 'boy'	oy	heute	*hoyte*
i	i in 'hit'	i	bitte	*bitte*
or	ee in 'meet'	ee	ihn	*een*
ie	ee in 'meet'	ee	dieser	*deezer*
o	o in 'lot'	o	Woche	*voke*
or	o in 'bone'	oh	Monat	*mohnaat*
ö	er in 'fern'	er	können	*kernnen*
u	oo in 'room'	oo	gut	*goot*
ü	ew in 'dew'	ew	für	*fewr*
y	ew in 'dew'	ew	typisch	*tewpish*

Consonants

	Approx. English equivalent	Shown in book as	Example	
b	b in 'but'	b	**Bad**	*baat*
c	c in 'can'	k	**Café**	*kafay*
ch	k in 'kit'	k	**brauche**	*browke*
or	sh in 'shut'	sh	**ich**	*ish*
or	c in 'can'	k	**Charakter**	*karakter*
d	d in 'dog'	d	**Dame**	*daame*
f	f in 'feet'	f	**fünf**	*fewnf*
g	g in 'got'	g	**grün**	*grewn*
h	h in 'hard'	h	**Hand**	*hant*
j	y in 'you'	y	**ja**	*yaa*
l	l in 'look'	l	**lang**	*lang*
m	m in 'mat'	m	**Mutter**	*mootter*
n	n in 'not'	n	**Name**	*naame*
p	p in 'pack'	p	**Person**	*perzohn*
qu	k + v	kv	**Quittung**	*kvittoong*
r	rolled at the back of the mouth	r	**Rücken**	*rewken*
s	s in 'set'	s	**es**	*es*
or	z in 'zoo'	z	**Sie**	*zee*
or	sh in 'shut'	sh	**Stunde**	*shtoonde*
sch	sh in 'shut'	sh	**schnell**	*shnell*
ß	ss in 'press'	ss	**heiß**	*hiyss*
t	t in 'tin'	t	**Tag**	*taag*
tsch	ch in 'church'	ch	**Deutsch**	*doych*
v	f in 'feet'	f	**vier**	*feer*
or sometimes	v in 'voice'	v	**Ventil**	*ventil*
w	v in 'voice'	v	**wo**	*voh*
x	x in 'taxi'	ks	**taxi**	*taksee*
z	ts in 'hits'	ts	**zeigen**	*tsiygen*

THE GERMAN ALPHABET

The **umlaut** means that there are three extra vowels in German: 'a' umlaut, 'o' umlaut' and 'u' umlaut.

The **ß** symbol represents a double 's' and is called 's,z' or 'scharfes s'.

Spelling

How is it spelt?
Wie schreibt man das?
vee shriybt man das

Letter	Pronounced	Letter	Pronounced
A	*aa*	O	*oh*
Ä	*ay*	Ö	*er*
B	*bay*	P	*pay*
C	*tsay*	Q	*koo*
D	*day*	R	*ayr*
E	*ay*	S	*es*
F	*ef*	ß	*es tset/sharfes es*
G	*gay*	T	*tay*
H	*haa*	U	*oo*
I	*ee*	Ü	*ew*
J	*yot*	V	*fow*
K	*kaa*	W	*vay*
L	*el*	X	*iks*
M	*em*	Y	*ewpsilon*
N	*en*	Z	*tset*

GENERAL CONVERSATION

● The Germans shake hands on meeting people and greeting friends much more than the British do.

● **Guten Tag** is a general greeting that can be used throughout the day. In Southern Germany and Austria you are much more likely to be greeted with **Grüß Gott!** You'll also hear **Servus!** in the south and in Austria which means hello and goodbye. You may also hear **Pfüeti!** or **Pfüetsi!** in Bavaria and Austria which literally means **Gott behüte dich/Sie** (God look after you) and is another way of saying goodbye. **Guten Morgen** and **Guten Abend** are both used to greet people at the appropriate time of the day and **Gute Nacht** is the equivalent of saying 'good night'.

● There are two ways of saying you – the formal and the informal way. **Sie** (always written with a capital letter) is formal and is used between people who are meeting for the first time or don't know each other well or between younger and older people. **Du** is informal and used between members of a family, friends, young people and to children. The form of the verb changes depending on whether you are addressing someone as **Sie** or **du**; where both forms are given in the phrases, the **Sie** form is given first. If in doubt about which form to use, stick to **Sie**.

Greetings

Hello	Good morning
Hallo	**Guten Morgen**
hallo	*gooten morgen*
Hello/goodbye	Good day/afternoon
Servus! *(S. Germany & Austria)*	**Guten Tag/Grüß Gott!**
servoos	*(S. Germany & Austria)*
	gooten taag/grewss gott

Good night	See you later
Gute Nacht	**Bis später**
goote naakt	*bis shpayter*

Good evening	(Hello), how are things?
Guten Abend	**Hallo, wie geht's?**
gooten aabent	*hallo vee gayts*

Goodbye	Fine, thanks
Auf Wiedersehen	**Gut, danke**
owf veederzayen	*goot danke*

'Bye	And you?
Tschüß	**Und Ihnen?** *(formal)*
chewss	*oont eenen*
	Und dir? *(informal)*
	oont deer

12 Introductions

My name is . . .	This my husband/son
Ich heiße . . .	**Das ist mein Mann/Sohn**
ish hiysse . . .	*das ist miyn mann/zohn*

This is . . .	This is my wife/daughter
Das ist . . .	**Das ist meine Frau/Tochter**
das ist . . .	*das ist miyne frow/toshter*

This is Mr Brown	Pleased to meet you
Das ist Herr Brown	**Sehr angenehm**
das ist herr brown	*zayr angenaym*

This is Mrs Clark	
Das ist Frau Clark	
das ist frow klark	

Talking about yourself and your family

(see Countries and nationalities, *page197)*

I am English
Ich bin Engländer *(male)*
ish bin englender
Ich bin Engländerin *(female)*
ish bin englenderin

I come from Scotland
Ich komme aus Schottland
ish komme ows shottlant

I come from Ireland
Ich komme aus Irland
ish komme ows eerlant

I come from Wales
Ich komme aus Wales
ish komme ows vales

We live in Newcastle
Wir wohnen in Newcastle
veer vohnen in newkasel

I am a student
Ich bin Student *(male)*
ish bin shtoodent
Ich bin Studentin *(female)*
ish bin shtoodentin

I am a nurse
Ich bin Krankenschwester
ish bin krankenshvester

I work in/for . . .
Ich arbeite bei . . .
ish arbiyte biy . . .

I work in a bank
Ich arbeite bei einer Bank
ish arbiyte biy iyner bank

I work for a computer firm
**Ich arbeite bei einer
 Computerfirma**
*ish arbiyte biy iyner
 kompewterfirma*

I work in an office/factory
**Ich arbeite in einem Büro/in
 einer Fabrik**
*ish arbiyte in iynem bewroh/in
 iyner fabreek*

I am unemployed
Ich bin arbeitslos
ish bin arbiytslohs

I am (not) married
Ich bin (nicht) verheiratet
ish bin (nisht) ferhiyraatet

I am separated
Ich lebe getrennt
ish laybe getrennt

I am divorced
Ich bin geschieden
ish bin gesheeden

I am a widower/widow
**Ich bin ein Witwer/eine
 Witwe**
ish bin iyn vitver/iyne vitve

I have a son/a daughter
Ich habe einen Sohn/eine Tochter
ish haabe iynen zohn/iyne toshter

I have three children
Ich habe drei Kinder
ish haabe driy kinder

I don't have any children
Ich habe keine Kinder
ish haabe kiyne kinder

I have one brother
Ich habe einen Bruder
ish haabe iynen brooder

I have three sisters
Ich habe drei Schwestern
ish haabe driy shvestern

I'm on holiday here
Ich bin im Urlaub hier
ish bin im oorlowp heer

I'm here on business
Ich bin auf Geschäftsreise hier
ish bin owf gesheftsriyze heer

I'm here with my husband/wife
Ich bin mit meinem Mann/meiner Frau hier
ish bin mit miynem man/miyner frow heer

I'm here with my family
Ich bin mit meiner Familie hier
ish bin mit miyner fameelye heer

I only speak a little German
Ich kann nur ein bißchen Deutsch sprechen
ish kan noor iyn bissyen doych shpreken

My husband/wife is . . .
Mein Mann/meine Frau ist . . .
miyn man/miyne frow ist . . .

My husband is a bus-driver
Mein Mann ist Busfahrer
miyn man ist boosfaarer

My wife is an accountant
Meine Frau ist Buchhalterin
miyne frow ist bookhalterin

My husband/wife works in . . .
Mein Mann/meine Frau arbeitet in . . .
miyn man/miyne frow arbiytet in . . .

My son is five years old
Mein Sohn ist fünf
miyn zohn ist fewnf

My daughter is eight years old
Meine Tochter ist acht
miyne toshter ist aakt

You may hear

Woher kommen Sie?
voher kommen zee
Where do you come from?

Wie heißen Sie?
vee hiyssen zee
What are you called?

Was sind Sie von Beruf?
vas zint zee fon beroof
What do you do?

Sind Sie verheiratet?
zint zee ferhiyraatet
Are you married?

Haben Sie Kinder?
haaben zee kinder
Do you have children?

Haben Sie Geschwister?
haaben zee geshvister
Do you have brothers and sisters?

Wie alt sind sie?
vee alt zint zee
How old are they?

Wie alt sind Sie/bist du?
vee alt zint zee/bist doo
How old are you?

Ist das Ihr Mann/Freund?
ist das eer man/froynd
Is this your husband/boyfriend?

Ist das Ihre Frau/Freundin?
ist das eere frow/froyndin
Is this your wife/girlfriend?

Er/Sie sieht sehr nett aus
er/zee zeet zayr nett ows
He/She looks very nice

Wohin fahren Sie?
vohin faaren zee
Where are you going?

Wo wohnen Sie?
voh vohnen zee
Where are you staying?

Wo wohnen Sie in Großbritannien?
voh vohnen zee in grohssbritannyen
Where do you live in Great Britain?

Talking about Germany, Austria or Switzerland and your own country

Germany is very beautiful
Deutschland ist sehr schön
doychlant ist zayr shern

It's the first time I have been to Germany
Ich bin zum ersten Mal in Deutschland
ish bin tsoom ersten mal in doychlant

I come to Austria often
Ich komme oft nach Österreich
ish komme oft naak ersterriysh

Do you live here?
Wohnen Sie hier?
vohnen zee heer

Have you ever been to England/Scotland/Ireland/Wales?
Waren Sie schon in England/Schottland/Irland/Wales?
varen zee shon in englant/shottlant/eerlant/vales

Did you like it?
Hat es Ihnen/dir gefallen?
hat es eenen/deer gefallen

You may hear

Gefällt Ihnen Deutschland/Österreich/die Schweiz?
gefellt eenen doychlant/ersterriysh/dee shviyts
Do you like Germany/Austria/Switzerland?

Waren Sie schon in Deutschland?
varen zee shon in doychlant
Have you been to Germany before?

Wie lange bleiben Sie hier?
vee lange bliyben zee heer
How long are you here for?

Was halten Sie von . . . ?
vas halten zee fon . . .
What do you think of . . . ?

Was halten Sie von Österreich?
vas halten zee fon ersterriysh
What do you think of Austria?

Ihr Deutsch ist sehr gut
eer doych ist zayr goot
Your German is very good

Likes and dislikes: food and people

I like . . .
Ich mag . . .
ish maag . . .

I like it . . .
Ich mag es . . .
ish maag es . . .

I like strawberries
Ich mag Erdbeeren
ish maag erdbeeren

I like her
Ich mag sie
ish maag zee

I don't like . . .
Ich mag . . . nicht
ish maag . . . nisht

I don't like it
Ich mag es nicht
ish maag es nisht

I don't like beer
Ich mag Bier nicht
ish maag beer nisht

Do you like it?
Mögen Sie's?/Magst du's?
mergen zeez/maagst dooz

Do you like ice cream?
Mögen Sie Eis?/Magst du Eis?
mergen zee iys/maagst doo iys

Likes and dislikes: activities

I like playing football
Ich spiele gern Fußball
ish shpeele gern foossball

I like swimming
Ich schwimme gern
ish shvimme gern

I don't like sailing
Ich segele nicht gern
ish zaygele nisht gern

Do you like travelling?
Reisen Sie gern?
riyzen zee gern

Invitations and replies

Would you like a drink?
Möchten Sie etwas trinken?
mershten zee etvas trinken

No, thank you
Nein danke
niyn danke

Would you like something to eat?
Möchten Sie etwas essen?
mershten zee etvas essen

That's very kind of you
das ist nett von Ihnen
das ist nett fon eenen

Yes, please
Ja bitte
yaa bitte

Please go away
Bitte gehen Sie weg!
bitte gayen zee vek

You may hear

Möchten Sie . . .
mershten zee . . .
Would you like . . .

Möchten Sie etwas trinken?
mershten zee etvas trinken
Would you like something to drink?

Möchten Sie etwas essen?
mershten zee etvas essen
Would you like something to eat?

Möchten Sie mitkommen?
mershten zee mitkommen
Would you like to come with us?

Was machen Sie heute abend?
vas maaken zee hoyte aabent
What are you doing tonight?

Möchten Sie tanzen gehen?
mershten zee tantsen gayen
Would you like to go dancing?

Möchten Sie essen gehen?
mershten zee essen gayen
Would you like to go for a meal?

Für wieviel Uhr sollen wir uns verabreden?
fewr veefeel oor zollen veer oons feraprayden
What time shall we meet?

Wo sollen wir uns verabreden?
voh zollen veer oons feraprayden
Where shall we meet?

Good wishes and exclamations

Congratulations!
Herzlichen Glückwunsch!
hertslishen glewkvoonsh

Happy Birthday!
**Herzlichen Glückwunsch
zum Geburtstag!**
*hertslishen glewkvoonsh tsoom
geboortstaag*

Happy Christmas!
Frohe Weihnachten!
frohe viynaakten

Happy New Year!
Guten Rutsch ins Neue Jahr!
gooten rootsh ins noye yaar

Good luck!
Viel Glück!
feel glewk

All the best!
Alles Gute!
alles goote

What a pity!
Schade!
shaade

Have a good evening!
Schön' Abend!
shern aabent

Have a good journey!
Gute Reise!
goote riyze

Safe journey home!
**Kommen Sie gut nach
Hause!**
kommen zee goot naak howze

Enjoy your meal!
Guten Appetit!
gooten appeteet

Thank you, same to you
Danke, gleichfalls
danke gliyshfalls

Cheers!
Prost!/Zum Wohl!
prost/tsoom vohl

Talking about the weather

The weather's very good/
 bad
**Das Wetter ist sehr schön/
 schlecht**
*das vetter ist zayr shern/
 shlesht*

It's very hot/cold
Est ist sehr warm/kalt
es ist zayr varm/kalt

It's good/bad
Es ist gut/schlecht
es ist goot/shlesht

It's a wonderful day
Es ist ein herrlicher Tag
es ist iyn herrlisher taag

I don't like the heat
Ich mag die Hitze nicht
ish maag dee hittse nisht

It's very windy
Es ist sehr windig
es ist zayr vindig

Is it going to rain?
Wird es regnen?
vird es raygnen

ARRIVING IN THE COUNTRY

● Whether you arrive by air, road or sea, the formalities (passport control and Customs) are quite straightforward; the only document you need is a valid passport.

● You will probably not need to say anything in German unless you are asked the purpose of your visit, or have something to declare at Customs. If you need to say what you have to declare (rather than just showing it), look up the words you need in the dictionary. EC duty-free allowances apply in West Germany – you can get a leaflet with the details at your point of departure.

● Duty-free allowances for Austria and Switzerland follow the EC pattern; details from the Swiss and Austrian National Tourist Offices.

You may see

Anmeldefreie Waren	Nothing to declare
Anmeldepflichtige Waren	Goods to declare
EG	EC
Grenze	Border
Grenzpolizei	Border police
Paßkontrolle	Passport control
Willkommen	Welcome
Zoll	Customs

You may want to say

I am here on holiday
Ich bin auf Urlaub hier
ish bin owf oorlowp heer

I am here on business
**Ich bin auf einer
   Geschäftsreise hier**
*ish bin owf iyner gesheftsriyze
   heer*

It's a joint passport
Es ist ein Familienpaß
es ist iyn fameelyenpass

I have something to declare
Ich habe etwas zu verzollen
ish haabe etvas tsoo fertsollen

I have this
Ich habe das
ish haabe das

I have two bottles of whisky
Ich habe zwei Flaschen Whisky
ish haabe tsviy flashen viskee

I have two cartons of
   cigarettes
**Ich habe zwei Stangen
   Zigaretten**
*ish haabe tsviy shtangen
   tsigarretten*

I have a receipt for this
Ich habe eine Quittung dafür
ish haabe iyne kvittoong daafewr

You may hear

Ihren Paß, bitte
eeren pass bitte
Your passport, please

Ihre Papiere, bitte
eere papeere bitte
Your documents, please

Was is der Zweck Ihres Besuchs?
vas ist der tsvek eeres bezooks
What is the purpose of your visit?

Sind Sie im Urlaub oder auf Geschäftsreise hier?
zint zee im oorlowp ohder owf gesheftsriyze heer
Are you here on holiday or business?

Wie lange bleiben Sie hier?
vee lange bliyben zee heer
How long are you going to stay here?

Wo fahren Sie hin?
voh faaren zee hin
Where are you going?

Bitte öffnen Sie diese Tasche/diesen Koffer
bitte erffnen zee deeze tashe/ deezen koffer
Please open this bag/ suitcase

Bitte öffnen Sie den Kofferraum
bitte erffnen zee dayn kofferrowm
Please open the boot

Wir müssen das Auto durchsuchen
veer mewssen das owto doorshzooken
We have to search the car

Haben Sie noch andere Gepäckstücke?
haaben zee nok andere gepekshtewke
Do you have any other luggage?

Sie müssen Zoll darauf zahlen
zee mewssen tsoll darowf tsaalen
There is duty to pay on this

Kommen Sie bitte mit mir/ mit uns
kommen zee bitte mit meer/mit oons
Come along with me/with us, please

DIRECTIONS

● Some general maps are available from the German National Tourist Office (address, page 208). A wide range of road maps and some more specialised maps, e.g. for walkers, are obtainable from bookshops and specialist mapsellers. Local tourist offices can provide town plans and regional maps.

● When you need to ask the way somewhere, the easiest thing is just to name the place you're looking for and add 'please', e.g. **Kurfürstendamm, bitte?** Or you can start with 'where is . . . ?' **Wo ist . . . ?**

● If you're looking for a particular address, have it written down. In Germany, addresses are written with the street name first and the number afterwards, e.g. **Hamburgerstraße 23**. The name of the town and postcode may be written before the street name.

● When you're being given directions, listen out for the important bits (such as whether to turn left or right), and try to repeat each bit to make sure you've understood it correctly. If you can't understand something, ask the person to say it again more slowly, prompting with **Wie bitte?** ('pardon?') if necessary.

You may see

Allee	Avenue
Bahnhof	Station
Burg	Castle, fortress
Bushaltestelle	Bus stop
Dom	Cathedral
Fußgänger	Pedestrians
Fußgängerüberweg	Pedestrian crossing
Fußgängerzone	Pedestrian precinct
Gasse	Alley
Hauptbahnhof	Main station
Hof	Court
Kirche	Church
Kunsthalle	Art gallery
Marktplatz	Market-place
Museum	Museum
Palast	Palace
Platz	Square
Privat	Private
Radweg	Cycle path
S-Bahn	Express underground or overground
Schloß	Castle, palace
Straße	Street
Straßenbahnhaltestelle	Tram stop
U-Bahn	Underground
Unbefügtes Betreten verboten	Trespassers will be prosecuted
Weg	Way
Zebrastreifen	Zebra crossing

You may want to say

Excuse me (please)
Entschuldigen Sie, bitte
entshooldigen zee bitte

Pardon?
Wie bitte?
vee bitte

Can you repeat that, please?
Noch einmal, bitte
nok iynmal bitte

More slowly, please
Langsamer, bitte
langzaamer bitte

Where are we?
Wo sind wir?
voh zint veer

Where does this road/street
lead to?
Wo führt diese Straße hin?
voh fewrt deeze shtraasse hin

Is this the right way to
Worpsweder?
**Ist das die Straße nach
Worpsweder?**
*ist das dee shtraasse naak
vorpsvayder*

Is this the footpath for
Seefeld?
**Ist das der Fußweg nach
Seefeld?**
*ist das der foossvayg naak
zayfelt*

Can you show me on the
map?
**Können Sir mir das auf der
Karte zeigen?**
*kernnen zee meer das owf der
karte tsiygen*

The station, please?
Der Bahnhof, bitte?
der baanhof bitte

The (town) centre, please?
Das Stadtzentrum, bitte?
das stattsentroom bitte

The road to Berchtesgaden?
Die Straße nach Berchtesgaden?
dee shtraasse naak bershtesgaaden

How do I/we get to. . . ?
Wie kommt man nach/zu . . . ?
vee kommt man naak/tsoo

How do I/we get to Freiburg?
Wie kommt man nach Freiburg?
vee kommt man naak friyboorg

How do I/we get to the airport?
Wie kommt man zum Flughafen?
vee kommt man tsoom flooghaafen

How do I/we get to the beach?
Wie kommt man zum Strand?
vee kommt man tsoom shtrant

Where is . . . ?
Wo ist . . . ?
voh ist

Where is this? *(if you've got an address written down)*
Wo ist das?
voh ist das

Where is the tourist office?
Wo ist das Fremdenverkehrsbüro?
voh ist das fremdenferkayrzbewroh

Where is the Post Office?
Wo ist die Post?
voh ist dee post

Where is this office/room?
Wo ist dieses Büro/Zimmer?
voh ist deezes bewroh/tsimmer

Where are the toilets?
Wo sind die Toiletten?
voh zint dee toyletten

Is it far?
Ist es weit?
ist es viyt

Is the airport far away?
Ist der Flughafen weit?
ist der flooghaafen viyt

How many kilometres?
Wie viele Kilometer?
vee feele kilomayter

How long does it take (on foot/by car)?
Wie lange dauert es (zu Fuß/mit dem Auto)?
vee lange dowert es tsoo fooss/mit daym owto

Is there a bus/train?
Gibt es einen Bus/einen Zug?
gipt es iynen boos/iynen tsoog

Can I/we get there on foot?
Kann man zu Fuß dorthinkommen?
kan man tsoo fooss dorthinkommen

Can I/we get there by car?
Kann man mit dem Auto dorthinkommen?
kan man mit daym owto dorthinkommen

Is there . . . ?
Gibt es . . . ?
gipt es

Is there a bank around here?
Gibt es eine Bank hier in der Nähe?
gipt es iyne bank heer in der naye

Is there a supermarket in the village?
Gibt es einen Supermarkt im Dorf?
gipt es iynen zoopermarkt im dorf

Where is the nearest service station?
Wo ist die nächste Tankstelle?
voh ist dee nekste tankshtelle

Where is the nearest bar?
Wo ist die nächste Bar?
voh ist dee nekste bar

You may hear

Sie haben sich geirrt
zee haaben zish ge-eert
You've made a mistake

Wir sind hier
veer zint heer
We are here

Hier
heer
Here

Da, dort
daa, dort
There

Hier entlang
heer entlang
This way, Along here

Da entlang
daa entlang
That way, Along there

Rechts
reshts
(To the) right

Links
links
(To the) left

(Immer) geradeaus
immer geraadeows
Straight on

Die erste (Straße)
dee erste shtraasse
The first (street/turning)

Die zweite (Straße)
dee tsviyte shtraasse
The second (street/turning)

Die dritte (Straße)
dee dritte shtraasse
The third (street/turning)

Am Ende der Straße
am ende der shtraasse
At the end/bottom of the street

Auf der anderen Seite des Platzes
owf der anderen ziyte des plattses
On the other side of the square

An der Ecke
an der eke
On the corner

Unten
oonten
Down, Downstairs

Oben
ohben
Up, Upstairs

Dort unten
dort oonten
Down there

Da oben
daa ohben
Up there

Da hinten
daa hinten
Behind there

Unter
oonter
Under

Über
ewber
Over

Vor der Ampel
for der ampel
Before the traffic lights

Nach dem Dom
naak daym dohm
After/Past the cathedral

Gegenüber
gegenewber
Opposite

Vor
for
In front of

Hinter
hinter
Behind

In der Nähe von . . .
in der naye fon
Near, Close to . . .

Es ist auf dem Platz
es ist owf daym platts
It's in the square

An der Siemensallee
an der zeemenzallay
At (When you get to)
   Siemensallee

Richtung Stadtzentrum
rishtoong shtattsentroom
Towards the town centre

Bis zur Kreuzung
bis tsoor kroytsoong
As far as the crossroads

Es ist im dritten Stock
es ist im dritten shtock
It's on the third floor

Die erste/zweite Tür
dee erste/tsviyte tewr
The first/second door

Es ist (nicht) weit
es ist (nisht) viyt
It's (not) far away

Sehr weit, ziemlich weit
zayr viyt, tseemlish viyt
Very far, Quite far

Es ist in der Nähe
es ist in der naye
It's close by

Sehr nah, ziemlich nah
zayr naa, tseemlish naa
Very close, Quite close

Es ist fünf Minuten von hier
es ist fewnf minooten fon heer
It's five minutes away

Es ist zwanzig Kilometer von hier
es ist tsvantsig kilomayter fon heer
It's twenty kilometres away

Sie müssen den Bus/den Zug nehmen
zee mewssen dayn boos/dayn tsoog naymen
You have to catch the bus/train

You may also hear phrases like these:

Gehen Sie . . .
gayen zee
Go . . .

Fahren Sie . . .
faaren zee
Drive . . .

Fahren Sie dort entlang
faaren zee dort entlang
Drive along there

Fahren Sie die Straße entlang
faaren zee dee shtraasse entlang
Drive along the street

Fahren Sie dort hinüber
faaren zee dort hinewber
Drive over there

Fahren Sie über die Brücke
faaren zee ewber dee brewke
Drive over the bridge

Nehmen Sie . . .
naymen zee
Take . . .

Nehmen Sie die dritte Ausfahrt
naymen zee dee dritte owsfaart
Take the third exit

Biegen Sie an der Ampel ab
beegen zee an der ampel ap
Turn off at the traffic lights

ROAD TRAVEL

● Consult the motoring organisations for information on driving in Germany. The German motoring organisations include **ADAC (Allgemeiner Deutscher Automobil Club)** and **AvD (Automobil Club von Deutschland)**.

● To take a car to Germany you need a valid driving licence and the green international insurance card. Drivers without this must take out short-term third party insurance. Insurance policies can be renewed at any **ADAC** office.

● You drive on the right in Germany. Traffic from the right has priority on roads, even on roundabouts, unless otherwise indicated. Seatbelts are compulsory, both in the front and the back (if you have them). Crash helmets are compulsory for both drivers and passengers of motorbikes and scooters.

● Speed limits are generally: 50 km per hour in towns and 100 km per hour on ordinary roads. There is no speed limit on motorways but 130 km per hour is the recommended speed.

● Main roads are as follows:
Autobahn – motorway
Bundesstraße – main 'A' road
Landstraße – 'B' road

● There are no tolls on German motorways.

● The main grade of petrol is **Super** (4-star). Unleaded petrol (**bleifreies Benzin**) is very widely available. Diesel is easily obtainable.

● Service stations are open on motorways round the clock and many have very good toilet and restaurant facilities. They normally take credit cards as do service stations in big cities. It's always best to check, though. Self-service garages are indicated by the sign **Selbsttanken** or **Selbstbedienung**.

● Parking within towns and cities is allowed on the right-hand side of the road unless otherwise indicated by 'no parking' signs. Some car parks have an attendant, and there are meters, underground car parks and multi-storey car parks in most cities.

In a Blue Zone (**Blaue Zone**) parking time is limited and you must display a parking disc or ticket to show the time you parked. Discs are available from newsagents.

If you park illegally you are likely to be fined on the spot or have your car towed away.

● You can arrange car hire in Britain with the large international car hire firms. They also have offices at airports and elsewhere in Germany (and there will often be someone who speaks English). There are local companies too in most towns and cities – look for the sign **Autovermietung**. You may be able to hire bicycles, especially in tourist areas.

● If you have to tell a mechanic what's wrong with your vehicle, the easiest way is to indicate the part affected and say 'This isn't working': **Das funktioniert nicht**, or **Das ist kaputt**. Otherwise, look up the word for the appropriate part.

ADAC and **AvD** run a patrol service on motorways and main roads. There are emergency telephones every 2 km on the motorways. When you get through, ask for the **Straßenwachthilfe**. This recovery service is free of charge, motorists only pay for the materials used in repairs. Both organisations have offices in major cities to ring in an emergency for repairs. The German National Tourist Office has a list of numbers. Don't hang up if you don't get through as the calls are stored. **ADAC** operates an urban breakdown service too.

Accidents

Accidents involving injury must be reported to the police. If a third party is involved, the insurance company of the appropriate country must be informed.

● Many drivers in Germany take part in the **Mitfahrgelegenheit** system and offer lifts to people going to the same destination as they are. The system is a cheap and reliable way of getting round the country if you are travelling without a car and is coordinated by a **Mitfahrzentrale** ('lift centre'). Passengers pay a small fee to the centre to organise a lift for them and then split the petrol costs with the driver. There are **Mitfahrzentralen** in most big towns and in some places there are women-only centres, **Frauenmitfahrzentralen**.

Austria and Switzerland

The rules and regulations are much the same as for Germany. A green card is recommended for both countries.

● The speed limits for both countries are:
Austria: 50 km/h in built-up areas, 100 km/h on normal roads and 130 km/h on motorways.
Switzerland: 50 km/h in built-up areas, 80 km/h on normal roads and 120 km/h on motorways.

● There is no leaded two-star petrol, **Normal**, available in Switzerland or in Austria. **Eurosuper** or **Euro-95** is four-star unleaded petrol available in some service stations in Austria.

● Take care on mountain roads. In Switzerland a yellow posthorn on a blue rectangle on some mountain roads indicates that post vans have precedence. You must switch your headlights on in mountain road tunnels.

● A motorway sticker, a **vignette**, is required to travel on Swiss motorways. You can buy these at the border from the **ACS (Automobil Club der Schweiz)** or from motoring organisations in this country. There are tolls on mountain passes and tunnels in Switzerland and Austria.

● In Austria the **ÖAMTC (Österreichischer Automobil und Motorräder Touring Club)** operates a 24-hour recovery service. The number to dial is **120**. The Austrian motoring organisations also rent out snow chains for use in the winter.

You may see

Achtung	Caution
Anlieger frei	Access to residents only
Ausfahrt	Exit
Autobahn	Motorway
Autovermietung	Car hire
Bahnübergang	Level crossing
Bewachte/Tiefgarage	Supervised/underground car park
Blaue Zone	Blue Zone
DB	German Railways
Durchfahrt verboten	No through traffic
Durchgangsverkehr	Through traffic
Einbahnstraße	One-way street
Einfahrt freihalten	Allow free access
Einordnen	Get in lane
Ende der Autobahn	End of motorway
Erste Hilfe	First Aid
Frostschäden	Frost damage
Fußgänger	Pedestrians
Fußgängerzone	Pedestrian precinct
Fußgängerüberweg	Pedestrian crossing
Gefahr	Danger
Gefährliche Kurve	Dangerous bend
Gegenverkehr	Two-way traffic
Geschwindigkeitsgrenze	Speed limit

Glatteisgefahr	Black ice
Halt	Stop
Halten verboten	No stopping
Hochgarage/Parkhaus	Multi-storey car park
Höchstgeschwindigkeit	Maximum speed
Hupen verboten	No hooting
Kein Durchgang für Fußgänger	No pedestrians
Langsam	Slow
Letzte Tankstelle vor der Autobahn	Last petrol station before the motorway
Links fahren/Rechts fahren	Drive on the left/right
Mautgebühr	Toll
Messegelände	Exhibition centre
Motor abschalten	Switch your engine off
Notrufsäule	Emergency telephone (on motorway)
P	Parking
Parken verboten/beschränkt	Parking prohibited/limited
Paß geschlossen	(Mountain) pass closed
Radweg	Cycle path
Radweg kreuzt	Cycle path crossing
Reparaturwerkstatt	Car repairs/Garage
Rollsplit	Loose grit
Sackgasse	Cul-de-sac, no through road
Scheinwerfer anschalten (im Tunnel)	Use headlights (in tunnel)
Schleudengefahr bei Nässe	Slippery surface in damp weather
Schritttempo	Dead slow
Schule	School
Stadtzentrum	Town/city centre
Straße gesperrt	Road closed
Straßenbauarbeiten	Road works
Straßenschäden	Uneven road surface
Steinschlag	Falling rocks
Tankstelle	Service/petrol station
Überholen verboten	No overtaking

Umleitung	Diversion
Unbeschränkter Bahnübergang	Unguarded level crossing
Viehpfad	Cattle track
Vorfahrt achten	Give way
Vorsicht	Caution
Vorsicht vor den Zügen	Beware of trains
Zollamt	Customs
Zutritt verboten	No entry

You may want to say

Petrol

Where is the nearest petrol
station?
Wo ist die nächste Tankstelle?
voh ist dee nekste tankshtelle

4-star
Super
zooper

Unleaded petrol
Bleifreies Benzin
bliyfriyes bentseen

Diesel
Diesel
deezel

20 litres of 4-star, please
Zwanzig Liter Super, bitte
tsvantsig leeter zooper bitte

30 marks' worth of
unleaded, please
**Dreißig Mark bleifreies
Benzin, bitte**
*driyssig mark bliyfriyes
bentseen bitte*

Fill it up with 4-star please
Volltanken mit Super bitte
folltanken mit zooper bitte

A (litre) can of oil, please
Einen Kanister Öl, bitte
iynen kanister erl bitte

A (half-litre) can of oil, please
Eine Dose Öl, bitte
iyne dohze erl bitte

A can of petrol, please
**Einen Reservekanister
Benzin, bitte**
iynen reservekanister bentseen bitte

Water, please
Wasser, bitte
vasser bitte

Can you check the pressure
in the tyres?
**Können Sie den Reifendruck
prüfen?**
*kernnen zee dayn riyfendrook
prewfen*

Can you change the tyre?
Können Sie den Reifen wechseln?
kernnen zee dayn riyfen vekseln

Can you clean the windscreen?
Können Sie die Windschutzscheibe waschen?
kernnen zee dee vintshootsshiybe vashen

Parking

Where can I/we park?
Wo kann man parken?
voh kann man parken

Can I/we park here?
Kann man hier parken?
kan man heer parken

How long can I/we park here?
Wie lange kann man hier parken?
vee lange kan man heer parken

Where is the air, please?
Wo ist die Luft, bitte?
voh ist dee looft bitte

How does the car wash work?
Wie funktioniert die Autowäsche?
vee foonktsyoneert dee owtoveshe

How much is it?
Was kostet das?
vas kostet das

How much is it per hour?
Was kostet es die Stunde?
vas kostet es dee shtoonde

A parking disc, please
Eine Parkscheibe, bitte
iyne parkshiybe bitte

Hiring a car

(see Days, months, dates*, page 189)*

I want to hire a car
Ich möchte ein Auto mieten
*ish **mershte** iyn **owto meeten***

A small car, please
Ein kleines Auto, bitte
*iyn **kliynes owto** bitte*

A medium-sized car, please
Ein mittelgroßes Auto, bitte
*iyn **mittelgrohsses owto** bitte*

A large car, please
Ein großes Auto, bitte
*iyn **grohsses owto** bitte*

An automatic car, please
Ein Auto mit Automatik, bitte
*iyn **owto** mit **owtomaatik** bitte*

For three days
Für drei Tage
*fewr driy **taage***

For a week
Für eine Woche
*fewr iyne **voke***

For two weeks
Für zwei Wochen
*fewr tsviy **voken***

From . . . to . . .
Von . . . bis . . .
fon . . . bis

From Monday to Friday
Von montag bis freitag
*fon **mohntaag** bis **friytaag***

From 10 to 17 August
**Vom zehnten bis zum
siebzehnten August**
*fom **tsaynten** bis tsoom
zeebtsaynten owgoost*

How much is it?
Was kostet das?
vas kostet das

Per day
Pro Tag
proh taag

Per week
Pro Woche
proh voke

Per kilometre
Pro Kilometer
proh kilomayter

Is mileage (kilometrage)
included?
**Ist die Kilometerzahl
inbegriffen?**
*ist dee **kilomaytertsaal**
inbegriffen*

Is petrol included?
Ist das Benzin inbegriffen?
*ist das **bentseen** inbegriffen*

Is insurance included?
Ist die Versicherung inbegriffen?
*ist dee **ferzisheroong** inbegriffen*

Comprehensive insurance cover
Vollkasko(versicherung)
follkaskoh(verzisheroong)

My husband/wife is driving too
Mein Mann/Meine Frau fährt auch
miyn mann/miyne frow fayrt owk

Is there a deposit?
Muß ich Geld hinterlegen?
mooss ish gelt hinterlaygen

Do you take credit cards?
Nehmen Sie Kreditkarten?
naymen zee kredeetkarten

Do you take traveller's cheques?
Nehmen Sie Reiseschecks?
naymen zee riyzeshecks

Can I leave the car in Hamburg?
Kann ich das Auto in Hamburg lassen?
kan ish das owto in Hamboorg lassen

Can I leave the car at the airport?
Kann ich das Auto am Flughafen lassen?
kan ish das owto am flooghaafen lassen

How do the . . . work?
Wie funktionieren die . . . ?
vee foonktsyoneeren dee

How do the gears work?
Wie funktionieren die Gänge?
vee foonktsyoneeren dee genge

Breakdowns and repairs

(*See also list of* car parts *on page 43*.)

My car has broken down
Ich habe eine Panne
ish haabe iyne panne

Can you telephone a garage?
Können Sie eine Reparaturwerkstatt anrufen?
kernnen zee iyne reparatoorverkshtatt anroofen

I've run out of petrol
Der Tank ist leer
der tank ist layr

Where is the nearest garage?
Wo ist die nächste Reparaturwerkstatt?
voh ist dee nekste reparatoorverkshtatt

Can you send a mechanic?
Können Sie einen Mechaniker schicken?
kernnen zee iynen mekaniker shiken

Do you do repairs?
Nehmen Sie Reparaturen vor?
naymen zee reparatooren for

I don't know what's wrong
Ich weiß nicht, was los ist
ish viyss nisht was lohs ist

I think ...
Ich glaube ...
ish glowbe

It's the clutch
Es ist die Kupplung
es ist dee kooploong

It's the radiator
Es ist der Kühler
es ist der kewler

It's the brakes
Es sind die Bremsen
es zint dee bremzen

The car won't start
Das Auto startet nicht
das owto shtartet nisht

The battery is flat
Die Batterie ist leer
dee batteree ist layr

The engine is overheating
Das Motor überhitzt
das mohtor ewberhitzt

It's losing water/oil
Es verliert Wasser/Öl
es ferleert vasser/erl

I have a puncture
Ich habe einen Platten
ish haabe iynen platten

The ... doesn't work
Der/die/das ... funktioniert nicht
der/dee/das ... foonktsyoneert nisht

I need ... *(for other car parts, see page 43)*
Ich brauche ...
ish browke

Is it serious?
Ist es schlimm?
ist es shlimm

Can you repair it (today)?
Können Sie es (heute) reparieren
kernnen zee es hoyte repareeren

When will it be ready?
Wann wird es fertig sein?
van virt es fertig ziyn

How much will it cost?
Was wird es kosten?
vas virt es kosten

You may hear

Petrol

Was möchten Sie?
*vas **mershten** zee*
What would you like?

Wieviel möchten Sie?
*veefeel **mershten** zee*
How much do you want?

Den Schlüssel, bitte
*dayn **shlewssel** bitte*
The key, please

Parking

Sie können hier nicht parken
*zee **kernnen** heer nisht **parken***
You can't park here

Es kostet zehn Mark die Stunde
*es **kostet** tsayn mark dee **shtoonde***
It's DM 10 an hour

Es kostet nichts
*es **kostet** nishts*
You don't pay

Es ist umsonst/gratis
*es ist **oomzonst/graatis***
It's free

Es gibt dort drüben einen Parkplatz
*es gipt dort **drewben** iynen **parkplatts***
There's a car park over there

Hiring a car

Was für ein Auto möchten Sie?
*vas fewr iyn **owto mershten** zee*
What kind of car do you want?

Für wie lange?
*fewr vee **lange***
For how long?

Für wie viele Tage?
*fewr vee **feele** taage*
For how many days?

Wer fährt?
ver fayrt
Who is driving?

Wer ist der Hauptmieter?
ver ist der howptmeeter
Who is the main driver?

**Es gibt eine Anzahlung von
hundert Mark**
*es gipt iyne antsaaloong fon
hoondert mark*
There is a deposit of DM 100

Haben Sie eine Kreditkarte?
haaben zee iyne kredeetkarte
Have you got a credit card?

**Es kostet siebzig Mark/
zweihundertfünfzig Mark**
*es kostet zeebtsig mark/
tsviyhoondertfewnftsig mark*
It costs DM 70/250

Pro Tag
proh taag
Per day

Pro Woche
proh voke
Per week

Ihr Führerschein, bitte
eer fewrershiyn bitte
Your driving licence, please

Was ist Ihre Adresse?
vas ist eere adresse
What is your address?

Hier ist der Schlüssel
heer ist der shlewssel
Here is the key

**Bitte bringen Sie das Auto
mit vollem Tank zurück**
*bitte bringen zee das owto mit
vollem tank tsoorewk*
Please return the car with a
full tank

**Bitte bringen Sie das Auto
vor sechs Uhr zurück**
*bitte bringen zee das owto for
zeks oor tsoorewk*
Please return the car before
six o'clock

**Wenn das Büro geschlossen
ist, können Sie den
Schlüssel im Briefkasten
lassen**
*venn das bewroh geshlossen
ist, kernnen zee dayn
shlewssel im breefkasten
lassen*
If the office is closed, you
can leave the key in the
letterbox

Breakdowns and repairs

Was ist los?
vas ist lohs
What's wrong with it?

**Ich habe die nötigen
  Ersatzteile nicht**
*ish haabe dee nertigen
erzatstiyle nisht*
I don't have the necessary
parts

**Ich muß die Ersatzteile
  bestellen**
*ish mooss dee erzatstiyle
beshtellen*
I will have to order the parts

**Kommen Sie nächsten
  Dienstag zurück**
*kommen zee neksten deenztaag
tsoorewk*
Come back next Tuesday

Es wird bis Montag fertig sein
es virt bis mohntaag fertig ziyn
It will be ready on Monday

**Es wird fünfundvierzig Mark
  kosten**
*es virt fewnfoontfeertsig mark
kosten*
It will cost DM 45

Car and bicycle parts

Accelerator	**das Gaspedal**	*gaspaydaal*
Air filter	**der Luftfilter**	*looftfilter*
Alternator	**die Lichtmaschine**	*lishtmasheene*
Battery	**die Batterie**	*batteree*
Bonnet	**die Motorhaube**	*mohtorhowbe*
Boot	**der Kofferraum**	*kofferrowm*
Brakes	**die Bremsen**	*bremzen*
Front wheel brake	**die Vorderrad-bremse**	*forderraatbremze*
Rear wheel brake	**die Hinterrad-bremse**	*hinterraatbremze*
Brake cable	**der Bremskabel**	*bremzkaabel*
Brake fluid	**die Bremsflüssigkeit**	*bremzflewssigkiyt*
Brake hose	**der Bremsschlauch**	*bremzshlowk*
Disc brakes	**die Scheiben-bremsen**	*shiybenbremzen*
Carburettor	**der Vergaser**	*fergaazer*

Chain	die Kette	*kette*
Choke	der Choke	*chohke*
Clutch	die Kupplung	*koopploong*
Distributor	der Zündverteiler	*tsewndfertiyler*
Electrical system	die Electric	*elayktrik*
Engine	der Motor	*mohtor*
Exhaust pipe	der Auspuff	*owspoof*
Fanbelt	der Keilriemen	*kiylreemen*
Frame	der Rahmen	*raamen*
Fuel gauge	die Tankanzeige	*tankantsiyge*
Fuel pump	die Benzinpumpe	*bentseenpoompe*
Fuses	die Sicherungen	*zisheroongen*
Gears	die Gänge	*genge*
Gearbox	das Getriebe	*getreebe*
Gear lever	der Schalthebel	*shalthaybel*
Handbrake	die Handbremse	*hantbremze*
Handlebars	die Lenkstange	*lenkshtange*
Headlights	die Scheinwerfer	*shiynverfer*
Heater	die Heizung	*hiytsoong*
Horn	die Hupe	*hoope*
Ignition	die Zündung	*tsewndoong*
Ignition key	der Zündschlüssel	*tsewndshlewssel*
Indicators	die Blinker	*blinker*
Inner tube	der Schlauch	*shlowk*
Lights	das Licht	*lisht*
Front lights	das Vorderlicht	*forderlisht*
Rear lights	das Rücklicht	*rewklisht*
Side lights	das Standlicht	*shtantlisht*
Lock	das Schloß	*shloss*
Oil filter	der Ölfilter	*erlfilter*
Oil gauge	die Ölanzeige	*erlantsiyge*
Pedal	das Pedal	*paydaal*
Points	die Unterbrecher-kontakte	*oonterbresher-kontakte*
Pump	die Pumpe	*poompe*
Radiator	der Kühler	*kewler*

Radiator hose (top/bottom)	der Kühlerschlauch (oberer/unterer)	kewlershlowk (ohberer/oonterer)
Reversing lights	die Rückfahrschein- werfer	rewkfaarshiyn- verfer
Rotor arm	der Verteilerfinger	fertiylerfinger
Saddle	der Sattel	sattel
Silencer	der Schalldämpfer	shaaldempfer
Spare wheel	der Ersatzreifen	erzattsriyfen
Spark plugs	die Zündkerzen	tsewndkertsen
Speedometer	der Tachometer	takohmayter
Spokes	die Speichen	shpiyken
Starter motor	der Anlasser	anlasser
Steering	die Lenkung	lenkoong
Steering wheel	das Lenkrad	lenkraat
Transmission (automatic)	das Schaltgetriebe	shaltgetreebe
Tyre	der Reifen	riyfen
Front tyre	der Vorderreifen	forderriyfen
Back tyre	der Rückreifen	rewkriyfen
Valve	das Ventil	venteel
Warning light	das Blinklicht	blinklisht
Wheel (front/rear)	das Rad	raat
Front wheel	das Vorderrad	forderraat
Back wheel	das Rückrad	rewkraat
Wheel rim	der Radkranz	raatkrants
Window	das Fenster	fenster
Windscreen	die Windschutz- scheibe	vintshootsshiybe
Windscreen washer	Der Scheibenspül- apparat	shiybenshpewl- apparaat
Windscreen wipers	die Scheibenwischer	shiybenvisher

TAXIS

● It's not usual in Germany to hail a taxi in the street. Go to a taxi rank or phone a **Taxizentrale**, taxi centre, the number will be in the telephone book. If a taxi is free the sign on top of the car will be lit up.

● All taxis have meters and the driver usually rounds the fare up so a tip isn't obligatory. There is a basic starting fare and supplements may be added for luggage or journeys to the airport.

● Write down clearly the address of your destination if it's at all complicated so that you can show it to the taxi driver.

● Taxis are beige in most German cities.

● **Swiss** taxi drivers expect a tip.

● In **Austria** taxis are metered in the larger cities. In smaller towns there are fixed charges for certain destinations. In Vienna a supplement is added for trips to the airport. Tips are at your discretion.

You may want to say

(see also Directions, *page 24)*

Is there a taxi rank around here?
Gibt es einen Taxistand in der Nähe?
gipt es iynen taksishtant in der naye

I need a taxi
Ich brauche ein Taxi
ish browke iyn taksi

Can you call me a taxi?
Können Sie ein Taxi für mich bestellen?
kernnen zee iyn taksi fewr mish beshtellen

Immediately
Bitte jetzt gleich
bitte yettst gliysh

For tomorrow at nine o'clock
Für morgen um neun Uhr
fewr morgen oom noyn oor

I'm going to the airport
Ich möchte zum Flughafen
ish mershte tsoom flooghaafen

Can I order a taxi, please
**Kann ich ein Taxi bitte
  bestellen**
*kan ish iyn taksi bitte
  beshtellen*

My address is . . .
Meine Adresse ist . . .
miyne adresse ist . . .

The airport, please
Zum Flughafen, bitte
tsoom flooghaafen bitte

The station, please
Zum Bahnhof, bitte
tsoom baanhof bitte

The Hotel Bellevue, please
Hotel Bellevue, bitte
hotel bellvew bitte

To this address, please
Zu dieser Adresse, bitte
tsoo deezer adresse bitte

Is it far?
Ist es weit?
ist es viyt

How much will it cost?
Wieviel wird es kosten?
veefeel virt es kosten

I am in a hurry
Ich bin in Eile
ish bin in iyle

Stop here, please
Halten Sie bitte hier
halten zee bitte heer

That's fine here, thanks
Das geht hier schon
das gayt heer shon

Can you wait (a few
  minutes), please?
**Können Sie bitte (ein paar
  Minuten) warten?**
*kernnen zee bitte (iyn paar
  minooten) varten*

How much is it?
Was macht das?
vas maakt das

I think there is a mistake
**Ich glaube, hier stimmt etwas
  nicht**
*ish glowbe heer shtimmt etvas
  nisht*

On the meter it's DM 7,50
**Es ist sieben Mark fünfzig
  auf dem Zähler**
*es ist zeeben mark fewnftsig
  owf daym tsayler*

Keep the change
Behalten Sie den Rest
behalten zee dayn rest

That's all right
Ist gut so/Es stimmt so
ist goot zoh/es shtimmt zoh

Can you give me a receipt?
Können Sie mir eine Quittung geben?
kernnen zee meer iyne kvittoong gayben

For DM 9
Für Neun Mark
fewr noyn mark

You may hear

Es ist zehn Kilometer von hier
es ist tsayn kilomayter fon heer
It's ten kilometres away

Es wird ungefähr fünfzehn Mark kosten
es virt oongefayr fewnftsayn mark kosten
It will cost approximately DM 15

(Das macht) achtzehn Mark
(das maakt) aakttsayn mark
(It's) DM 18

Dazu kommt ein Zuschlag
daatsoo kommt iyn tsooshlaag
There is a supplement

Für das Gepäck
fewr das gepek
For the luggage

Für jeden Koffer
fewr yayden koffer
For each suitcase

Für die Fahrt zum Flughafen
fewr dee faart tsoom flooghaafen
For the journey to the airport

AIR TRAVEL

• There are regular shuttle services between all the big German cities. The major German airport is Frankfurt.

• At airports and airline offices you'll generally find someone who speaks English, but be prepared to say a few things in German.

• Signs at major airports will be in English and German.

• Approximate flight times from Frankfurt to some other main cities:

Hamburg – 55 minutes	Düsseldorf – 45 minutes
Hanover – 50 minutes	Berlin – 55 minutes
Cologne/Bonn – 40 minutes	Stuttgart – 45 minutes
Munich – 55 minutes	

Frankfurt is an hour and 35 minutes from London.

• There are more than 20 flights a day from Frankfurt and Hamburg to Berlin and flights from all other airports. All flights land at Tegel airport, 5 miles from the city centre. There is a regular and direct bus link to the centre.

• Frankfurt airport has its own station with connecting trains to the Inter City Network and regular services into the centre of the city. All German airports have good connections to the local transport system.

• There are **DB** offices at all airports from which luggage can be sent to any station.

• The international car hire firms have offices at major airports where you can arrange to hire or pick up cars.

- The main airports in **Switzerland** are Zürich and Geneva. There are good links between the airports and the city centre. Zürich airport has its own station with through services to many major towns.

- There are airports in **Austria** in Vienna, Salzburg, Graz, Linz and Klagenfurt with regular shuttle services between them.

You may see

Abflughalle	Departure lounge
Abflug	Departures
Anmeldefreie Waren	Nothing to declare
Ankunft	Arrivals
Anmeldepflichtige Waren	Goods to declare
Ausgang	Exit
Auskunft	Information
Ausland	International departures
Autovermietung	Car hire
Bitte anschnallen	Fasten seatbelts
Bus (zum Stadtzentrum)	Buses (to the town/city centre)
EG	EC
Eingang	Entrance
Filmsicher	Film safe
Gepäckausgabe	Luggage reclaim
Inland	Domestic departures
Paßkontrolle	Passport control
Rauchen verboten	No smoking
Toiletten	Toilets
Taxis	Taxis
Wechselstube	Bureau de change
Zoll	Customs

You may want to say

(see Numbers, *page 211;* Days, months, dates, *page 189;* Time, *page 193)*

Is there a flight (from Frankfurt) to Hamburg?
Gibt es einen Flug (von Frankfurt) nach Hamburg?
gipt es iynen floog (fon frankfoort) naak hamboorg

Today
Heute
hoyte

This morning/afternoon
Heute morgen/Heute nachmittag
hoyte morgen/hoyte naakmittag

Tomorrow (morning/afternoon)
Morgen (früh/nachmittag)
morgen (frew/naakmittag)

Do you have a timetable of flights to Hanover?
Haben Sie einen Flugplan für Hannover?
haaben zee iynen floogplaan fewr hannohver

What time is the first flight to Berlin?
Um wieviel Uhr ist der erste Flug nach Berlin?
oom veefeel oor ist der erste floog naak berleen

The next flight
Der nächste Flug
der nekste floog

The last flight
Der letzte Flug
der lettste floog

What time does it arrive (at Berlin)?
Um wieviel Uhr kommt es (in Berlin) an?
oom veefeel oor kommt es (in berleen) an

A ticket/Two tickets to Stuttgart, please
Eine Fahrkarte/Zwei Fahrkarten nach Stuttgart, bitte
iyne faarkarte/tsviy faarkarten naak shtoottgart bitte

Single
Ein Hinflug
iyn hinfloog

Return
Ein Hin- und Rückflug
iyn hin oont rewkfloog

First class/Business class
Erste Klasse/Business Klasse
erste klasse/bizness klasse

For the eleven o'clock flight
Für den Flug um elf Uhr
fewr dayn floog oom elf oor

I want to change/cancel my reservation
Ich möchte meine Reservierung ändern/stornieren
ish mershte miyne rezerveeroong endern/shtorneeren

What is the number of the flight?
Was ist die Flugnummer?
vas ist dee floognoommer

What time do I/we have to check in?
Um wieviel Uhr muß man einchecken?
oom veefeel oor mooss man iyncheken

Which gate is it?
Welcher Flugsteig ist es?
velsher floogshtiyg ist es

Is there a delay?
Ist es verspätet?
ist es fershpaytet

I don't want to put my camera/bag through the machine
Ich möchte meinen Photoapparat/meine Tasche nicht durchleuchten lassen
ish mershte miynen fohtoapparaat/miyne tashe nisht doorshloyshten lassen

You can hand search it
Sie können es bei Hand durchsuchen
zee kernnen es biy hant doorshzooken

Where is the luggage from the flight to London?
Wo ist das Gepäck vom Flug aus London?
voh ist das gepek fom floog ows london

My luggage is not here
Mein Gepäck ist nicht da
miyn gepek ist nisht da

Is there a bus to the centre of town?
Gibt es einen Bus zum Stadtzentrum?
gipt es iynen boos tsoom shtattsentroom

You may hear

Möchten Sie einen Fensterplatz?
mershten zee iynen fensterplatts
Would you like a seat by the window?

Möchten Sie einen Gangplatz?
mershten zee iynen gangplatts
Would you like a seat on the aisle?

Raucher oder Nichtraucher?
rowker ohder nishtrowker
Smoking or non-smoking?

Der Flug wird um . . . aufgerufen
der floog virt oom . . . owfgeroofen
The flight will be called/board at . . . (time)

Flugsteig Nummer sieben
floogshtiyg noommer zeeben
Gate number seven

Ihre Flugticket, bitte
eere floogticket bitte
Your ticket, please

Ihren Paß, bitte
eeren pass bitte
Your passport, please

Wie sieht Ihr Gepäck aus?
vee zeet eer gepek ows
What does your luggage look like

Ihre Bordkarte, bitte
eere bordkarte bitte
Your boarding card, please

Haben Sie das Gepäcketikett?
haaben zee das gepeketikett
Do you have the reclaim tag?

Words to listen out for

Aufruf	*owfroof*	Call
Flug	*floog*	Flight
Flugsteig	*floogshtiyg*	Gate
Letzter Aufruf	*lettster owfroof*	Last call
Verspätung	*fershpaytoong*	Delay

TRAVELLING BY TRAIN

● The German State Railway is the **Deutsche Bundesbahn**.

● There are various types of train, including, in reverse order of speed:

Nahverkehrszug – short-distance, suburban train

Personenzug – slow, local train which stops at every station

Eilzug – stops at stations in bigger towns

D-Zug
Schnellzug
Express
Inter City } All fast trains, often travelling between countries, only stopping at principal stations

TEE – Trans-European Express. Luxury, high-speed train with first-class accommodation only

● Sleepers and couchettes must be booked in advance. Tourists can opt for either 2- or 3-berth sleeper compartments – many of which are equipped with showers.

● You can send bicycles in advance by train and pick them up at your destination. There are bicycles for hire at many **DB** stations.

● Single tickets for distances up to 100 km are only valid for a day. For longer distances, single tickets are valid for four days and returns for a month.

● Holders of standard single and return tickets travelling 51 km or over can go on express and Inter City trains without paying the supplement.

● There are also various types of tickets available to tourists:

Tourist cards are recommended for tourists who are undertaking extensive train travel in Germany. They are available for periods of 4, 9 or 16 days or for young people for 9 or 16 days. The card entitles the holder to unlimited travel in first-

or second-class accommodation. (Young Persons' cards are second class only.) Tourist cards are also valid on some bus routes and on boats of the **Deutsche Rheinschiffahrt** on the Rhine and Moselle. The cards are obtainable from British Rail Travel Centres and from travel agents which deal with train travel. It's best to buy the card before you go.

Other discounts include:
Reductions for families, young people and senior citizens.
'Saver' and 'Super Saver' tickets.
Details from British Rail Travel Centres.

● Children under 4 travel free on the German railways (though they are not entitled to a seat at peak times) and children between 4 and 11 travel for half price.

● Refreshments are available in the buffet car or 'minibar' on long journeys.

● Information centres at large stations may be able to book accommodation for you. You can also change money at large stations, though the exchange rate may not be as good as in a bank.

● There is an extensive Motorail service within Germany. Further details from the German National Tourist Office.

● The **Swiss** railways offer various concessions to rail travellers. These include the **Swiss Pass** which operates along the same lines as the German tourist card (see above) and regional passes which are valid for 15 days for tourists visiting a particular region during the summer.

● The Austrian State Railway is the **Österreichische Bahn** (**ÖB**). Their special offers include the **Rabbitkarte** which is valid for ten days, four of which can be travelled on.

You may see

Abfahrt	Departure
Ankunft	Arrival
Ausgang	Exit
Auskunft	Information
Bahnsteig	Platform
Bahnhof	Railway station
Bahnhofsmission	Travellers' Aid
Damen	Ladies
Deutsche Bundesbahn (DB)	German State Railway
Eingang	Entrance
Fahrkarten	Tickets
Fahrkartenschalter	Ticket office
Fahrplan	Train timetable
Fundbüro	Lost property office
Geldwechsel	Change office
Gepäckabfertigung/ Gepäckannahme	Luggage office
Gepäckaufbewahrung	Left luggage
Gleise	Platforms, Tracks
Herren	Gentlemen
Kein Zutritt	No access
Liegewagen	Couchettes
Nicht hinauslehnen	Do not lean out
Reiseziel	Destination
Reservierungen	Reservations
Schlafwagen	Sleeping-car
Schliessfächer	Luggage lockers
Speisewagen	Dining-car
Täglich	Daily
Toiletten	Toilets
Wartesaal	Waiting room
Zimmernachweis	Accommodation information
Zu den Bahnsteigen	To the platforms

Information

(see Time, page 193)

Is there a train to Hanover?
Gibt es einen Zug nach Hannover?
gipt es iynen tsoog naak hannohver

Do you have a timetable of trains to Regensburg?
Haben Sie einen Fahrplan für Züge nach Regensburg?
haaben zee iynen faarplan fewr tsooge naak raygenzboorg

What time . . . ?
Um wieviel Uhr . . . ?
oom veefeel oor

What time is the train to Munich?
Um wieviel Uhr fährt der Zug nach München?
oom veefeel oor fayrt der tsoog naak mewnchen

What time is the first train to Salzburg?
Um wieviel Uhr fährt der erste Zug nach Salzburg?
oom veefeel oor fayrt der erste tsoog naak saltsboorg

The next train
Der nächste Zug
der nekste tsoog

The last train
Der letzte Zug
der lettste tsoog

What time does it arrive (in Bremen)?
Um wieviel Uhr kommt er (in Bremen) an?
oom veefeel oor kommt er (in braymen) an

What time does the train from Stuttgart arrive?
Um wieviel Uhr kommt der Zug von Stuttgart an?
oom veefeel oor kommt der tsoog fon shtoottgart an

Which platform (for Freiburg)?
Von welchem Gleis fährt der Zug (nach Freiburg)?
fon velshem gliys fayrt der tsoog (naak friyboorg)

Does this train go to Augsburg?
Fährt dieser Zug nach Augsburg?
fayrt deezer tsoog naak owksboorg

Is this right for Constance?
Ist das hier der Zug nach Konstanz?
ist das heer der tsoog naak konstants

Do I have to change trains?
Muß ich umsteigen?
mooss ish oomshtiygen

Where?
Wo?
voh

Tickets

(see Time, page 193; Numbers, page 211)

One/two tickets to Vienna, please
Eine Fahrkarte/Zwei Fahrkarten nach Wien, bitte
iyne faarkarte/tsviy faarkarten naak veen, bitte

Single
Einfach
iynfaak

Return
Hin und zurück
hin oont tsoorewk

For one adult/two adults
Für einen Erwachsenen/zwei Erwachsene
fewr iynen ervaksenen/tsviy ervaksene

(And) one child/two children
(Und) ein Kind/zwei Kinder
oont iyn kint/tsviy kinder

First/second class
Erste Klasse/zweite Klasse
erste klasse/tsviyte klasse

For the 10.00 train to Düsseldorf
Für den Zug um zehn nach Düsseldorf
fewr dayn tsoog oom tsayn naak dewsseldorf

For the Inter City to Cologne
Für den Inter City nach Köln
fewr dayn inter city naak kerln

I want to reserve a seat/two seats
Ich möchte einen Platz/zwei Plätze buchen
ish mershte iynen platts/tsviy plettse booken

I want to reserve a sleeper
Ich möchte einen Platz im Schlafwagen buchen
ish mershte iynen platts im shlaafvaagen booken

I want to reserve a couchette
Ich möchte einen Platz im Liegewagen buchen
ish mershte iynen platts im leegevaagen booken

I want to book tickets on the car-train to Geneva
Ich möchte Plätze auf dem Autozug nach Genf buchen
ish mershte plettse owf daym owtotsoog naak genf booken

For the car and two passengers
Für ein Auto und zwei Passagiere
fewr ein owto oont tsviy passajeere

The car is a Volkswagen Beetle
Das Auto ist ein Käfer
das owto ist iyn kayfer

Can I send my bicycle on to Nuremberg?
Kann ich mein Fahrrad nach Nürnberg aufgeben?
kan ish miyn faarraat naak newrnberg owfgayben

How much is it?
Was kostet das?
vas kostet das

Is there a supplement?
Muß ich einen Zuschlag bezahlen?
mooss ish iynen tsooshlaag betsaalen

Left luggage

Can I leave this?
Kann ich das hinterlassen?
kan ish das hinterlassen

Can I leave these two suitcases?
Kann ich diese zwei Koffer hier lassen?
kan ish deeze tsviy koffer heer lassen

Until three o'clock
Bis drei Uhr
bis driy oor

What time do you close?
Um wieviel Uhr schließen Sie?
oom veefeel oor shleessen zee

How much is it?
Was kostet das?
vas kostet das

On the train

I have reserved a seat
Ich habe einen Platz gebucht
ish haabe iynen platts gebookt

I have reserved a sleeper/couchette
Ich habe einen Platz im Schlafwagen/Liegewagen gebucht
ish haabe iynen platts im shlaafvaagen/leegevaagen gebookt

Is this seat taken?
Ist dieser Platz frei?
ist deezer platts friy

Excuse me, may I get by?
Entschuldigung/Pardon
entshooldigoong/pardon

Where is the dining-car?
Wo ist der Speisewagen?
voh ist der shpiyzevaagen

Where is the sleeping-car?
Wo ist der Schlafwagen?
voh ist der shlaafvaagen

May I open the window?
Darf ich das Fenster öffnen?
darf ish das fenster erffnen

May I smoke?
Darf ich rauchen?
darf ish rowken

Where are we?
Wo sind wir?
voh zint veer

Are we at Basel?
Sind wir in Basel?
zint veer in baazel

How long does the train
   stop here?
Wie lange bleibt der Zug hier?
vee lange bliypt der tsoog heer

Can you tell me when we
   get to Kaiserslauten?
**Können Sie mir bitte sagen,
   wenn wir in Kaiserslauten
   ankommen?**
*kernnen zee meer bitte zaagen
   ven veer in kiyzerslowten
   ankommen*

You may hear

Information

(see Time, *page 193;* Numbers, *page 211)*

**Er fährt um zehn Uhr
   dreißig ab**
*er fayrt oom tsayn oor
   driyssig ap*
It leaves at 10.30

**Er kommt um zehn nach
   vier an**
*er kommt oom tsayn naak
   feer an*
It arrives at ten past four

**Sie müssen in Trier
   umsteigen**
zee moossen in tree-er oomshtiygen
You have to change trains
   at Trier

Es ist Gleis vier
es ist gliys feer
It's platform number four

Tickets

Für wann möchten Sie die Fahrkarte?
fewr van mershten zee dee faarkarte
When do you want the ticket for?

Wann wollen Sie fahren?
van vollen zee faaren
When do you want to travel?

Einfach oder hin und zurück?
iynfaak oder hin oont tsoorewk
Single or return?

Wann möchten Sie zurückkommen?
van mershten zee tsoorewkkommen
When do you want to return?

Raucher oder Nichtraucher?
rowker oder nishtrowker
Smoking or non-smoking?

(Das macht) dreißig Mark
das maakt driyssig mark
(It's) DM 30

Dazu kommt ein Zuschlag von fünf Mark
daatsoo kommt iyn tsooshlaag fon fewnf mark
There is a supplement of DM 5

Der Zug hat nur erste Klasse
der tsoog hat noor erste klasse
That train's first class only

BUSES AND COACHES

● You usually pay as you enter on buses in towns and cities. There may be automatic ticket machines at bus stops. Tickets for some long-distance services can be bought at bus station ticket offices.

● If you intend to use the buses a lot in a town or city, you can buy **eine Tageskarte**, a day card, which is valid on buses, trams and the underground. You can buy them from machines in underground stations or from kiosks. Most cities are divided into zones; make sure all the zones you want to travel in are stamped on your ticket.

● You can also buy tickets which are valid for shorter periods such as two hours.

● There are on-the-spot fines for travelling without a valid ticket.

● A good way to see Germany by coach is to go on one of the **DB**'s (German Railways) coach tours. There are excursions in the Rhine area and in the Alps. More information from the German National Tourist Office or the main railway station in any big city.

● **Switzerland** has several Postbus routes. Further information on Postbus services, including the Alpine services, and excursions is available from local tourist offices. A **Swiss Pass** ticket is valid for buses as well as trains.

● **Austria** There are plenty of local bus services operating throughout the country to take tourists on excursions and between towns and cities.

You may see

Bedarfhaltestelle	Request stop
Busbahnhof	Bus station
Bushaltestelle	Bus stop
Eingang	Entrance
Hinten einsteigen	Enter by the back door
Kein Ausstieg	No exit
Kein Einstieg	No entry
(Not)ausgang	(Emergency) exit
Rauchen verboten	No smoking
Während der Fahrt nicht mit dem Fahrer sprechen	Do not talk to the driver
Vorne aussteigen	Exit by the front door

You may want to say

(for sightseeing bus tours, see Sightseeing, *page 142)*

Where is the bus stop?
Wo ist die Bushaltestelle?
*voh ist dee **boos**halteshtelle*

Where is the bus station?
Wo is der Busbahnhof?
*voh ist der **boos**baanhof*

Is there a bus to the lake?
Gibt es einen Bus zum See?
*gipt es **iy**nen boos tsoom zay*

What number is the bus to the station?
Welche Buslinie fährt zum Bahnhof?
*velshe **boos**leenye fayrt tsoom **baan**hof*

Do they go often?
Fahren sie oft?
faaren zee oft

What time is the bus to Berlin?
Um wieviel Uhr fährt der Bus nach Berlin?
oom veefeel oor fayrt der boos naak berleen

What time is the first bus to Celle?
Um wieviel Uhr fährt der erste Bus nach Celle?
oom veefeel oor fayrt der erste boos naak zelle

The next bus
Der nächste Bus
der nekste boos

The last bus
Der letzte Bus
der lettste boos

What time does it arrive?
Um wieviel Uhr kommt er an?
oom veefeel oor kommt er an

Where can I buy tickets?
Wo kann ich Fahrkarten kaufen?
voh kan ish faarkarten kowfen

Where can I get a day ticket?
Wo kann ich eine Tageskarte kaufen?
voh kan ish iyne taageskarte kowfen

Where does the bus to the town centre leave from?
Wo fährt der Bus zum Stadtzentrum ab?
voh fayrt der boos tsoom shtattsentroom ap

Does the bus to the airport leave from here?
Fährt der Bus zum Flughafen von hier ab?
fayrt der boos tsoom flooghaafen fon heer ap

Does this bus go to Blankenese?
Fährt dieser Bus nach Blankenese?
fayrt deezer boos naak blankeneze

Can you tell me where to get off?
Können Sie mir sagen, wo ich aussteigen muß?
kernnen zee meer zaagen voh ish owsshtiygen mooss

The next stop, please
Die nächste Haltestelle, bitte
dee nekste halteshtelle bitte

Can you open the door, please?
Bitte die Tür öffnen!
bitte dee tewr erffnen

Excuse me, may I get by?
Pardon
pardon

Tickets

One/two to the centre, please
Eins/zwei zum Zentrum, bitte
iyns/tsviy tsoom tsentroom bitte

A day card, please
Eine Tageskarte, bitte
iyne taageskarte bitte

How much is it?
Was kostet das?
vas kostet das

You may hear

Der Bus zum Stadtzentrum fährt von dieser Haltestelle da ab
*der boos tsoom **shtattsentroom** fayrt fon **dee**zer **halteshtelle** daa ap*
The bus to the town centre leaves from that stop there

Der siebenundfünfziger fährt zum Bahnhof
*der zeebenoond**fewnftsiger** fayrt tsoom **baan**hof*
The 57 goes to the station

Sie fahren alle zehn Minuten
*zee **faaren** alle tsayn **minooten***
They go every ten minutes

Sie können eine Tageskarte bei einem Kiosk kaufen
*zee **kernnen** iyne **taages**karte biy iynem **kee**osk **kowfen***
You can buy a day ticket from a kiosk

Wie viele Zonen möchten Sie?
*vee **feele** **tsohnen** **mershten** zee*
How many zones do you want?

Sie zahlen beim Fahrer
*zee **tsaalen** biym **faarer***
You pay the driver

Steigen Sie hier aus?
***shtiygen** zee heer ows*
Are you getting off here?

Sie müssen an der nächsten Haltestelle aussteigen
*zee **mewssen** an der **neksten** **halteshtelle** **owsshtiygen***
You have to get off at the next stop

Sie haben die Haltestelle verpaßt
*zee **haaben** dee **halteshtelle** fer**passt***
You've missed the stop

UNDERGROUND TRAVEL

● The underground is called the **U-Bahn**, and there are systems in most large cities. The **S-Bahn** is an express underground, or overground, which goes further afield. You can buy tickets for your journey at an automatic machine in the station. In most large cities tickets for the bus (and tram) are also valid on the **U-Bahn**, though not always on the **S-Bahn**.

● Children under 4 travel free, and there are concessions for children under 14.

● In **Austria** tourists can buy a **Wochenkarte**, weekly card, for the underground and buses.

You may see

Ausgang	Exit
Eingang	Entrance
Hinweis	Information
S-Bahn	Express underground or overground
Rauchen verboten	No smoking
U-Bahn	Underground

You may want to say

Do you have a map of the underground?
Haben Sie einen Zonenplan?
haaben zee iynen tsohnenplaan

One/Two, please
Eins/Zwei, bitte
iyns/tsviy bitte

Which line is it for Dammtor station?
Welche Linie fährt zum Dammtor?
velshe leenye fayrt tsoom dammtor

Which stop is it for the Theresienwiesen?
Wo muß ich für die Theresienwiesen aussteigen?
voh mooss ish fewr dee terayzyenveezen owsshtiygen

Where are we?
Wo sind wir?
voh zint veer

Is this the right stop for the Fish Market?
Ist das hier richtig für den Fischmarkt?
ist das heer rishtig fewr dayn fishmarkt

Does this train go to the Rathaus?
Fährt dieser Zug zum Rathaus?
fayrt deezer tsoog tsoom raathows

You may hear

Es ist die Linie S zwei
es ist dee leenye s tsviy
It's line number S2

Es ist die nächste Station
es ist dee nekste shtatsyon
It's the next stop

Es war die letzte Station
es vaar dee lettste shtatsyon
It was the last stop

BOATS AND FERRIES

• The **Rheinschiffahrt** company organises long- and short-distance cruises on the Rhine and the Moselle and there are boat trips and cruises on all the major German rivers. There are cruises and excursions on Lake Constance (**der Bodensee**) and also a car ferry service. If you have a Lake Constance pass you are entitled to concessions.

• If you want to visit the German North Sea Islands or the Baltic island of Fehmarn, one rail ticket will cover you for travel to the coast, the ferry across and transport the other side. There are also motorail services to the islands.

• There are steam cruises on the Danube (**Donau**) and on the larger Austrian and Swiss lakes all through the summer. Further information is available from local tourist offices.

Signs you may see

Anlegestelle	Pier, embarkation point
Autodeck	Car deck
Bootfahrten	Cruises
Bootrundfahrt	Round trip
Dampfer	Steamer
Dampferfahrten	Steam cruises
Fähre	Ferry
Flußfahrten	River trips
Hafen	Port, harbour
Kabinen	Cabins
Luftkissenfahrzeug	Hovercraft
Rettungsring	Lifebelt
Rheinfahrten	Rhine cruises

You may want to say

Information

(see Time, *page 193)*

Is there a boat to Weltenburg (today)?
Fährt (heute) ein Schiff nach Weltenburg?
fayrt hoyte iyn shiff naak veltenboorg

Is there a car ferry to Constance?
Fährt eine Fähre nach Konstanz?
fayrt iyne fayre naak konstants

Are there any boat trips?
Gibt es Schiffahrten?
gipt es shiffaarten

What time is the boat to Passau?
Um wieviel Uhr fährt das Schiff nach Passau ab?
oom veefeel oor fayrt das shiff naak passow ap

What time is the first boat?
Um wieviel Uhr fährt das erste Schiff?
oom veefeel oor fayrt das erste shiff

The next boat
Das nächste Schiff
das nekste shiff

The last boat
Das letzte Schiff
das lettste shiff

What time does it arrive?
Um wieviel Uhr kommt es an?
oom veefeel oor kommt es an

What time does it return?
Um wieviel Uhr kommt es zurück?
oom veefeel oor kommt es tsoorewk

How long is the cruise?
Wie lange dauert die Fahrt?
vee lange dowert dee faart

Where does the boat to Koblenz leave from?
Wo fährt das Schiff nach Koblenz ab?
voh fayrt das shiff naak koblents ap

Where can I buy tickets?
Wo kann ich Karten kaufen?
voh kan ish karten kowfen

What is the lake like today?
Wie ist der See heute?
vee ist der zay hoyte

Tickets

(see Numbers, *page 211)*

Four tickets to Mainz, please
Vier Fahrkarten nach Mainz, bitte
feer faarkarten naak miynts bitte

Two adults and two children
Zwei Erwachsene und zwei Kinder
tsviy ervaksene oont tsviy kinder

Single
Einfach
iynfaak

Return
Hin und zurück
hin oont tsoorewk

I want to book tickets for the ferry to Fehmarn
Ich möchte Fahrkarten für die Fähre nach Fehmarn buchen
ish mershte faarkarten fewr dee fayre naak faymarn booken

For a car and two passengers
Für ein Auto und zwei Passagiere
fewr iyn owto oont tsviy passajeere

I want to book a cabin
Ich möchte eine Kabine buchen
ish mershte iyne kabeene booken

For two people
Für zwei Personen
fewr tsviy perzohnen

For one person
Für eine Person
fewr iyne perzohn

How much is it?
Was kostet das?
vas kostet das

On board

I have reserved a cabin
Ich habe eine Kabine gebucht
ish haabe iyne kabeene gebookt

I have reserved a two-berth cabin
Ich habe eine Zweierkabine gebucht
ish haabe iyne tsviyerkabeene gebookt

Where are the cabins?
Wo sind die Kabinen?
voh zint dee kabeenen

Where is cabin number 20?
Wo ist Kabine Nummer zwanzig?
voh ist kabeene noommer tsvantsig

Can I/we go out on deck?
Kann man auf das Deck gehen?
kan man owf das deck gayen

Schiffe fahren dienstags und freitags
shiffe faaren deenstaags oond friytaags
There are boats on Tuesdays and Fridays

Das Schiff nach Konstanz fährt um neun Uhr ab
das shiff naak konstants fayrt oom noyn oor ap
The boat to Constance leaves at nine o'clock

Es kommt um halb fünf zurück
es kommt oom halp fewnf tsoorewk
It returns at half past four

Das Schiff nach Mainz fährt von Anlegestelle zwei ab
das shiff naak miynts fayrt fon anlaygeshtelle tsviy ap
The boat to Mainz leaves from pier number two

Der See ist still
der zay ist shtil
The lake is calm

Der See ist stürmisch
der zay ist shtewrmish
The lake is rough

AT THE TOURIST OFFICE

● There are tourist information offices in most towns and cities – look for any of the words listed below. There will usually be someone who speaks English.

● Tourist offices have leaflets about sights worth seeing, lists of hotels, town plans and regional maps, and can supply information about opening times and local transport. They can also book hotel rooms for you for a small fee.

● Tourist offices have the same sort of opening hours as shops (*see page 127*).

You may see

Any of these signs means tourist information:

Fremdenverkehrsamt
Fremdenverkehrsbüro
Fremdenverkehrsverein
Verkehrsamt
Verkehrsverein

You may want to say

(see Directions, *page 24;* Sightseeing, *page 142;* Time, *page 193)*

Where is the tourist office?
Wo ist das Fremdenverkehrsbüro?
voh ist das fremdenferkayrzbewroh

Do you have . . . ?
Haben Sie . . . ?
haaben zee . . .

Do you have a plan of the town?
Haben Sie einen Stadtplan?
haaben zee iynen shtatplaan

Do you have a map of the town/village and surrounding area?
Haben Sie einen Plan von der Stadt/dem Dorf und der Umgebung?
haaben zee iynen plaan fon der shtat/daym dorf oont der oomgayboong

Do you have a list of hotels?
Haben Sie eine Hotelliste?
haaben zee iyne hotelliste

Do you have a list of campsites?
Haben Sie eine Liste von Campingplätzen?
*haaben zee iyne liste fon **kam**pingplettsen*

Can you recommend a cheap hotel?
Können Sie ein preiswertes Hotel empfehlen?
*kernnen zee iyn **priys**vertes hotel empfaylen*

Can you book a hotel room for me, please?
Können Sie für mich ein Hotelzimmer bitte buchen?
*kernnen zee fewr mish iyn hoteltsimmer bitte **booken***

Can you recommend a traditional restaurant?
Können Sie mir ein typisches Restaurant empfehlen?
*kernnen zee meer iyn **too**pishes restoron empfaylen*

Where can I/we hire a car?
Wo kann man ein Auto mieten?
voh kan man iyn owto meeten

What is there to see here?
Was gibt es hier für Sehenswürdigkeiten?
vas gipt es heer fewr zayenzvewrdigkiyten

Do you have any leaflets?
Haben Sie irgendwelche Prospekte?
haaben zee irgentvelshe prospekte

Where is the city art gallery?
Wo ist die Kunsthalle?
voh ist dee koonsthalle

Can you show me that on the map?
Können Sie mir das auf dem Stadtplan zeigen?
kernnen zee meer das owf daym shtatplaan tsiygen

When is the museum open?
Wann ist das Museum offen?
van ist das moozayoom offen

Are there any excursions?
Gibt es irgendwelche Ausflüge?
gipt es irgentvelshe owsflewge

You may hear

Kann ich Ihnen helfen?
kan ish eenen helfen
Can I help you?

Sind Sie Englisch?
zint zee english
Are you English?

Französisch?
frantserzish
French?

Wie lange ist Ihr Aufenthalt?
vee lange ist eer owfenthalt
How long are you going to be here?

Wo wohnen Sie?
voh vohnen zee
Where are you staying?

Was für ein Hotel möchten Sie?
vas fewr iyn hotel mershten zee
What kind of hotel do you want?

Was für ein Zimmer möchten Sie?
vas fewr iyn tsimmer mershten zee
What kind of room do you want?

Es ist in der Altstadt
es ist in der altshtat
It's in the old part of town

ACCOMMODATION

● There is a wide range of hotels, inns and guest houses in West Germany.

● **Hotels** are not officially graded but standards conform to the usual European star system. Prices are always displayed in the rooms.

● A **Hotel garni** offers bed and breakfast. A **Pension** is a guest house and a **Gasthof** is like a country inn and offers good food and a limited amount of accommodation. The sign **Zimmer frei** indicates rooms to let in a private house.

● There are motels along major routes. The 'International Motel Guide', available in Germany from **ADAC** (the German motoring organisation) offices, has a list.

● The German National Tourist Office has information about accommodation in castles and stately homes. The organisation that runs these hotels is **Gast im Schloss**.

● Some hotels in **Switzerland** offer special facilities for convalescence, rest and relaxation. A list is available from the Swiss National Tourist Office.

● There are plenty of campsites all over Germany, including special winter campsites. Further information and a list of sites is available from the German National Tourist Office. It is best to book in good time during the busy summer season. There are reductions at **DCC (Deutscher Camping Club)** sites for holders of international carnets. The same applies to many campsites in **Austria**, where there are also reductions for children. Wild camping is allowed with the landowner's permission.

• There are over 600 Youth Hostels, **Jugendherbergen**, in Germany which are open to members of any organisation affiliated to the IYHF. The YHA in London has further information and the International Youth Hostel Handbook. In **Switzerland** hostels are open to young people under 25 and to the over-25s if there is room. Foreign visitors must have a membership card of an organisation affiliated to the International Youth Hostelling Federation for hostels in Switzerland and Austria.

• When you book in somewhere you will usually be asked for your passport. In a hotel, you may have to fill in a registration card, **ein Anmeldeschein**, which will usually have an English translation. You may also have to leave your passport at reception overnight.

• There are plenty of chalets, villas and apartments for rent throughout the year – some of them in holiday villages. The German National Tourist Office has a brochure and you can make bookings through regional tourist offices in Germany and travel agents too. Many farms, **Bauernhöfe**, offer accommodation and holidays to tourists.

Information requested on a registration card

Vorname	First name
Familienname	Surname
Wohnort/Straße/Nr.	Home address/Street/Number
Nationalität	Nationality
Beruf	Occupation
Geburtsdatum	Date of birth
Geburtsort	Place of birth
Paßnummer	Passport number
Letzter Aufenthaltsort/ Reiseziel	Coming from/going to
Ausgestellt	Issued at
Datum	Date
Unterschrift	Signature

You may see

Aufenthaltsraum	Lounge
Ausgebucht	Full up
Bitte läuten	Please ring the bell
Campingplatz/Zeltplatz	Campsite
Camping verboten	No camping
Chemische Toilette hier abladen	Empty chemical toilets here
Duschen	Showers
Das Abladen von Abfällen ist untersagt	Do not dump rubbish
Empfang/Rezeption	Reception
Erdgeschoß	Ground floor
Erster Stock	First floor
Eßzimmer	Dining-room
Fahrstuhl	Lift
Fernsehraum	Television room
Frühstücksbüffet	Breakfast bar
Garage	Garage
Gasthof	Inn, hotel
Gaststätte	Restaurant
Halbpension	Half board
Hotel	Hotel
Hotel garni	Bed and breakfast
Jugendherberge	Youth hostel
Keine Lagerfeuer anzünden	Do not light fires
Luxus Hotel	Five-star, luxury hotel
Müll	Rubbish
(Not)ausgang	(Emergency) exit
Pension	Guest house
Strom	Electricity
Toiletten	Toilets
Trinkwasser	Drinking water
Vollpension	Full board
Wäscherei	Laundry

Wohnwagen verboten	No caravans
Zimmerservice	Room service
Zimmer frei	Rooms vacant (often in a private house)
Zweiter Stock	Second floor

You may want to say

Booking in and out

I've reserved a room
Ich habe ein Zimmer reservieren lassen
ish haabe iyn tsimmer rezerveeren lassen

I've reserved two rooms
Ich habe zwei Zimmer reservieren lassen
ish haabe tsviy tsimmer rezerveeren lassen

I've reserved a place
Ich habe einen Platz reservieren lassen
ish haabe iynen platts rezerveeren lassen

My name is . . .
Mein Name ist . . .
miyn naame ist

Do you have a room?
Haben Sie ein Zimmer?
haaben zee iyn tsimmer

A single room
Ein Einzelzimmer
iyn iyntseltsimmer

A double room
Ein Doppelzimmer
iyn doppeltsimmer

A twin-bedded room
Ein Zimmer mit zwei Einzelbetten
iyn tsimmer mit tsviy iyntselbetten

For one night
Für eine Nacht
fewr iyne naakt

For two nights
Für zwei Nächte
fewr tsviy nekte

With bath/shower
Mit Bad/Dusche
mit baat/dooshe

Do you have space for a tent?
Haben Sie Platz für ein Zelt?
haaben zee platts fewr iyn tselt

Do you have space for a caravan?
Haben Sie Platz für einen Wohnwagen?
haaben zee platts fewr iynen vohnvaagen

How much is it?
Was kostet das?
vas kostet das

Per night
Pro Nacht
proh naakt

Per week
Pro Woche
proh voke

Is there a reduction for children?
Gibt es eine Ermäßigung für Kinder?
gipt es iyne ermaysigoong fewr kinder

Is breakfast included?
Ist das Frühstück inbegriffen?
ist das frewshtewk inbegriffen

It's too expensive
Es ist zu teuer
es ist tsoo toyer

Do you have anything cheaper?
Haben Sie etwas Billigeres?
haaben zee etvas billigeres

Do you have anything bigger/smaller?
Haben Sie etwas Größeres/Kleineres?
haaben zee etvas grersseres/kliyneres

I'd like to stay another night
Ich möchte noch eine Nacht bleiben
ish mershte nok iyne naakt bliyben

I am leaving tomorrow morning
Ich fahre morgen früh ab
ish faare morgen frew ap

Thank you, it's been very nice here
Vielen Dank, es hat uns hier gut gefallen
feelen dank es hat oons heer goot gefallen

The bill, please
Die Rechnung, bitte
dee reshnoong bitte

Do you take credit cards?
Nehmen Sie Kreditkarten?
naymen zee kredeetkarten

Do you take traveller's cheques?
Nehmen Sie Reiseschecks?
naymen zee riyzeshecks

Can you recommend a hotel in Würzburg?
Können Sie ein Hotel in Würzburg empfehlen?
kernnen zee iyn hotel in vertsboorg empfaylen

Can you book a room for me there, please?
Können Sie bitte ein Zimmer für mich dort buchen?
kernnen zee bitte iyn tsimmer fewr mish dort booken

In hotels

(see Problems and complaints, page 170; Time, page 193)

Where can I/we park?
Wo kann man parken?
voh kan man parken

Do you have a cot for the baby?
Haben Sie ein Kinderbett für das Baby?
haaben zee iyn kinderbett fewr das baybee

Is there room service?
Gibt es Zimmerservice?
gipt es tsimmerservis

Do you have facilities for the disabled?
Bieten Sie Möglichkeiten für Behinderte?
beeten zee merglishkiyten fewr behinderte

A room with a view, please
Ein Zimmer mit Aussicht, bitte
iyn tsimmer mit owssisht bitte

Can I see the room, please?
Kann ich das Zimmer bitte sehen?
kan ish das tsimmer bitte zayen

What time is breakfast?
Um wieviel Uhr ist das Frühstück?
oom veefeel oor ist das frewshtewk

Can I/we have breakfast in the room?
Kann man im Zimmer frühstücken?
kan man im tsimmer frewshtewken

What time is dinner?
Um wieviel Uhr ist das Abendessen?
oom veefeel oor ist das aabentessen

What time does the hotel close?
Wann schließen Sie das Hotel ab?
van shleessen zee das hotel ap

I'll be back very late
Ich komme sehr spät zurück
ish komme zayr shpayt tsoorewk

Where is the bathroom?
Wo ist das Badezimmer?
voh ist das baadetsimmer

Where is the dining-room?
Wo ist das Eßzimmer?
voh ist das esstsimmer

(Key) number 42, please
(Schlüssel) Nummer zweiundvierzig, bitte
(shloossel) noommer tsviyoontfeertsig bitte

Are there any messages for me?
Hat jemand für mich angerufen?
hat yaymant fewr mish angeroofen

Can I leave this in the safe?
Kann ich das im Safe lassen?
kan ish das im sayf lassen

Can you give me my things from the safe?
Können Sie mir meine Sachen vom Safe geben?
kernnen zee meer miyne zaaken vom sayf gayben

Can you call me at eight o'clock?
Können Sie mich um acht Uhr wecken?
kernnen zee mish oom aakt oor veken

Can you order me a taxi?
Können Sie bitte ein Taxi bestellen?
kernnen zee bitte iyn taksi beshtellen

For right now
Gleich
gliysh

For tomorrow at nine o'clock
Für morgen um acht Uhr
fewr morgen oom aakt oor

Can you clean this jacket for me?
Können Sie diese Jacke für mich reinigen lassen?
kernnen zee deeze yake fewr mish riynigen lassen

Can you find me a babysitter?
Können Sie mir einen Babysitter besorgen?
kernnen zee meer iynen baybeesitter bezorgen

Can you put it on the bill, please?
Schreiben Sie es mir auf die Rechnung, bitte
shriyben zee es meer owf dee reshnoong bitte

Room number 21
Zimmer Nummer einundzwanzig
tsimmer noommer iynoonttsvantsig

I need another pillow
Ich brauche noch ein Kopfkissen
ish browke nok iyn kopfkissen

I need a towel
Ich brauche ein Handtuch
ish browke iyn hanttook

At campsites

Is there a campsite around here?
Gibt es einen Zeltplatz hier in der Nähe?
gipt es iynen tseltplatts heer in der naye

Where are the toilets?
Wo sind die Toiletten?
voh zint dee toyletten

Do we pay extra for the showers?
Müssen wir extra für die Duschen bezahlen?
mewssen veer ekstra fewr dee dooshen betsaalen

Can we camp here?
Können wir hier zelten?
kernnen veer heer tselten

Where are the showers?
Wo sind die Duschen?
voh zint dee dooshen

Is the water drinkable?
Ist das Wasser trinkbar?
ist das vasser trinkbar

Where is there an electric point?
Wo ist der Stromanschluß?
voh ist der shtromanshloos

Where are the dustbins?
Wo sind die Mülleimer?
voh zint dee mewlliymer

Self-catering accommodation

(see Directions, *page 24;* Problems and complaints, *page 170)*

I have rented a chalet
Ich habe ein Chalet gemietet
ish haabe iyn shalay gemeetet

I have rented an apartment
Ich habe eine Ferienwohnung gemietet
ish haabe iyne fayree-envohnoong gemeetet

We're in number 11
Wir sind in Nummer elf
veer zint in noommer elf

My name is . . .
Mein Name ist . . .
miyn naame ist . . .

What is the address?
Was ist die Adresse?
vas ist dee adresse

How do we get there?
Wie kommen wir dahin?
vee kommen veer daahin

Can you give me the key, please?

Können Sie mir bitte den Schlüssel geben?

kernnen zee meer bitte dayn shloossel gayben

Where is . . . ?

Wo ist . . . ?

voh ist

Where is the stopcock?

Wo ist der Abstellhahn?

voh ist der apshtellhaan

Where is the fusebox?

Wo ist der Sicherungskasten?

voh ist der zisheroongskasten

Are there any shops around here?

Gibt es irgendwelche Geschäfte hier in der Nähe?

gipt es irgentvelshe geshefte heer in der naye

How does the cooker work?

Wie funktioniert der Herd?

vee foonktsyoneert der hert

How does the water-heater work?

Wie funktioniert der Warmwasserbereiter?

vee foonktsyoneert der varmvasserberiyter

Is there air conditioning?

Gibt es eine Klimaanlaage?

gipt es iyne kleema-anlaage

Is there another gas bottle?

Gibt es eine andere Flasche Gas

gipt es iyne andere flashe gas

Are there any more blankets?

Gibt es noch Bettdecken?

gipt es nok bettdeken

When does the cleaning lady come?

Wann kommt die Putzfrau?

van kommt dee poottsfrow

Where do I/we put the rubbish?

Wo stelle ich/stellen wir den Müll hin?

voh shtelle ish/shtellen veer dayn mewll hin

When do they collect the rubbish?

Wann kommt die Müllabfuhr?

van kommt dee mewllapfoor

Where can I contact you?

Wo kann ich Sie erreichen?

voh kan ish zee erriyshen

You may hear

Kann ich Ihnen helfen?
kan ish eenen helfen
Can I help you?

Wie heißen Sie, bitte?
vee hiyssen zee bitte
What's your name, please?

Für wie viele Nächte?
fewr vee feele nekte
For how many nights?

Für wie viele Personen?
fewr vee feele perzohnen
For how many people?

Mit oder ohne Bad?
mit ohder ohne baat
With bath or without bath

Haben Sie ein großes oder ein kleines Zelt?
haaben zee iyn grohsses ohder iyn kliynes tselt
Have you got a big or a small tent?

Es tut mir leid, wir sind voll
es toot meer liyt veer zint foll
I'm sorry, we're full

Ihren Paß, bitte
eeren pass bitte
Your passport, please

Können Sie bitte hier unterschreiben?
kernnen zee bitte heer oontershriyben
Can you sign here, please?

Die Putzfrau kommt jeden (zweiten) Tag
dee poottsfrow kommt yayden (tsviyten) taag
The cleaning lady comes every (other) day

Sie kommen freitags
zee kommen friytaags
They come on Fridays

TELEPHONES

● National and international calls can be made in phone boxes with the sign **Ausland** and from post offices with coin-operated phones. Lift the receiver first and then put the money in; there are usually pictures giving operating instructions in the phone box.

● German speakers usually start a formal or business call by saying 'Here is Mr/Mrs. . .', **Hier ist Herr/Frau ...** They answer the phone by simply giving their surname.

● The number for the police is **110** and for the other emergency services, **112**. (See Emergency telephone numbers, page 288.)

● To call abroad, first dial **00**, then the code for the country – for the UK it's **44** from Germany, Austria and Switzerland. Follow this with the town code minus the 0, and then the number you want. For example: for a central London number, dial **00 44 71**, then the number.

● The numbers for directory enquiries are:
118 (for numbers within Germany)
00118 (for international numbers)

● The numbers for the emergency services in **Austria** are:
Police **133**
Fire **122**
Ambulance **144**

● It's cheaper to make calls after 6 pm and at weekends.

● If you make a call from a public telephone in Austria you may have to press an extra button, **der Zahlknopf**, to complete the connection.

● Useful telephone numbers in **Switzerland** are:
Police **117**
Fire **118**
Ambulance **144**
International Directory Enquiries **191**
Directory Enquiries **111**
Tourist Information and snow bulletin **120**
Avalanche bulletin **187**
International operator **114**

● Phone cards are available in both Austria and Switzerland
from newsagents, post offices and kiosks.

You may see

Ferngespräch	Long-distance
Inland/Ausland	Local and international calls
International	International calls
Bundespost	Telephone company
Telefon	Telephone

You may want to say

Is there a telephone?
Ist hier ein Telefon?
ist heer iyn telefohn

Where is the telephone?
Wo ist das Telefon?
voh ist das telefohn

May I use your telephone, please?
Kann ich Ihr Telefon bitte benutzen?
kan ish eer telefohn bitte benootsen

Do you have change for the telephone, please?
Haben Sie bitte Kleingeld fürs Telefon?
haaben zee bitte kliyngelt fewrz telefohn

A phone card, please
Eine Telefonkarte, bitte
iyne telefohnkarte bitte

Do you have the Bonn telephone directory?
Haben Sie das Bonner Telefonbuch?
haaben zee das bonner telefohnbook

I want to call England
Ich möchte ein Gespräch nach England machen
ish mershte iyn geshprek naak englant maaken

I want to make a reverse charge call
Ich möchte ein Rückgespräch machen
ish mershte iyn rewkgeshprek maaken

Mr Reimann, please
Herr Reimann, bitte
herr riymann bitte

Extension number 121, please
Apparat eins, zwei, eins, bitte
apparaat iyns tsviy iyns bitte

It's Mrs Stanley speaking
Hier ist Frau Stanley
heer ist frow stanley

It's Robert speaking
Hier ist Robert
heer ist rohbert

My name is . . .
Mein Name ist . . .
miyn naame ist

When will he/she be back?
Wann kommt er/sie zurück?
van kommt er/zee tsoorewk

I'll call later
Ich werde später zurückrufen
ish verde shpayter tsoorewkroofen

Can I leave a message?
Können Sie etwas für mich ausrichten?
kernnen zee etvas fewr mish owsrishten

Please tell him/her that . . . called
Bitte, sagen Sie ihm/ihr, *(your name)* **hat angerufen**
bitte zaagen zee eem/eer, . . . hat angeroofen

I am in the Hotel Bellevue
Ich wohne bei Hotel Bellevue
ish vohne biy hotel bellvew

My telephone number is . . .
Meine Telefonnummer ist . . .
miyne telefohnnoommer ist

Can he/she call me?
Kann er/sie mich anrufen?
kan er/zee mish anroofen

I beg your pardon?
Wie bitte?
vee bitte

More slowly, please
Langsamer, bitte
langzamer bitte

We were cut off
Wir sind unterbrochen worden
veer zint oonterbroken vorden

How much is the call?
Was kostet der Anruf?
vas kostet der anroof

Can you give me a number to call a taxi?
Können Sie mir eine Nummer für ein Taxi geben?
kernnen zee meer iyne noommer fewr iyn taksi gayben

You may hear

Hallo
hallo
Hello?

Reimann
riymann
Herr/Frau Reimann speaking

(Ja, ich bin) am Apparat
(yaa ich bin) am apparaat
Speaking

Wer spricht?
ver shprikt
Who's calling?

Augenblick, bitte
owgenblick bitte
One moment, please

Er/Sie ist nicht hier
er/zee ist nisht heer
He/She is not in

Bitte warten Sie einen Moment
bitte varten zee iynen mohment
Please wait

Ich verbinde Sie
ish ferbinde zee
I'm putting you through

Es ist besetzt
es ist bezettst
The line's engaged

Möchten Sie warten?
mershten zee varten
Do you want to hold?

Es meldet sich niemand
es meldet zish neemant
There's no answer

Sie haben sich verwählt
zee haaben zish fervaylt
You've got the wrong number

CHANGING MONEY

● The German unit of currency is the **Deutschmark** (abbreviated as **DM**). There are coins of 1, 2, 5, 10 and 50 **Pfennige (Pf)** and 1, 2 and 5 **DM**. There are 100 **Pfennige** in a **Deutschmark**. There are notes of 5, 10, 20, 50, 100, 500 and 1000 **DM**.

● You can change money, travellers' cheques or Eurocheques into Deutschmarks at banks and other places (hotels, travel agencies, main railway stations and airports) where you see a **Wechsel** sign. You'll probably get the best rate in a bank.

● Banks are open from 8.30 am – 12.30 pm and 2 pm – 4 pm on Mondays to Fridays. On Thursdays they stay open until 5.30 pm. They are closed on Saturdays.

● In banks you go first to the **Wechsel** desk where a form is filled in for you to sign. You then get your money from the cashier (**Kasse**). You'll need your passport to change any money.

● You can get money from banks on credit cards.

● The currency in **Austria** is the Austrian **Schilling (Sch)**. There are coins of 1, 5, 10, 20, 25, 50, 100, 500 and 1000 **Schillings** and notes of 20, 50, 100, 500 and 1000 **Schillings**. There are also 2, 5, 10 and 50 **Groschen** coins. There are 100 **Groschen** in a **Schilling**. Banks are open from 8 am to midday and from 1.30 pm – 3 pm Mondays to Fridays with late opening to 5.30 pm on Thursdays.

● The currency in **Switzerland** is the Swiss **franc**. There are coins of 5, 10, 20 and 50 **centimes**, and 1, 2 and 5 **francs**, and banknotes of 10, 20, 50, 100, 500 and 1000 **francs**. There are 100 **centimes** in a **franc**. Check locally, but normal opening times for banks are Mondays to Fridays from 7.30 am to midday and 1.45 pm – 6 pm. On Saturdays they are generally open from 7.30 am – 11 am.

You may see

Ausgang	Exit
Bank	Bank
Drücken	Press
Eingang	Entrance
EC Automat	Cash dispenser
Geöffnet	Open
Geschäftszeiten	Business hours
Geschlossen	Closed
Sparkasse	Savings bank
Wechsel	Exchange
Wechselstube	Exchange office
Ziehen	Pull

You may want to say

I'd like to change some pounds sterling
Ich möchte Sterling wechseln
ish mershte sterling vekseln

I'd like to change some travellers' cheques
Ich möchte Reiseschecks wechseln
ish mershte riyzeshecks vekseln

I'd like to change a Eurocheque
Ich möchte einen Euroscheck wechseln
ish mershte iynen oyrosheck vekseln

I'd like to get some money with my credit card
Ich möchte mit meiner Kreditkarte Geld abheben
ish mershte mit miyner kredeetkarte gelt ap-hayben

What's the exchange rate today, please?
Wie ist heute der Wechselkurs, bitte?
vee ist hoyte der vekselkoors bitte

Can you give me some change, please?
Können Sie mir bitte Kleingeld geben
kernnen zee meer bitte kliyngelt gayben

Can you give me two ten-Mark notes?
Können Sie mir bitte zwei zehn Mark Scheine geben?
kernnen zee meer bitte tsviy tsayn mark shiyne gayben

I'm at the Vierjahreszeiten
Ich wohne im Hotelvierjahreszeiten
ish vohne im hotelfeerjaarestsiyten

I'm staying with friends
Ich wohne bei Freunden
ish vohne biy froynden

The address is Steinstraße 23
Die Adresse ist Steinstraße dreiundzwanzig
dee adresse ist shtiynshtraasse driyoondtsvantsig

Here's the address
Hier ist die Adresse
heer ist dee adresse

You may hear

Ihren Paß, bitte
eeren pass bitte
Your passport, please

Wieviel möchten Sie wechseln?
veefeel mershten zee vekseln
How much do you want to change?

Ihre Adresse, bitte?
eere adresse bitte
Your address, please

Der Name Ihres Hotels, bitte?
der naame eeres hotels bitte
The name of your hotel, please

Bitte hier unterschreiben
bitte heer oontershriyben
Please sign here

Bitte zur Kasse gehen
bitte tsoor kasse gayen
Please go to the cashier

EATING AND DRINKING

● To order something, all you need do is name it, and say 'please', adding 'for me', 'for him' or 'for her' if you're ordering for several people to show who wants what.

● In bars and cafés you often pay for all your drinks and so on when you leave, though in the larger, busy bars you will probably have to pay for each round. There is always waiter service in cafés, pubs and wine bars and even though service is included in your bill, it's usual to leave a tip for your waiter or waitress. It's cheaper to drink at the bar in a pub. In restaurants service at 10 or 15 per cent is usually included, but again a tip is normal practice.

● Cafés usually open early in the morning and close at about 6.00 pm unless they're a **Bistro** as well in which case they stay open until ten or eleven at night. Restaurants serve hot meals from around midday to 2.00 pm and from 6.00 pm to nine or ten at night. Some are open all the way through the afternoon too.

● Meal times in all three countries are roughly the same as in Britain. Lunch, **Mittagessen**, is the largest meal of the day. Many Germans only have a light supper, **Abendbrot**, in the evening, unless they are eating out.

● Bars and cafés serve all kinds of drinks – alcohol, soft drinks, coffee and tea etc. Cafés usually serve cakes or flans and perhaps omelettes in the way of food. Sandwiches and rolls are often sold to take away at a **Metzgerei**, a **Feinkostgeschäft** or a **Bäckerei**. (See Shopping, page 127.)

● **Schnellimbiß, Imbißstube, Würstchenbude**: all offer a cheap but filling hot meal which might mean a plate of chips with mayonnaise, a sausage such as a **Bratwurst** or **Currywurst**, soup, omelette or potato salad. You can also get tea, coffee, bottled and canned beer and soft drinks in any of them. You can often get similar snacks in a **Kneipe** or **Wirtschaft**, including **Bratkartoffeln**, fried potatoes. In Switzerland these are known as **Rösti**. A **Weinstube** usually serves more up-market food.

● Most restaurants have waiter service. The menu should be displayed outside or in the window to give you some idea of prices before you go in. They will often provide children's portions, look for **Kinderteller** on the menu. Many of them do a special set menu, **Touristen-Menü**, and they may offer late night snacks, ask for the **kleine Karte**.

● The Germans drink excellent black and white coffee, **schwarzer Kaffee** or **Kaffee mit Sahne** (cream or tinned milk). **Cappuccinos** are popular too. In **Switzerland** coffee is usually served with warm, fresh milk.

● **Vienna** is the coffee house capital of Europe and there is such a wide selection of coffee on the menu that you need to specify when you make your order. An **Einspänner** comes in a glass with **Schlagobers** (whipped cream – known as **Schlagsahne** in Germany.) **Mokka** is strong and black, **Großer Brauner** and **Kleiner Brauner** both come with a dash of milk or cream. **Melange** is half coffee and half warm milk.

● If you ask for tea with milk, **Tee mit Milch**, you'll probably be given a little pot of long-life milk. Herbal teas such as **Kamillentee** (camomile tea), **Hagebutten** (rose-hip tea), and **Pfefferminztee** (peppermint tea) are common.

● **Heiße Schokolade**, hot chocolate, with or without whipped cream is delicious, especially in Southern Germany and Austria.

- All three countries produce their own wines. German wines include **Rheinhessen** and **Rheinpfalz**, sweet and white, and **Badischer Wein**, which is dry and white. **Veltliner** is a red or white Austrian wine.

- The German equivalent to Champagne is **Sekt**.

- **Heurigenlokale** are peculiar to Vienna and are wine bars or gardens where you can drink the year's wine harvest. Most Heurigenlokale only serve cold snacks, but you can bring your own food.

- There are all sorts of different beers and lagers in Germany. **Dunkles Bier** is dark and like brown ale. **Altbier** is like bitter; **Weizenbier** is a bitter made from barley and **Malzbier** is a dark, sweet malt beer. Draught beer is **Bier vom Faß**. The best-known lagers are probably **Pilsener**, which has quite a bitter taste, and **Export**. **Berliner Weisser** is light Berlin ale with raspberry juice and makes a very refreshing drink.

Swiss and Austrian beer are more of the lager type.

- All three countries have a wide range of fiery spirits. **Schnapps** and **Korn** are both distilled from grain and there are various different flavours. **Kirschwasser** is Black Forest brandy distilled from cherries.

- Regional food specialities vary from country to country and region to region within the different countries. **Swiss** specialities include **Raclette** and **Fondue**, both cheese dishes, and delicious pastries and cakes. **Austria** has inherited its cuisine from its once vast Empire and this is reflected in the variety of dishes on the menus. **Wiener Schnitzel** is escalope of veal in breadcrumbs. Desserts include a good choice of pancakes, **Palatschinken**, and cakes include the delicious, chocolate **Sachertorte**. **Sauerkraut**, pickled white cabbage, is eaten all over Germany and fish is popular in the north. **Aalsuppe**, eel soup, is a Hamburg speciality.

You may see

Wir nehmen Kreditkarten	We accept credit cards
Selbstbedienung	Self-service
Bar	Bar
Beisel	Pub (*Austria*)
Biergarten	Beer garden
Bierkeller	Beer cellar
Café	Café
Eisdiele	Ice-cream café
Fischrestaurant	Fish restaurant
Garderobe	Cloakroom
Gasthof	Inn
Gaststätte	Restaurant/Pub
Gastwirtschaft	Inn, guest house
Grillstube	Steak house
Hähnchen-Grill	Roast chicken takeaway
Heurigenlokal	Wine bar, garden (*Austria*)
Imbißstube	Snack bar
Kneipe	Pub
Lokal	Pub
Kaffeehaus	Café
Pizzeria	Pizzeria, eat in or takeaway
Rasthof	Motorway rest area and café
Ratskeller	Restaurant (often in basement of local town hall)
Rastplatz	Open-air snack bar; picnic area
Restaurant	Restaurant
Schnellimbiß	Snack bar
Toiletten	Toilets
Touristen-Menü	Tourist menu/set meal
Weinstube	Wine bar
Wirtschaft	Pub
Würstchenbude	Sausage and burger stand

You may want to say

General phrases

Is there an inexpensive
    restaurant around here?
(see Directions, page 24)
**Gibt es ein preiswertes
    Restaurant in der Nähe?**
*gipt es iyn priysvertes resteron
in der naye*

A (one) . . ., please
Ein/Eine . . ., bitte
iyn/iyne . . . bitte

Another . . ., please
Noch ein/eine . . ., bitte
nok iyn/iyne . . . bitte

A little more . . ., please
Ein bißchen mehr, bitte
iyn bissyen mayr bitte

A little less . . .
Ein bißchen weniger . . ., bitte
iyn bissyen vayniger, bitte

For me
Für mich
fewr mish

For him
Für ihn
fewr een

For her
Für sie
fewr zee

For them
Für sie
fewr zee

This, please
Das, bitte
das bitte

Two of these, please
Zwei davon, bitte
tsviy daafon, bitte

Do you have . . .?
Haben Sie . . .?
haaben zee

Is/Are there any . . .?
Gibt es . . .?
gipt es

What do you have for . . ./
    what kind of . . . do you
    have?
Was für . . . haben Sie?
vas fewr haaben zee

What do you have for dessert?
Was für Nachspeisen haben Sie?
vas fewr naakshpiyzen haaben zee

What kind of soups do you
    have?
Was für Suppen haben Sie ?
vas fewr zooppen haaben zee

What do you recommend?
Was können Sie mir empfehlen?
vas kernnen zee meer empfaylen

Do you have any typical
  local dishes?
**Haben Sie irgendwelche
  Spezialitäten?**
*haaben zee irgendvelshe
  shpetsee-alitayten*

What is this?
Was ist das?
vas ist das?

How do you eat this?
Wie ißt man das?
vee isst man das

Cheers!
Prost!/Zum Wohl!
prost/tsoom vohl

Enjoy your meal!
Guten Appetit!
gooten appeteet

Thank you, same to you
Danke gleichfalls
danke gliyshfalls

Where are the toilets?
Wo sind die Toiletten?
voh zint dee toyletten

Nothing else, thanks
Sonst nichts, danke
zonzt nishts danke

The bill, please
Die Rechnung, bitte
dee reshnoong bitte

Bars, cafés and snack bars

A black coffee, please
Einen schwarzen Kaffee, bitte
iynen shvartsen kaffay bitte

Two cappuccinos, please
Zwei Cappuccinos, bitte
tsviy kappoocheenos bitte

A tea with milk/lemon, please
**Einen Tee mit Milch/
  Zitrone, bitte**
iynen tay mit milsh/tsitrohne bitte

A coffee with cream, please
Einen Kaffee mit Sahne, bitte
iynen kaffay mit zaane bitte

A hot chocolate, please
Eine heiße Schokolade, bitte
iyne hiysse shokolaade bitte

Mineral water, please
Ein Mineralwasser, bitte
iyn mineraalvasser bitte

Fizzy or still?
Mit oder ohne Kohlensäure?
mit ohder ohne kohlenzoyre

A lemonade, please
Eine Limonade, bitte
iyne limonaade bitte

What fruit juices do you have?
Was für Säfte haben Sie?
vas fewr zefte haaben zee

An orange juice, please
Einen Orangensaft, bitte
iynen oronjenzaft bitte

A milk shake, please
Ein Milchshake, bitte
iyn milshshake bitte

A coke and lemonade, please
Ein Spezi, bitte
iyn shpaytsee bitte

A beer, please
Ein Bier, bitte
iyn beer bitte

A glass of red wine, please
Ein Glas Rotwein, bitte
iyn glas rohtviyn bitte

A gin and tonic, please
Ein Gin-Tonik, bitte
iyn gin-tonik bitte

With ice
Mit Eis
mit iys

A glass of water, please
Ein Glas Wasser, bitte
iyn glas vasser bitte

A cake, please
Einen Kuchen, bitte
iynen kooken bitte

A piece of cheesecake, please
Ein Stück Käsekuchen, bitte
iyn shtewk kayzekooken bitte

A piece of Black Forest
gateau, please
**Ein Stück Schwarzwälder
Kirschtorte, bitte**
*iyn shtewk shwartsvelder
kirshtorte, bitte*

A Bratwurst (spicy sausage),
please
Eine Bratwurst, bitte
iyne braatvoorst bitte

A Frankfurter, please
Eine Bockwurst, bitte
iyne bokvoorst bitte

Chips with mayonnaise and
ketchup, please
Pommes Rot-Weiß, bitte
pomm-es roht viyss bitte

What sandwiches do you have?
Was für Brötchen haben Sie?
vas fewr brertyen haaben zee

A ham roll, please
Ein Schinkenbrötchen, bitte
iyn shinkenbrertyen bitte

Two cheese rolls, please
Zwei Käsebrötchen, bitte
tsviy kayzebrertyen bitte

Do you have ice-creams?
Haben Sie Eis?
haaben zee iys

Two chocolate ice creams, please
Zwei Schokoladeneis, bitte
tsviy shokolaadeniys bitte

Booking a table

I want to reserve a table for two people
Ich möchte einen Tisch für zwei Personen reservieren lassen
ish mershte iynen tish fewr tsviy perzohnen rezerveeren lassen

For nine o'clock
Für neun Uhr
fewr noyn oor

For tomorrow evening at half past eight
Für morgen abend um halb neun
fewr morgen aabent oom halp noyn

I have booked a table
Ich habe einen Tisch reservieren lassen
ish haabe iynen tish rezerveeren lassen

My name is . . .
Mein Name ist . . .
miyn naame ist

In restaurants

A table for four, please
Ein Tisch für vier Personen, bitte
iyn tish fewr feer perzohnen bitte

Outside/On the terrace, if possible
Draußen/Auf der Terrasse, wenn's möglich ist
drowssen/owf der terrasse venns merglish ist

Excuse me!
Entschuldigen Sie bitte!
entshooldigen zee bitte

The menu, please
Die Speisekarte, bitte
dee shpiyzekarte bitte

The wine list, please
Die Weinkarte, bitte
dee viynkarte bitte

Do you have an à la carte menu?
Haben Sie eine Speisekarte?
haaben zee iyne shpiyzekarte

Do you have vegetarian dishes?
Haben Sie vegetarische Gerichte?
haaben zee vegetarishe gerishte

The tourist menu, please
Das Touristen-Menü, bitte
das tooristen menew bitte

For the starter . . .
Als Vorspeise . . .
als forshpiyze

Onion soup, please
Zwiebelsuppe, bitte
tsveebelzooppe bitte

Pickled herring, please
Rollmops, bitte
rollmops bitte

For the meat/fish course . . .
Als Hauptgericht . . .
als howptgerisht

The Wiener Schnitzel, please
Das Wienerschnitzel, bitte
das veenershnittsel bitte

The trout, please
Die Forelle, bitte
dee forelle bitte

Are vegetables included?
Kommt das mit Gemüse?
kommt das mit gemewze

Is there a salad with it?
Ist da Salat dabei?
ist da zalaat daabiy

With chips
Mit Pommes frites
mit pomme freet

And a mixed/green salad
Und ein gemischter/grüner Salat
oont iyn gemishter/grewner zalaat

For dessert . . .
Als Nachspeise . . .
als naakshpiyze

Pancake with raisins and almonds, please
Kaiserschmarren, bitte
kiyzershmarren bitte

Ice cream with hot raspberries
Vanilleeis mit heißen Himbeeren
vanilleniys mit hyssen himbeeren

What cheeses are there?
Was für Käse haben Sie ?
vas fewr kayze haaben zee

Excuse me, where is my meal?
**Entschuldigung, wo bleibt
mein Essen?**
*entshooldigoong voh bliypt
miyn essen*

More bread, please
Noch etwas Brot, bitte
nok etvas broht bitte

More chips, please
Noch Pommes frites, bitte
nok pomme freet bitte

A glass of water
Ein Glas Wasser
iyn glas vasser

A bottle of red wine
Eine Flasche Rotwein
iyne flashe rohtviyn

A bottle of white wine
Eine Flasche Weißwein
iyne flashe viyssviyn

Half a litre of white wine
Einen halben Liter Weißwein
iynen halben leeter viyssviyn

A carafe of red wine
Eine Karaffe Rotwein
iyne karaffe rohtviyn

(for ordering coffee,
see page 106)

It's very good
Es ist sehr gut
es ist zayr goot

It's really delicious
Es ist ausgezeichnet
es ist owsgetsiyshnet

This is burnt
Es ist angebrannt
es ist angebrannt

This is not cooked
Das ist nicht gar
das ist nisht gar

No, I ordered the chicken
**Nein, ich habe das Hähnchen
bestellt**
*niyn ish haabe das haynchen
beshtellt*

The bill, please
Die Rechnung, bitte
dee reshnoong bitte

Do you accept credit cards?
Nehmen Sie Kreditkarten?
naymen zee kredeetkarten

Do you accept travellers'
  cheques?
Nehmen Sie Reiseschecks?
naymen zee riyzesheks

Excuse me, there is a
  mistake here
**Entschuldigung, Sie haben
  sich hier geirrt**
*entshooldigoong zee haaben
  zish heer ge-eert*

You may hear

Bars, cafés and snack bars

Ja, bitte
yaa bitte
What can I do for you?

Sofort
zohfort
Right away

Was hätten Sie gern?
vas hetten zee gern
What would you like?

Wir haben . . .
veer haaben
We have . . .

Mit Eis?
mit iys
Would you like ice?

Welche(r)?
velshe(r)
Which one?

Mit oder ohne Kohlensäure?
mit ohder ohne kohlenzoyre
Fizzy or still?

Mit Sahne?
mit zaane
With whipped cream?

Groß oder klein?
grohss ohder kliyn
Large or small?

**Bezahlen Sie zusammen oder
  getrennt?**
*betsaalen zee tsoozammen
  ohder getrennt*
Are you paying together or
  separately?

Schoppen oder viertel?
shoppen ohder feertel
Large or small? (*wine*)

Restaurants

Für wie viele Personen?
fewr vee feele perzohnen
For how many people?

Einen Moment
iynen mohment
Just a moment

Haben Sie einen Tisch reserviert?
haaben zee iynen tish rezerveert
Have you booked a table?

Sie müßten zehn Minuten warten
zee mewssten tsayn minooten varten
You'd have to wait ten minutes

Möchten Sie warten?
mershten zee varten
Would you like to wait?

Was hätten Sie gern?
vas hetten zee gern
What would you like?

Haben Sie sich entschieden?
haaben zee zish entsheeden
Have you decided?

Wir empfehlen . . .
veer empfaylen
We recommend . . .

Als Vorspeise
als forshpiyze
For the starter

Als Hauptgericht
als howptgerisht
For the main course

Als Nachspeise
als naakshpiyze
For dessert

Was möchten Sie trinken?
vas mershten zee trinken
To drink?

Für wen war . . .?
fewr vayn var
Who was the . . . for?

Schmeckt es Ihnen?
shmekt es eenen
Are you enjoying your food?

Möchten Sie eine Nachspeise?
mershten zee iyne naakshpiyze
Would you like a dessert?

Sind Sie fertig?
zint zee fertig
Have you finished?

Sonst noch etwas?
zonst nok etvas
Anything else?

Haben Sie noch einen Wunsch?
haaben zee nok iynen voonsh
Anything else?

112

MENU READER

General Phrases

Abendessen	Dinner
Bedienung inbegriffen	Service included
Beilage	Side dish or garnish
Eintopfgerichte	Stews
Eierspeisen	Egg dishes
Eis	Ice cream
Extraaufschlag	Supplementary charge
Fischgerichte	Fish dishes
Fleischgerichte	Meat dishes
Frühstück	Breakfast
Gemüse	Vegetables
Getränke	Drinks
Im Preis inbegriffen	Included in the price
Käse	Cheese
Mehlspeisen	Desserts *(Austria)*
Mehrwertsteuer inklusiv	VAT inclusive
Mittagessen	Lunch
Nachspeisen	Desserts
Nach Wahl	According to choice
Obst	Fruit
Salatteller	Salads
Schoppenkarte	Wine list
Spezialität des Hauses	Speciality of the house
Suppen	Soups
Süßspeisen	Desserts
Vorspeisen	Starters
Tagesgedeck	Set menu
Tagesgericht	Dish of the day
Touristen-Menü	Tourist menu
Weinkarte	Wine list
Wild und Geflügel	Game and poultry

Drinks

Bier	Beer
Alsterwasser	Shandy *(north Germany)*
Altbier	Bitter with high hop content
Altbierbowle	Bitter punch with bits of pineapple
Berliner Weisser	Light Berlin ale with raspberry juice
Bockbier	Strong, malt beer
Doppelbock	Strong, malt Munich beer
dunkles Bier	Dark, strong beer
Kupferbier	Dark, malt beer
Malzbier	Dark, sweet malt beer
Märzen	Strong, malt, Munich beer
Pilsener	Strong, hoppy lager
Radler(maß)	(a litre of) Shandy
Weißbier	Yeasty beer brewed with wheat
Weizenbier	Light beer brewed with wheat
Bommerlunder	Caraway brandy
Danziger Goldwasser	Aniseed liqueur
Dornkaat	German gin
Fruchtsaft	Fruit juice
Apfelsaft	Apple juice
Johannisbeersaft	Red- or blackcurrant juice
Orangensaft	Orange juice
Tomatensaft	Tomato juice
Traubensaft	Grape juice
Eierlikör	Egg nog
Gespritzter Wein (süß oder sauer)	White wine with lemonade (süß) or mineral water (sauer)
Glühwein	Mulled wine
Heidelbeergeist	Blueberry brandy
Heiße Schokolade	Hot chocolate

Himbeergeist	Raspberry brandy
Kaffee	Coffee
Einspänner	Black coffee with whipped cream
Expresso	Strong, black espresso coffee
großer Brauner	Large black coffee with a dash of milk
großer Schwarzer	Large black coffee
kleiner Brauner	Small black coffee with a dash of milk
koffeinfrei	Decaffeinated
Melange	Half coffee, half warm milk
mit Sahne	With cream (white coffee)
Mokka	Strong black coffee
Kirschwasser	Cherry brandy
Korn	Distilled grain spirit
Weizenkorn	Distilled wheat spirit
Limonade	Lemonade
Milchmixgetränk	Milk shake
Mineralwasser	Mineral water
mit Kohlensäure	Fizzy
ohne Kohlensäure	Still
Orangeade	Orangeade
Pflümliwasser	Plum brandy
Sekt	German equivalent to Champagne
Schnapps	Brandy
Apfelschnapps	Apple brandy
Steinhäger	Juniper berry brandy (like gin)

Tee	Tea
Eistee	Iced tea
Hagebuttentee	Rose-hip tea
Kamillentee	Camomile tea
Kräutertee	Herb tea
mit Milch	With milk (usually condensed milk)
mit Zitrone	With lemon
Wein	
Auslese	Medium dry wine made with late grapes
Beerenauslese	Medium sweet wine made with overripe grapes
herb	Dry
lieblich	Sweet
Rotwein	Red wine
Spätlese	Dry wine made with late grapes
süß	Sweet
trocken	Dry
Trockenbeerenauslese	Sweet dessert wine made with dried grapes
vollmundig	Full bodied
Weißwein	White wine
Schaumwein	Sparkling wine
Weinbrand	Brandy

Food

Aal	Eel
Räucheraal	Smoked eel
Altenburger	Mild goat's cheese
Ananas	Pineapple
Apfel	Apple
Apfelmus	Apple sauce
Apfelsine	Orange

Apfelstrudel	Apple, nuts and raisins sandwiched between thin layers of pastry
Appenzeller	Mild, firm Swiss cheese
Aprikose	Apricot
Artischocke	Artichoke
Aubergine	Aubergine
Auflauf	Soufflé
Aufschnitt	Sliced cold meat and sausage
Austern	Oysters
Backpflaumen	Prunes
Backsteinkäse	Strong, Bavarian cheese
Bananen	Bananas
Barsch	Freshwater perch
Basilikum	Basil
Bauernfrühstück	*(lit. farmer's breakfast)* Egg, bacon and potatoes
Bauernomelett	Bacon and onion omelette
Bauernschmaus	Sauerkraut with bacon, sausages, pork, dumpling and potatoes
Belegtes Brot	Open sandwich
Berliner	Jam doughnut
Berner Platte	Sauerkraut (or green beans) with various cooked meats (pork, beef, sausages, bacon)
Bienenstich	Honey and almond cake
Birne	Pear
Bismarckhering	Pickled herring with onions
Blumenkohl	Cauliflower
Bohnen	Beans
grüne Bohnen	Green (French) beans
Bouillon	Broth, consommé
Bratkartoffeln	Fried potatoes

Braten	Roast meat
Hackbraten	Meatloaf
Jungfernbraten	Roast pork with bacon
Rostbraten	Rump steak
Sauerbraten	Marinated, braised beef
Brombeeren	Blackberries
Brot	Bread
Roggenbrot	Rye bread
Schwarzbrot	Black bread, pumpernickel
Vollkornbrot	Wholemeal bread
Brötchen	Bread roll
Brühe	Broth
Champignons	Button mushrooms
Datteln	Dates
Deutschesbeefsteak	Hamburger
Dorsch	Cod
Eier	Eggs
Rührei	Scrambled egg
Spiegelei	Fried egg
Eintopf	Stew
Eis	Ice cream
Eisbecher	Ice cream sundae
Eisbein	Pig's knuckle
Eisbombe	Ice bomb
Emmentaler	Mild, Swiss cheese
Ente	Duck
Erbsen	Peas
Erdapfel	Potato *(Austria)*
Erdbeeren	Strawberries
Fasan	Pheasant
Feigen	Figs
Fisolen	French beans *(Austria)*
Fondue	Hot melted cheese dip with white wine, kirsch and a touch of garlic *(Switzerland)*

Forelle	Trout
Frikadellen	Meatballs
Froschschenkel	Frogs' legs
Frucht	Fruit
nach Jahreszeit	Seasonal fruit
Gans	Goose
Gedämpft	Steamed
Gedünstet	Steamed
Gefüllt	Stuffed
Geräuchert	Smoked
Gewürzt	Spicy
Götterspeise	*(lit. food of the gods)* Jelly
Granatrührei	Scrambled egg with prawns
Hackfleisch	Mince
Hähnchen	Chicken
Hase	Hare, rabbit
Hausfrauenart	Served with apple, sour cream and onions
Hausgemacht	Homemade
Heilbutt	Halibut
Hendl	Chicken *(Austria)*
Hering	Herring
Himbeeren	Raspberries
Himmel und Erde	*(lit. heaven and earth)* Bacon and meat casserole with apple sauce
Hoppel-Poppel	Scrambled egg with diced bacon and sausage
Hühnchen	Chicken
Hummer	Lobster
Hummerkrabben	King prawns
Ingwer	Ginger
Jägerart	*(lit. hunter's style)* Served in red wine sauce with mushrooms
Jakobsmuscheln	Scallops
Johannisbeeren	Red or Blackcurrants

Kabeljau	Cod
Kaiserschmarren	Shredded sweet pancake with raisins
Kalbfleisch	Veal
Kalbmilch	Veal sweetbreads
Kalbsrolle	Braised stuffed veal roll
Kaninchen	Rabbit
Karfiol	Cauliflower
Karpfen	Carp
Karotten	Carrots
Kartoffeln	Potatoes
Pellkartoffeln	Potatoes boiled in their skins
Petersilienkartoffeln	Boiled potatoes with parsley and butter
Salzkartoffeln	Boiled potatoes
Kartoffelbrei	Mashed potatoes
Kartoffelpuffer mit Apfelmus	Potato pancakes with apple sauce
Käse	Cheese
Käsesahne	Fresh creamy curd cheese gateau
Käseschnitte	Open, melted cheese sandwich
Käseteller	Plate of assorted cheeses, probably including Emmentaler
Käsewähe	Hot cheese tart
Kasseler Rippen	Roast smoked loin of pork
Kastanien	Chestnuts
Kirschen	Cherries
Knoblauch	Garlic
Klöße	Dumplings
Knödel	Dumplings
Kohl	Cabbage
Kohlroulade	Cabbage leaves stuffed with minced meat

Kohlrabi	Kohlrabi (cross between cabbage and turnip)
Kompott	Stewed fruit
Königinpastete	Puff pastry filled with chopped meat and mushrooms
Königsberger Klopse	Meatballs in white caper sauce
Kotelett	Chop
Sülzkotelett	Pork chop in aspic
Krabben	Prawns
Kraftbrühe	Beef consommé
mit Einlage	With a garnish
Kräuter	Herbs
Kräuterbutter	Garlic butter
Krebs	Crab, crayfish
Kren	Horseradish *(Austria)*
Kuchen	Cake
Kümmelkäse	Mild cheese with caraway seeds
Kürbis	Pumpkin
Labskaus	Thick stew of minced meat with mashed potatoes
Lachs	Salmon
Lammfleisch	Lamb
Lammkeule	Leg of lamb
Lauch	Leek
Lende	Loin
Mais	Sweetcorn
Makrele	Mackerel
Mandeln	Almonds
Marillen	Apricots *(Austria)*
Mark	Bone marrow
Matjeshering	Young, salted herring
Meeresfrüchte	Sea food
Meerrettich	Horseradish

Melone	Melon
Möhren	Carrots
Mohrrüben	Carrots
Mus	Puréed stewed fruit
Nelken	Cloves
Nieren	Kidneys
Nockerl	Dumpling
Grießnockerl	Semolina dumpling
Salzburgernockerl	Sweet egg soufflé flavoured with vanilla
Nürnbergerbratwurst	Nuremberg sausage cooked on a charcoal grill
Nudeln	Pasta
Nuß	Nut
Haselnuß	Hazelnut
Muskatnuß	Nutmeg
Walnuß	Walnut
Nußstrudel	Flaky pastry with nuts and honey
Oliven	Olives
Palatschinken	Pancakes *(Austria)*
Pampelmuse	Grapefruit
Paniert	Cooked in egg and breadcrumbs
Paradeiser	Tomatoes
Petersilie	Parsley
Pfannkuchen	Pancakes
Pfeffersteak	Steak covered with half peppercorns
Pfirsich	Peach
Pflaumen	Plums
Pichelsteiner Fleisch	Mixed meat and vegetable stew
Pilze	Mushrooms
Pommes frites	Chips
Porree	Leek
Powidl	Plum

Powidltatschkerln	Pancake with a plum filling
Preiselbeeren	Cranberries
Pudding	Blancmange
Pute	Turkey
Quark	Curd cheese (fromage frais)
Quarkspeise	Dessert made with quark and (usually) fruit
Rahm	Cream
Rebhuhn	Partridge
Reh	Venison
Rehrücken	Saddle of venison
Reis	Rice
Rhabarber	Rhubarb
Rindfleisch	Beef
Rohschinken	Cured ham
Rollmops	Pickled herring wrapped round slices of onion
Rosenkohl	Brussels sprout
Rosinen	Raisins
Rösti	Fried potatoes *(Switzerland)*
Rote Beete	Beetroot
Rote Grütze	Red fruit jelly
Rotkohl	Red cabbage
Rouladen	Slices of rolled beef or veal in gravy
Russische Eier	Hard boiled eggs with mayonnaise
Sahne	Cream
Schlagsahne	Whipped cream
Salat	Salad
gemischter Salat	Mixed salad
grüner Salat	Green salad
Kopfsalat	Lettuce salad
Obstsalat	Fruit salad
russischer Salat	Diced vegetables in mayonnaise

Salbei	Sage
Sardellen	Anchovies
Sauerkraut	Pickled white cabbage
Schinken	Ham
Schlachtplatte	Assorted cold meat and sausages
Schlagobers	Whipped cream *(Austria)*
Schmelzkäse	Soft cheese, used in cooking
Schnitzel	Escalope (usually veal)
Holsteiner Schnitzel	Veal cutlet in breadcrumbs with vegetables and a fried egg on top
Rahmschnitzel	Escalope of veal in cream sauce
Wienerschnitzel	Escalope of veal cooked in egg and breadcrumbs
Schnecken	Snails
Weinbergschnecken	Snails with garlic, herbs and butter
Schnittlauch	Chives
Schokolade	Chocolate
Scholle	Plaice
Schwarzwälderkirschtorte	Black Forest gateau
Schweinefleisch	Pork
Seebarsch	Sea bass
Sellerie	Celery
Semmel	Bread roll *(Austria)*
Soße	Sauce
Spargel	Asparagus
Spargelspitzen	Asparagus tips
Spätzle	Tiny dumplings
Speck	Smoked bacon
Spinat	Spinach
Stachelbeeren	Gooseberries
Steinbutt	Turbot
Stelze	Pig's knuckle *(Austria)*

Stollen	Cake with almonds, nuts and candied and dried fruits (often eaten at Christmas)
Strammer Max	Raw ham and fried eggs served on rye bread
Streuselkuchen	Cake with a butter, sugar, flour and cinammon topping
Suppe	Soup
Aalsuppe	Eel soup
Baselermehlsuppe	Thick soup with grated cheese *(Switzerland)*
Bohnensuppe	Bean soup
Fischbeuschelsuppe	Fish roe and vegetable soup
Frühlingssuppe	Spring vegetable soup
Königinsuppe	Soup with beef, sour cream and almonds
Leberknödelsuppe	Soup with liver dumplings
Linsensuppe	Lentil soup
Ochsenschwanzsuppe	Oxtail soup
Paradeissuppe	Tomato soup
Schildkrötensuppe	Turtle soup
Serbischebohnensuppe	Spicy Serbian bean soup
Tomatensuppe	Tomato soup
Teig	Dough
Teigwaren	Pasta
Thunfisch	Tuna fish
Tomaten	Tomatoes
Topfen	Curd cheese *(Austria)*
Topfenstrudel	Thin layers of pastry filled with curd cheese
Torte	Gateau, flan
Linzertorte	Almond flan with a raspberry topping
Sachertorte	Rich chocolate cake (from Sacher's café in Vienna)
Truthahn	Turkey

Überbacken	Baked
Weintrauben	Grapes
Wildschwein	Wild boar
Windbeutel	Cream puff
Wurst	Sausage
Bierwurst	Smoked pork and beef sausage
Blutwurst	Black pudding
Bockwurst	Frankfurter
Bratwurst	Spicy, fried sausage
Currywurst	Curry sausage
Jagdwurst	Smoked sausage with garlic and mustard
Rauchwurst	Smoked sausage
Weißwurst	Veal, bacon, parsley and onion sausage
Wienerli	Vienna-style frankfurter
Zervelat	Spicy smoked sausage
Zimt	Cinnamon
Zitrone	Lemon
Zucchini	Courgettes
Zwetschken	Plums *(Austria)*
Zwiebel	Onion

SHOPPING

● There are local variations in shop opening times, but in general shops are open from 9.00 am–6.30 pm on Mondays to Fridays, and from 9.00 am–2.00 pm on Saturdays. On the first Saturday of every month, **langer Samstag**, shops stay open until 6.00 pm. Shops in towns and cities don't usually close for lunch.

● Chemists, **Apotheken**, have the same opening hours as shops, though they are closed on Wednesdays. Addresses of emergency and late chemists can be found in the local newspapers or on the door. You need a prescription to get medicines from an **Apotheke**. No prescription is needed in a **Drogerie** which also sells cosmetics, perfumes and health foods. A **Parfümerie** only sells perfume and cosmetics.

● Films can be developed at photo shops, in a **Drogerie** or in large department stores. Films tend to be cheaper in Germany but developing more expensive.

● You can buy stamps at Post Offices or anywhere where you buy postcards. There are sometimes stamp machines next to post boxes.

● There are regular fruit and vegetable markets in most towns. At weekends there are flea markets, **Flohmärkte**, in many of the big cities. You can pick up bargains in the way of clothes, jewellery, antiques, books and memorabilia.

● Shops are open in **Austria** from seven or eight in the morning until six or six-thirty at night. Outside the cities they usually close at lunch times. Saturday opening hours vary but are generally from 8.00 am to midday. Some shops in Austria display a 'tax free' sticker which means that customers are entitled to a VAT refund on goods bought there. To claim the refund, fill in a customs declaration form on leaving the country.

● In **Switzerland** shops are open from 8.00 am to midday and then from 1.30 pm to 6.30 pm or 4.00 pm on Saturdays. Shops may close on Monday afternoons. You can only buy stamps from Post Offices which are open from 7.30 am–midday and from 1.45 pm to 6.30 pm. Most close at 11.00 am on Saturdays. There are stamp machines at railway stations and airports.

You may see

Antiquitäten	Antiques
Andenkenladen	Souvenirs
Ausverkauf	Sale
Bäckerei	Baker's
Bitte nicht berühren	Please do not touch
Boutique	Clothes/Fashions
Buchhandlung	Bookshop
Delikatessen	Delicatessen
Drogerie	Drugstore
Duchgehend geöffnet	Open all day
Eingang	Entrance
Eisenwarenhandlung	Ironmonger's/Hardware
Elektrogeschäft	Electrical goods
Feinkostgeschäft	Delicatessen
Fischladen	Fishmonger's
Fleischerei	Butcher's
Friseursalon	Hairdresser's
Geöffnet	Open
Geschäftszeiten	Business hours
Geschenkartikel	Gift shop/Souvenirs
Geschlossen	Closed
Haushaltswarenhandlung	Hardware
Juwelier	Jeweller's
Im Angebot	On offer
Kasse	Cashier
Kein Ausgang	No exit
Kein Eingang	No entry

Konditorei	Cake shop
Lebensmittelgeschäft	Groceries
Lederwaren	Leather goods
Metzgerei	Butcher's
Möbelgeschäft	Furniture
Modegeschäft	Clothes/Fashions
Nachtdienst/Sontagsdienst	Duty Chemist's (or doctor's)
(Not)ausgang	(Emergency) Exit
Obst- und Gemüsehandlung	Fruit/Fruiterer's
Optiker	Optician's
Parfümerie	Perfumery
Photogeschäft	Photo shop
Postamt	Post Office
Reformhaus	Health foods
Reinigung	Dry-cleaner's
Schallplatten	Records
Schlußverkauf	Sale
Schreibwarengeschäft	Stationer's
Schuhgeschäft	Shoe shop
Selbstbedienungsladen	Self-service shop
Spielwarengeschäft	Toy shop
Sportgeschäft	Sports goods
Supermarkt	Supermarket
Süßwarenladen	Confectioner's
Tabakladen	Tobacconist's
Uhrmacher	Watchmaker's
Umkleidekabine	Fitting rooms
Warenhaus	Department store
Weinhandlung	Wine shop
Zeitungshändler	Newsagent's

You may want to say

General phrases

(See also Directions, *page 24*; Problems and complaints, *page 170*; Numbers, *page 211)*

Where is . . .
Wo ist . . .
voh ist

Where is the main shopping area?
Wo ist die Einkaufsstraße?
voh ist dee iynkowfsshtraasse

Where is the chemist's?
Wo ist die Apotheke?
voh ist dee apotayke

Is there a food shop around here?
Gibt es ein Lebensmittel-geschäft in der Nähe?
gipt es iyn laybenzmittelgesheft in der naye

Where can I buy batteries?
Wo kann ich Batterien kaufen?
voh kan ish batteree-en kowfen

I'd like . . .
Ich möchte . . .
ish mershte

Have you got . . .?
Haben Sie . . .?
haaben zee

Have you got stamps?
Haben Sie Briefmarken?
haaben zee breefmarken

How much is it?/How much does it cost?
Was kostet es . . .?
vas kostet es

How much do they cost?
Was kosten sie?
vas kosten zee

How much does it come to?
Was macht das?
vas maakt das?

I don't understand
Ich verstehe nicht
ish fershtaye nisht

Can you write it down please?
Können Sie es bitte aufschreiben?
kernnen zee es bitte owfshriyben

It's too expensive
Es ist zu teuer
es ist tsoo toyer

Have you got anything cheaper?
Haben Sie etwas Billigeres?
haaben zee etvas billigeres

I don't have enough money
Ich habe nicht genug Geld
ish haabe nisht genoog gelt

Can you keep it for me?
Können Sie es für mich zurücklegen?
kernnen zee es fewr mish tsoorewklaygen

When do you open in the morning?
Wann machen Sie morgens auf?
van maaken zee morgenz owf

When do you close?
Wann machen Sie zu?
van maaken zee tsoo

What time . . .?
Um wieviel Uhr . . .?
oom veefeel oor

What time does the Post Office open?
Um wieviel Uhr macht die Post auf?
oom veefeel oor maakt dee post owf

Do you close for lunch?
Schließen Sie mittags?
shleessen zee mittaags

I'm just looking
Ich sehe mich nur um
ish zaye mish noor oom

I'll have to think about it
Ich muß darüber nachdenken
ish muss darewber naakdenken

That one there, please
Das da bitte
das daa bitte

This one here, please
Dies hier bitte
dees heer bitte

Two of those, please
Zwei von denen bitte
tsviy fon daynen bitte

Some of these, please
Einige von diesen bitte
iynige fon deezen bitte

A bit of that, please
Ein bißchen von dem bitte
iyn bissyen fon daym bitte

What is this?
Was ist das?
vas ist das

Can I try it?
Kann ich das probieren?
kan ish das probeeren

Not that one – this one here
Nicht das – dieser hier
nisht das – deezer heer

There's one in the window
Es ist im Schaufenster
es ist im showfenster

A bag please
Eine Tüte bitte
iyne tewte bitte

The receipt please
Die Quittung bitte
dee kvittoong bitte

It's a gift
Es ist ein Geschenk
es ist iyn geshenk

I'm taking it to England
Ich nehme es nach England mit
ish nayme es naak englant mit

Can you wrap it please?
Können Sie es bitte verpacken?
kernnen zee es bitte ferpaken

With lots of paper, please
Mit viel Papier bitte
mit feel papeer bitte

Where is the cash desk?
Wo ist die Kasse?
voh ist dee kasse

Do you take credit cards?
Nehmen Sie Kreditkarten?
naymen zee kredeetkarten

Do you take travellers' cheques?
Nehmen Sie Reiseschecks?
naymen zee riyzesheks

I'm sorry, I don't have any change
Es tut mir leid, ich habe kein Kleingeld
es toot meer liyt ish haabe kiyn kliyngelt

That's fine
Das ist in Ordnung
das ist in ortnoong

I'll take it
Ich nehme es
ish nayme es

Nothing else, thank you
Das ist alles
das ist alles

Buying food and drink

A kilo of . . . please
Ein Kilo . . . bitte
iyn keeloh . . . bitte

A kilo of cherries, please
Ein Kilo Kirschen, bitte
iyn keeloh keershen bitte

2 kilos of apples, please
Zwei Kilo Äpfel, bitte
tsviy keeloh epfel bitte

Half a kilo of courgettes, please
Ein halbes Kilo Zucchini, bitte
iyn halbes keeloh tsookeenee bitte

A pound of tomatoes, please
Ein Pfund Tomaten, bitte
iyn pfoont tomaaten bitte

A hundred grams of . . . please
Hundert Gramm . . . bitte
hoondert gramm . . . bitte

A hundred grams of olives,
    please
Hundert Gramm Oliven, bitte
hoondert gramm oleeven bitte

Two hundred grams of liver
    sausage, please
**Zweihundert Gramm
    Leberwurst, bitte**
*tsviyhoondert gramm
    laybervoorst bitte*

A piece of cheese, please
Ein Stück Käse, bitte
iyn shtewk kayze bitte

Five slices of ham, please
**Fünf Scheiben Schinken,
    bitte**
fewnf shiyben shinken bitte

A bottle of water, please
Eine Flasche Wasser, bitte
iyne flashe vasser bitte

A litre of wine, please
Ein Liter Wein, bitte
iyn leeter viyn bitte

Half litre of milk, please
Einen halben Liter Milch, bitte
iynen halben leeter milsh bitte

A crate of beer, please
Einen Kasten Bier, bitte
iynen kasten beer bitte

A bit more, please
Ein bißchen mehr, bitte
iyn bissyen mayr bitte

A bit less, please
Ein bißchen weniger, bitte
iyn bissyen vayniger bitte

That's enough, thank you
Das ist genug, danke
das ist genoog danke

That's all, thank you
Das wär's, danke
das vayrz danke

What's this like?
Wie ist das?
vee ist das

What's this made of?
Aus was ist das gemacht?
ows vas ist das gemaakt

At the chemist's

Aspirins/plasters, please
Aspirin/Pflaster, bitte
aspeereen/pflaster, bitte

Have you got something for . . .
Haben Sie etwas für . . .
haaben zee etvas fewr . . .

Have you got something for
sunburn?
**Haben Sie etwas für
Sonnenbrand**
*haaben zee etvas fewr
zonnenbrannt*

Have you got something for
diarrhoea?
**Haben Sie etwas für
Durchfall?**
*haaben zee etvas fewr
doorshfall*

Have you got something for
period pains?
**Haben Sie etwas für
Regelschmerzen?**
*haaben zee etvas fewr
raygelshmertsen*

Buying clothes and shoes

I'd like a skirt
Ich möchte einen Rock
ish mershte iynen rok

I'm looking for a suit
Ich möchte einen Anzug
ish mershte iynen antsoog

My size is . . .
Meine Größe ist . . .
miyne grersse ist

Can I try it on?
Kann ich das anprobieren?
kan ish das anprohbeeren

Can I try them on?
Kann ich sie anprobieren
kan ish zee anprohbeeren

Is there a mirror?
Gibt es einen Spiegel?
gipt es iynen shpeegel

I like it
Es gefällt mir
es gefellt meer

I don't like it
Es gefällt mir nicht
es gefellt meer nisht

It's very nice
Es ist sehr schön
es ist zayr shern

They're very nice
Sie sind sehr schön
zee zint zayr shern

Fine
Sehr gut
zayr goot

It's too big
Es ist zu groß
es ist tsoo grohss

They're too big
Sie sind zu groß
zee zint tsoo grohss

It's too small
Es ist zu klein
es ist tsoo kliyn

They're too small
Sie sind zu klein
zee zint tsoo kliyn

What size is it?
Welche Größe ist es?
velshe grersse ist es

Have you got size 42?
Haben Sie Größe zweiundvierzig?
haaben zee grersse tsviyoontfeertsig

Have you got a smaller size?
Haben Sie es kleiner?
haaben zee es kliyner

Have you got a bigger size?
Haben Sie es größer?
haaben zee es grersser

Have you got another colour?
Haben Sie eine andere Farbe?
haaben zee iyne andere farbe

Can you measure me, please?
Können Sie meine Größe bitte messen?
kernnen zee miyne grersse bitte messen

Miscellaneous

Five stamps for England, please
Fünf Briefmarken für England bitte
fewnf breefmarken fewr englant bitte

For letters/postcards
Für Briefe/Postkarten
fewr breefe/postkarten

Three postcards, please
Drei Postkarten bitte
driy postkarten bitte

Have you got an English newspaper?
Haben Sie eine englische Zeitung?
haaben zee iyne englishe tsiytoong

Matches, please
Streichhölzer bitte
shtriykherltser bitte

A film for this camera, please
Ein Film für diese Kamera bitte
iyn film fewr deeze kamera bitte

You may hear

Darf ich Ihnen helfen?
darf ish eenen helfen
May I help you?

Haben Sie Kleingeld?
haaben zee kliyngelt
Have you got any change?

Was möchten Sie?
vas mershten zee
What would you like?

Bezahlen Sie bar?
betsaalen zee bar
Are you paying cash?

Wieviel möchten Sie?
veefeel mershten zee
How much would you like?

Sie brauchen dafür ein Rezept
zee browken daafewr iyn raytsept
You need a prescription for that

Wie viele möchten Sie?
vee feele mershten zee
How many would you like?

Welche Größe haben Sie?
velshe grersse haaben zee
What size are you?

Sonst noch etwas?
zonst nok etvas
Anything else?

Postkarte oder Brief?
postkarte ohder breef
Postcard or letter?

Es tut mir leid, wir sind ausverkauft
es toot meer liyt veer zint owsferkowft
I'm sorry, we're sold out

Was für . . .
vas fewr
What sort of . . .

Was für eine Kamera haben Sie
vas fewr iyne kamera haaben zee
What sort of camera do you have?

Es tut mir leid, wir sind jetzt zu
es toot meer liyt veer zint jetst tsoo
I'm sorry, we're closed now

Was für einen Film möchten Sie?
vas fewr iynen film mershten zee
What sort of film do you want?

Soll ich das verpacken?
zoll ish das ferpaken
Shall I wrap it for you?

BUSINESS TRIPS

● You'll probably be doing business with the help of interpreters or in a language everyone speaks, but you may need a few German phrases to cope at a company's reception desk.

● Women are usually referred to as **Frau** whether they are married or not. If someone has **Doktor** in their title they are referred to as either **Herr Doktor . . .** or **Frau Doktor . . . .** The same applies to **Professor**.

● When you arrive for an appointment, all you need do is say who you've come to see and give your name or hand over your business card. However, if you're not expected you may need to make an appointment or leave a message.

● It is important to be punctual for business appointments in Germany.

You may see

AG (Aktiengesellschaft)	Joint stock company
Außer Betrieb	Out of order
Drücken	Press, push
Eingang	Entrance
Erdgeschoß	Ground floor
Erster Stock	1st floor
Fahrstuhl	Lift
Gesellschaft	Company
G.m.b.H. = Gesellschaft mit beschränkter Haftung	Limited company
Rauchen verboten	No smoking
Treppe	Stairs
Zutritt verboten	No entry
Empfang/Rezeption	Reception
(Not)Ausgang	(Emergency) exit
Ziehen	Pull
Zweiter Stock	2nd floor

You may want to say

(See also Days, months, dates, *page 189;* Time, *page 193*)

Mr Kochmann, please
Herr Kochmann, bitte
herr kokmann bitte

Dr Paulick, please
Frau Doktor Paulick, bitte
frow doktor powlick bitte

Mrs Gromm, please
Frau Gromm, bitte
frow gromm bitte

The manager, please
Den Geschäftsführer, bitte
dayn gesheftsfewrer bitte

My name is ...
Mein Name ist ...
miyn naame ist

I work for ...
Ich arbeite bei ...
ish arbiyte biy

I have an appointment with
Mr Dieter Kochmann
**Ich habe einen Termin mit
Herrn Dieter Kochmann**
*ish haabe iynen termeen mit
herrn deeter kokmann*

I don't have an appointment
Ich habe keinen Termin
ish haabe kiynen termeen

I'd like ...
Ich möchte ...
ish mershte

I'd like to make an
appointment with Mrs
Gromm
**Ich möchte einen Termin mit
Frau Gromm vereinbaren**
*ish mershte iynen termeen mit
frow gromm feriynbaren*

I'd like to talk to the export
manager
**Ich möchte den
Exportmanager sprechen**
*ish mershte dayn
eksportmanager shpreken*

What is his/her name?
Wie heißt er/sie?
vee hiysst er/zee

When will he/she be back?
Wann kommt er/sie zurück?
van kommt er/zee tsoorewk

I am free this afternoon at
five o'clock
**Ich bin heute nachmittag um
fünf Uhr frei**
*ish bin hoyte naakmittag oom
fewnf oor friy*

Can I leave a message?
Können Sie etwas ausrichten?
kernnen zee etvas owsrishten

Can he/she call me?
Kann er/sie mich anrufen?
kan er/zee mish anroofen

My telephone number is . . .
Meine Telefonnummer ist . . .
miyne telefohnnoommer ist

I am staying at the Hotel Excelsior
Ich wohne im Hotel Excelsior
ish vohne im hotel exchelsior

Where is his/her office?
Wo ist sein/ihr Büro?
voh ist ziyn/eer bewroh

I am here for the exhibition
Ich bin für die Ausstellung hier
ish bin fewr dee owsshtelloong heer

I am here for the trade fair
Ich bin für die Messe hier
ish bin fewr dee messe heer

I am attending the conference
Ich besuche die Konferenz
Ish bezooke dee konferents

I need to make a phone call (to Britain)
Ich muß (nach Großbritannien) telefonieren
ish mooss (naak grossbritannee-en) telefohneeren

I need to send a telex
Ich muß ein Telex schicken
ish moos iyn teleks shiken

I need to send this by fax
Ich muß das mit Telefax schicken
ish moos das mit telefaks shiken

I need to send this by post
Ich muß das mit der Post schicken
ish moos das mit der post shiken

I need to send this by courier
Ich muß das mit dem Kurier schicken
ish mooss das mit daym koorier shiken

I need a photocopy (of this)
Ich brauche (davon) eine Fotokopie
ish browke (daafon) iyne fotokopee

I need an interpreter
Ich brauche einen Dolmetscher
ish browke iynen dolmecher

Can someone type a letter for me?
Kann jemand einen Brief für mich tippen?
kan yaymant iynen breef fewr mish tippen

You may hear

Ihr Name bitte?
eer naame bitte
Your name, please?

Wie heißen Sie, bitte?
vee hiyssen zee bitte
What is your name, please?

Wie heißt Ihre Gesellschaft?
vee hiysst eere gezellshaft
The name of your company, please?

Haben Sie einen Termin?
haaben zee iynen termeen
Do you have an appointment?

Haben Sie eine Geschäftskarte?
haaben zee iyne gesheftskarte
Do you have a card?

Werden Sie erwartet?
verden zee ervartet
Is he/she expecting you?

(Warten Sie) einen Augenblick bitte
(varten zee) iynen owgenblick bitte
(Wait) one moment, please

Ich sage ihm/ihr, daß Sie hier sind
ish zaage eem/eer dass zee heer zint
I'll tell him/her you're here

Er/sie kommt gleich
er/zee kommt gliysh
He/she's just coming

Bitte nehmen Sie Platz
bitte naymen zee platts
Please sit down

Möchten Sie sich setzen?
mershten zee zish zettsen
Would you like to sit down?

Gehen Sie bitte hinein
gayen zee bitte hiniyn
Go in, please

Kommen Sie bitte mit
kommen zee bitte mit
Come with me, please

Herr Kochmann ist nicht da
herr kokmann ist nisht daa
Mr Kochmann isn't in

Frau Doktor Paulick kommt um elf zurück
frow doktor powlick kommt oom elf tsoorewk
Dr Paulick will be back at eleven

In einer halben Stunde/in einer Stunde
in iyner halben shtoonde/in iyner shtoonde
In half an hour/an hour

Nehmen Sie den Fahrstuhl zum dritten Stock
naymen zee dayn faarshtool tsoom dritten shtock
Take the lift to the third floor

Gehen Sie den Gang entlang
gayen zee dayn gang entlang
Go along the corridor

Es ist die erste/die zweite Tür
es ist dee erste/dee tsviyte tewr
It's the first/second door

Links/rechts
links/reshts
On the left/right

Es ist Zimmer Nummer dreihundertzwanzig
es ist tsimmer noommer driyhoonderttsvantsig
It's room number 320

Herein!
heriyn
Come in!

SIGHTSEEING

● Opening hours vary for historic buildings, museums, galleries and so on, but most close for several hours in the afternoons and most are shut on Mondays.

● The German National Tourist Office has details of national parks and nature reserves.

● Sightseeing tours by coach with English-speaking guides are available in many cities and tourist areas.

You may see

142

Betreten des Rasens verboten	Keep off the grass
Bitte nicht berühren	Do not touch
Geöffnet	Open
Geschlossen (für Restaurierung)	Closed (for restoration)
Führungen	Guided tours
Öffnungszeiten	Visiting hours
Privat	Private
Zutritt verboten	No entry

You may want to say

(*See* At the tourist office, *page 76, for asking for information brochures, etc*)

Opening times

(*See* Time, *page 193*)

When is the museum open?	Is it open on Sundays?
Wann ist das Museum geöffnet?	**Ist es sonntags geöffnet?**
van is das moozayoom ge-erffnet	*ist es zonntaags ge-erffnet*

What time does the castle open?
Um wieviel Uhr öffnet das Schloß?
oom veefeel oor erffnet das shloss

What time does the palace close?
Um wieviel Uhr schließt der Palast?
oom veefeel oor shleesst der palast

Can I/we visit the monastery?
Kann man das Kloster besuchen?
kan man das klohster bezooken

Is it open to the public?
Ist es der Öffentlichkeit zugänglich?
ist es der erffentlishkiyt tsoogenglish

Can we look round?
Können wir herumsehen?
kernnen veer heroomzayen

Visiting places

One/Two, please
Eins/Zwei, bitte
iyns/tsviy bitte

Two adults and one child
Zwei Erwachsene und ein Kind
tsviy ervaksene oont iyn kint

Is there a reduction for children?
Gibt es eine Ermäßigung für Kinder?
gipt es iyne ermayssigoong fewr kinder

For pensioners?
Für Rentner?
fewr rentner

For the disabled?
Für Behinderte?
fewr behinderte

For students?
Für Studenten?
fewr shtoodenten

For groups?
Für Gruppen?
fewr grooppen

Are there guided tours (in English)?
Gibt es Führungen (auf Englisch)?
gipt es fewroongen (owf english)

Can I/we take photos?
Kann man photografieren?
kan man fotografeeren

Can you take a photo of us, please?
Können Sie uns bitte photografieren?
kernnen zee oons bitte fotografeeren

When was this built?
Wann wurde das gebaut?
van voorde das gebowt

Who painted that picture?
Wer hat das Bild gemalt?
ver hat das bilt gemaalt

In what year?
(*See* Days, Months, Dates,
page 189)
In welchem Jahr?
in velshem yaar

What time is mass?
Um wieviel Uhr ist die Messe?
oom veefeel oor ist dee messe

What time is the church
service?
**Um wieviel Uhr ist der
Gottesdienst?**
*oom veefeel oor ist der
gottesdeenst*

Is there a priest who speaks
English?
**Gibt es einen Geistlichen, der
Englisch spricht?**
*gipt es iynen giystlishen der
english shprikt*

What kind of flower is that?
Was für eine Blume ist das?
vas fewr iyne bloome ist das

What is that bird called?
Was für einen Vogel ist das?
vas fewr iynen fohgel ist das

Is there a picnic area (in the
park)?
**Gibt es einen Rastplatz (im
Park)?**
*gipt es iynen rastplatts (im
park)*

Sightseeing excursions

What excursions are there?
Was gibt es für Ausflüge?
vas gipt es fewr owsflewge

Are there any excursions to
Berlin?
Gibt es Ausflüge nach Berlin?
gipt es owsflewge naak berleen

What time does it leave?
Um wieviel Uhr geht es los?
oom veefeel oor gayt es lohs

How long does it last?
Wie lange dauert es?
vee lange dowert es

What time do we get back?
**Um wieviel Uhr kommen wir
zurück?**
*oom veefeel oor kommen veer
tsoorewk*

Where does it leave from?
Von wo fährt der Bus ab?
fon voh fayrt der boos ap

Does the guide speak English? How much is it?
Kann der Führer Englisch? **Was kostet das?**
kann der fewrer english *vas kostet das*

You may hear

Das Museum ist jeden Tag außer montags geöffnet
das moozayoom ist yayden taag owsser mohntaags ge-erffnet
The museum is open every day except Mondays

Sonntags ist es geschlossen
zonntaags ist es geshlossen
It's closed on Sundays

Das Schloß wurde siebzehnhundertzwölf gebaut
das shloss voorde zeebtsaynhoondertzwerlf gebowt
The castle was built in 1712

Der Maler war . . .
der maaler var
The painter was . . .

Der Künstler war . . .
der koonstler var
The artist was . . .

Der Architekt war . . .
der arsheetekt var
The architect was . . .

Die Ausflüge sind jeden Dienstag und Donnerstag
dee owsflewge zint yayden deenztaag oont donnerstaag
There are excursions every Tuesday and Thursday

Der Bus fährt um zehn vom Marktplatz ab
der boos fayrt oom tsayn fom marktplatts ap
The bus leaves at ten o'clock from the market square

ENTERTAINMENTS

● Films are categorised as suitable for people over 16, **ab 16**, or 18, **ab 18. Kinderfilme** are suitable for children. Many American and British films are shown in German and Austrian cinemas, most of them dubbed but sometimes with subtitles (**Untertitel**).

● The main cities for theatre in Germany are Hamburg, Berlin and Munich. Berlin and Munich in particular have a strong cabaret tradition.

● **Austria** has a famous music tradition. The Salzburg festival takes place every July and August. Vienna's musical attractions include a famous opera house and the Vienna Boys' Choir, **der Wiener Knabenchor**.

● The most popular spectator sport is football.

You may see

Abendvorstellung	Evening performance
Ausverkauft	Sold out
Diskothek	Discothèque
Durchgehende Vorstellung	Continuous performance
Einlaß ab 18	Under-18s not allowed
Eintritt für heute	Tickets for today's performances
Erster Rang	Dress circle
Erste Reihe	Orchestra stalls
Filmclub	Film club
Frühvorstellung	Matinee
Haupttribüne	Stand, grandstand
Kino	Cinema
Kein Einlaß während der Vorstellung	No entry once the performance has begun

Keine Pausen	No intervals
Konzertsaal	Concert hall
Logen	Boxes
Opernhaus	Opera house
Parkett	Stalls
Reihe	Row, tier
Rennbahn	Racecourse
Stadium	Stadium
Tanzsaal	Dance hall
Theater	Theatre
Tür	Door
Vorverkaufsstelle	Advance booking
Zirkus	Circus
Zutritt	Entry

You may want to say

What's on

(*See* Time, *page 193*)

What is there to do in the evenings?
Was kann man abends tun?
vas kan man aabents toon

Is there a disco around here?
Gibt es eine Diskothek in der Nähe?
gipt es iyne diskotayk in der naye

Is there any entertainment for children?
Gibt es Unterhaltung für Kinder?
gipt es oonterhaltoong fewr kinder

What's on tonight?
Was wird heute abend gespielt?
vas veert hoyte aabent geshpeelt

What's on tomorrow?
Was wird morgen gespielt?
vas veert morgen geshpeelt

At the cinema
Im Kino
im keeno

At the theatre
Im Theater
im tayaater

Who is playing? *(music)*
Wer spielt?
ver shpeelt

Who is singing?
Wer singt?
ver zingt

Who is dancing?
Wer tanzt?
ver tantst

Does the film have subtitles?
Ist der Film mit Untertiteln?
ist der film mit oonterteeteln

Is there a football match on Sunday?
Gibt es am Sonntag ein Fußballspiel?
gipt es am zonntaag iyn foossballshpeel

Who's playing? *(sport)*
Wer spielt?
ver shpeelt

Where can I/we get tickets?
Wo kann man Karten kaufen?
voh kan man karten kowfen

What time does the show start?
Um wieviel Uhr beginnt die Vorstellung?
oom veefeel oor beginnt dee forshtelloong

What time does the concert start?
Um wieviel Uhr beginnt das Konzert?
oom veefeel oor beginnt das kontsert

How long does the performance last?
Wie lange dauert die Vorstellung?
vee lange dowert dee forshtelloong

When does it end?
Um wieviel Uhr wird es zu Ende sein?
oom veefeel oor veert es tsoo ende ziyn

Tickets

Can you get me tickets for the ballet?
Können Sie mir Karten für das Ballett besorgen?
kernnen zee meer karten fewr das ballett bezorgen

For the football match
Für das Fußballspiel
fewr das foossballshpeel

For the theatre
Für das Theater
fewr das tayaater

Two, please
Zwei, bitte
tsviy bitte

Two for tonight, please
Zwei für heute abend, bitte
tsviy fewr hoyte aabent bitte

Two for the 11 o'clock screening, please
Zwei für die Vorstellung um elf Uhr, bitte
tsviy fewr dee forshtelloong oom elf oor bitte

Are there any seats left for Saturday?
Haben Sie noch Karten für Samstag?
haaben zee nok karten fewr zamztaag

I want to book a box for four people
Ich möchte eine Loge für vier Personen buchen
ish mershte iyne loje fewr feer perzohnen booken

I want to book two seats
Ich möchte zwei Plätze buchen
ish mershte tsviy plettse booken

For Friday
Für Freitag
fewr friytaag

In the stalls
Im Parkett
im parkett

In the circle
Im ersten Rang
im ersten rang

Do you have anything cheaper?
Haben Sie etwas Billigeres?
haaben zee etvas billigeres

How much are the seats?
Wieviel kosten die Plätze?
veefeel kosten dee plettse

That's fine
Gut/In Ordnung
goot/in ortnoong

At the show/game

Where is this, please?
(showing your ticket)
Wo ist das, bitte?
voh ist das bitte

A programme, please
Ein Programm, bitte
iyn prohgramm bitte

Where is the cloakroom?
Wo ist die Garderobe?
voh ist dee garderohbe

Where can I/we get a programme?
Wo kann man ein Programm kaufen?
voh kan man iyn prohgramm kowfen

Where is the bar?
Wo ist die Bar?
voh ist dee bar

Where are the toilets?
Wo sind die Toiletten?
voh zint dee toyletten

Is there an interval?
Gibt es eine Pause?
gipt es iyne powze

You may hear

Sie können Karten hier im Hotel vorbestellen
zee kernnen karten heer im hotel forbeshtellen
You can get tickets here in the hotel

Am Stadium
am shtaadyum
At the stadium

Es fängt um sieben Uhr an
es fengt oom zeeben oor an
It begins at seven o'clock

Es dauert zweieinviertel Stunden
es dowert tsviyiynfeertel shtoonden
It lasts two and a quarter hours

Es wird um halb zehn zu Ende sein
es veert oom halp tsayn tsoo ende ziyn
It ends at half past nine

Es gibt eine Pause von fünfzehn Minuten
es gipt iyne powze fon fewnftsayn minooten
There is a fifteen-minute interval

Für wann möchten Sie die Karten?
fewr van mershten zee dee karten
When would you like the tickets for?

Im Parkett oder im ersten Rang?
im parkett ohder im ersten rang
In the stalls or in the circle?

Es sind zwei Plätze hier im Parkett *(indicating on seating plan)*
es zint tsviy plettse heer im parkett
There are two here, in the stalls

Es tut mir leid, wir sind ausverkauft
es toot meer liyt veer zint owsferkowft
I'm sorry, we're sold out

Kann ich Ihre Karte sehen?
kan ish eere karte zayen
May I see your ticket?

SPORTS AND ACTIVITIES

● There are good facilities throughout Germany for golf, riding, tennis and other sports.

● **Fishing** There is plenty of fresh-water fishing in lakes, rivers and streams, particularly in Bavaria and the Black Forest. You need an angling permit, **Angelschein**, obtainable from the district administration or town council and a local angling permit from the owner or lessee of the waters. Local Tourist Offices will be able to supply further information. The national angling organisation is the **Verband Deutscher Sportfischer**.

● **Sailing** There are over 30 sailing schools on the North Sea, Baltic Coast and on the large inland lakes. The German National Tourist Office has a list of addresses and also further information on taking a boat on the network of inland waterways.

● **Walking and climbing** The **Verband Deutscher Gebirgs- und Wandervereine** looks after a network of well-signposted paths, mountain trails, hostels and shelters in the medium altitude ranges such as the Black Forest and the Bayrischer Wald. The **Deutscher Alpenverein (DAV)** runs huts in the Alps and runs mountaineering and ski courses.

● **Winter sports** There are resorts spread over the German Alps, the Harz, the Black Forest and the Bavarian Forest. There are Olympic skiing facilities at Garmisch-Patenkirchen. Cross-country skiing, **Langlauf**, is becoming more popular. Further information from local tourist offices.

● **Wine seminars and tastings** are held in the wine-producing areas. Tourists are welcome to join in. More information, plus details of the various wine festivals, from the German National Tourist Office.

● **Spas and health resorts** A **Kur** is a German speciality and there are registered spas in all sorts of locations from the mountains to the sea offering different treatments. More information from the German National Tourist Office.

● **Naturist holidays** The **FKK (Freikörperkultur)** offers holiday facilities at over 100 different sites.

● **Switzerland and Austria** Activities on offer are not limited to winter sports and climbing, but also include summer skiing, fishing, golf, tennis and water sports. Switzerland is a botanist's paradise, but many plants are protected. Check with local tourist offices for information on protected species.

You may see

Angeln verboten	No fishing
Drahtseilbahn	Cable car
Erste Hilfe	First Aid
Freibad	Outdoor swimming pool
Fußballplatz	Football pitch
Golfplatz	Golf course
Gefahr	Danger
Hallenbad	Indoor swimming pool
Lawinengefahr	Danger of avalanches
Piste	Ski run
Sportzentrum	Sports centre
Schwimmbad	Swimming pool
Schwimmen verboten	No swimming
Schlepplift	Drag lift
Sessellift	Chair lift
Skilift	Ski lift
Skischule	Ski school
Skiverleih	Ski hire
Strand	Beach
Tennisplatz	Tennis court
Unbefugtes Betreten verboten	Trespassers will be prosecuted

General phrases

Can I/we . . .?
Kann man . . .?
kan man

Can I/we hire bikes?
Kann man Fahrräder mieten?
kan man faarrayder meeten

Can I/we go fishing?
Kann man angeln gehen?
kan man angeln gayen

Can I/we go riding?
Kann man reiten gehen?
kan man riyten gayen

Where can I/we . . .
Wo kann man . . .
voh kan man

Where can I/we play tennis?
Wo kann man Tennis spielen?
voh kan man tennis shpeelen

Where can I/we go windsurfing?
Wo kann man windsurfen?
voh kan man vintsoorfen

Are there lessons?
Gibt es Unterricht?
gipt es oonterrisht

I'm a beginner
Ich bin Anfänger
ish bin anfenger

I'm quite experienced
Ich bin ziemlich erfahren
ish bin tseemlish erfaaren

How much does it cost per hour?
Wieviel kostet es pro Stunde?
veefeel kostet es proh shtoonde

How much does it cost per day?
Wieviel kostet es pro Tag?
veefeel kostet es proh taag

How much does it cost per round?
Wieviel kostet die Runde?
veefeel kostet dee roonde

Is there a reduction for children?
Gibt es eine Ermäßigung für Kinder?
gipt es iyne ermayssigoong fewr kinder

Can we hire equipment?
Können wir die Ausrüstung mieten?
kernnen veer dee owsrewstoong meeten

Can we hire rackets?
Können wir Schläger mieten?
kernnen veer shlayger meeten

Where can I/we get one?
Wo bekommt man das?
voh bekommt man das

Can we hire clubs?
Können wir Golfschläger mieten?
kernnen veer golfshlayger meeten

Is it necessary to be a member?
Muß man Mitglied sein?
mooss man mitgleet ziyn

Do we need a licence?
Brauchen wir eine Lizenz?
browken veer iyne leetsents

Beach, lake and pool

Can I/we swim here?
Kann man hier schwimmen?
kan man heer shvimmen

Is it safe for children?
Ist es sicher für Kinder?
ist es zisher fewr kinder

Can I/we swim in the river?
Kann man im Fluß schwimmen?
kan man im flooss shvimmen

When is high tide?
Wann ist Hochwasser?
van ist hohkvasser

Is it dangerous?
Ist es gefährlich?
ist es gefayrlish

Is the water clean?
Ist das Wasser sauber?
ist das vasser zowber

Skiing

What is the snow like?
Wie ist der Schnee?
vee ist der shnay

. . . for a week
. . . für eine Woche
fewr iyne voke

How much is the lift pass?
Was kostet der liftpass?
vas kostet der liftpass

. . . for a day
. . . für einen Tag
fewr iynen taag

What time is the last ascent?
Um wieviel Uhr ist der letzte Aufstieg?
oom veefeel oor ist der letste owfshteeg

Where is the nursery slope?
Wo ist der Anfängerhügel?
voh ist der anfengerhewgel

Is it steep?
Ist es steil?
ist es shtiyl

Is it icy?
Ist es eisig?
ist es iyzig

Is the run wide?
Ist die Piste breit?
ist dee peeste briyt

You may hear

Sind Sie ein Anfänger?
zint zee iyn anfenger
Are you a beginner?

Können Sie Ski fahren?
kernnen zee shee faaren
Can you ski?

Können Sie windsurfen?
kernnen zee vintsoorfen
Can you windsurf?

Es kostet zehn Mark die Stunde
es kostet tsayn mark dee shtoonde
It costs DM 10 per hour

Es gibt eine Anzahlung von fünfzig Mark
es gipt iyne antsaaloong fon fewnftsig mark
There is a deposit of DM 50

Es tut mir Leid, wir sind ausgebucht
es toot meer liyt veer zint owsgebookt
I'm sorry, we're booked up

Können Sie bitte einen Augenblick warten
kernnen zee bitte iynen owgenblik varten
Could you wait a moment, please

Kommen Sie ein bißchen später zurück
kommen zee iyn bissyen shpayter tsoorewk
Come back a bit later

Es ist sehr windig
es ist zayr vindig
It's very windy

Die Strömung ist sehr stark
dee shtrermoong ist zayr shtark
The current is very strong

Welche Größe haben Sie?
velshe grersse haaben zee
What size are you?

Sie brauchen ein Foto
zee browken iyn fohto
You need a photo

Der Schnee ist tief
der shnay ist teef
The snow is deep

Wir haben Pappschnee/ Pulverschnee
veer haaben pappshnay/ poolvershnay
The snow is soft/powdery

Wir haben nicht viel Schnee
veer haaben nisht feel shnay
There isn't much snow

HEALTH

Medical details – to show the Doctor

*(Tick where appropriate,
or fill in names/details*

| | Self
Ich | Other members
of family/party
Anderen | | |
|---|---|---|---|---|
| Blood group **Blutgruppe** | | | | |
| Asthmatic **Asthmatisch** | | | | |
| Blind **Blind** | | | | |
| Deaf **Schwerhörig** | | | | |
| Diabetic **Zuckerkrank** | | | | |
| Epileptic **Epileptisch** | | | | |
| Handicapped **Behindert** | | | | |
| Heart condition **Schwaches Herz** | | | | |

High blood pressure
Hoher Blutdruck				
Pregnant **Schwanger**				
Allergic to **Allergisch gegen**				
Antibiotics **Antibiotik**				
Penicillin **Penizillin**				
Cortisone **Kortison**				

Medicines **Medikamente**

Self **Ich** _____

Others **Anderen** _____

_____

_____

• Your local Department of Health office can provide information about medical care abroad. Within the EC you can obtain the local equivalent of NHS treatment by producing the required form – you may have to pay first and reclaim the payment when you return to Britain. Your travel insurance should also cover you for illness and accident.

• A chemist, **Apotheker**, will usually be qualified to treat minor disorders.

• In **Austria** information about the emergency medical service, **Ärztenodienst**, is available from the police.

• To indicate where the pain is you can simply point and say 'it hurts here' (**es tut hier weh**). Otherwise you'll need to look up the German for the appropriate part of the body.

You may see

159

Ambulanz	Surgery, Outpatients
Gift	Poison
Klinik	Clinic, hospital
Krankenhaus	Hospital
Praxis	Surgery
Sanitätswache	First aid post
Sprechstunden	Surgery hours
Unfallstation	Accident and Emergency ward

You may want to say

At the doctor's

I need a doctor
Ich brauche einen Arzt
ish browke iynen artst

Please call a doctor
Bitte, rufen Sie einen Arzt
bitte roofen zee iynen artst

My husband is ill
Mein Mann ist krank
miyn man ist krank

My wife is ill
Meine Frau ist krank
miyne frow ist krank

My friend is ill
Mein Freund *(male)*/**meine
Freundin** *(female)* **ist krank**
*miyn froynt/**miyne froyndin** ist
krank*

My son is ill
Mein Sohn ist krank
miyn zohn ist krank

My daughter is ill
Meine Tochter ist krank
miyne toshter ist krank

My baby is ill
Mein Baby ist krank
miyn baybee ist krank

Your symptoms

I feel unwell
Ich fühle mich nicht wohl
ish fewle mish nisht vohl

It hurts here
Es tut hier weh
es toot heer vay

My . . . hurts
Mein . . . tut weh
miyn . . . toot vay

My stomach hurts
Mein Bauch tut weh
miyn bowk toot vay

My back hurts
Mein Rücken tut weh
miyn rewken toot vay

My nose hurts
Meine Nase tut weh
miyne naaze toot vay

Someone else's symptoms

He/She feels unwell
Er/sie fühlt sich nicht wohl
er/zee fewlt zish nisht vohl

It hurts here
Es tut ihm/ihr hier weh
es toot eem/eer heer vay

His/Her . . . hurts
Sein/ihr . . . tut weh
ziyn/eer . . . toot vay

His/Her stomach hurts
Sein/ihr Bauch tut weh
ziyn/eer bowk toot vay

His/Her back hurts
Sein/ihr Rücken tut weh
ziyn/eer rewken toot vay

His/Her nose hurts
Seine/ihre Nase tut weh
ziyne/eere naaze toot vay

My . . . hurt
Meine . . . tun weh
miyne . . . toon vay

His/Her . . . hurt
Seine/ihre . . . tun weh
ziyne/eere . . . toon vay

My eyes hurt
Meine Augen tun weh
miyne owgen toon vay

His/Her eyes hurt
Seine/ihre Augen tun weh
ziyne/eere owgen toon vay

My feet hurt
Meine Füsse tun weh
miyne fewsse toon vay

His/Her feet hurt
Seine/ihre Füsse tun weh
ziyne/eere fewsse toon vay

I have a sore throat
Ich habe Halsschmerzen
ish haabe halsshmertsen

He/She has a sore throat
Er/sie hat Halsschmerzen
er/zee hat halsshmertsen

I have a temperature
Ich habe Fieber
ish haabe feeber

He/She has a temperature
Er/sie hat Fieber
er/zee hat feeber

I have diarrhoea
Ich habe Durchfall
ish haabe doorshfall

He/She has diarrhoea
Er/sie hat Durchfall
er/zee hat doorshfall

I feel dizzy
Mir ist schwindelig
meer ist shvindelig

He/She feels dizzy
Ihm/ihr ist es schwindelig
eem/eer ist es shvindelig

I have been sick
Ich habe mich übergeben
ish haabe mish ewbergayben

He/She has been sick
Er/sie hat sich übergeben
er/zee hat zish ewbergayben

I can't sleep
Ich kann nicht schlafen
ish kan nisht shlaafen

He/She can't sleep
Er/sie kann nicht schlafen
er/zee kan nisht shlaafen

I can't breathe
Ich kann nicht atmen
ish kan nisht aatmen

He/She can't breathe
Er/sie kann nicht atmen
er/zee kan nisht aatmen

My . . . is bleeding
Mein(e) . . . blutet
miyn/miyne . . . blootet

His/Her . . . is bleeding
Sein(e)/Ihr(e) . . . blutet
ziyn(e)/eer(e) . . . blootet

I think that . . .	He/she thinks that . . .
Ich glaube, . . .	**Er/sie glaubt, . . .**
ish glowbe	*er/zee glowbt*
It's my . . .	It's his/her . . .
Es ist mein(e) . . .	**Es ist sein(e)/ihr(e) . . .**
es ist miyn/miyne	*es ist ziyn(e)/eer(e)*
It's my arm	It's his/her leg
Es ist mein Arm	**Es ist sein/ihr Bein**
es ist miyn arm	*es ist ziyn/eer biyn*
It's my leg	It's his/her ankle
Es ist mein Bein	**Es ist sein/ihr Knöchel**
es ist miyn biyn	*es ist ziyn/eer knerkel*
It's broken	It's broken
Es ist gebrochen	**Es ist gebrochen**
es ist gebroken	*es ist gebroken*
It's sprained	It's sprained
Es ist verstaucht	**Es ist verstaucht**
es ist fershtowkt	*es ist fershtowkt*
I have cut myself	He/she has cut him/herself
Ich habe mich geschnitten	**Er/sie hat sich geschitten**
ish haabe mish geshnitten	*er/zee hat zish geshnitten*
I have burnt myself	He/she has burnt him/herself
Ich habe mich verbrannt	**Er/sie hat sich verbrannt**
ish haabe mish ferbrannt	*er/zee hat zish ferbrannt*
I have been stung by an insect	He/she has been stung by an in
Ein Insekt hat mich gestochen	**Ein Insekt hat ihn/sie gestochen**
iyn inzekt hat mish geshtoken	*iyn inzekt hat een/zee geshtoken*
I have been bitten by a dog	He/she has been bitten by a dog
Ein Hund hat mich gebissen	**Ein Hund hat ihn/sie gebissen**
iyn hoont hat mish gebissen	*iyn hoont hat een/zee gebissen*

You may hear

Wo tut es weh?
voh toot es vay
Where does it hurt?

Tut es hier weh?
toot es heer vay
Does it hurt here?

Sehr? Nur ein bißchen?
zayr, noor iyn bissyen
A lot? A little?

Seit wann fühlen Sie sich so?
ziyt van fewlen zee zish zoh
How long have you been feeling like this?

Wie alt sind Sie?
vee alt zint zee
How old are you?

Wie alt ist er/sie
vee alt ist er/zee
How is he/she?

Machen Sie bitte den Mund auf
maaken zee bitte dayn moont owf
Open your mouth, please

Ziehen Sie sich bitte aus
tsee-en zee zish bitte ows
Get undressed, please

Machen Sie sich oben frei
maaken zee zish ohben friy
Take your top off

Legen Sie sich bitte da drüben hin
laygen zee zish bitte daa drewben hin
Lie down over there, please

Nehmen Sie irgendwelche Medikamente?
naymen zee eergentvelshe maydikamente
Are you taking any medicines?

Sind Sie gegen irgendein Medikament allergisch?
zint zee gaygen eergentiyn maydikament allergish
Are you allergic to any medicine?

Sind Sie gegen Wundstarrkrampf geimpft?
zint zee gaygen voontshtarrkrampf geimpft
Have you been vaccinated against tetanus?

Was haben Sie (heute) gegessen?
vas haaben zee (hoyte) gegessen
What have you eaten (today)?

Ich gebe Ihnen ein Rezept
ish gaybe eenen iyn raytsept
I am going to give you a prescription

Nehmen Sie dreimal täglich eine Tablette
naymen zee driymal tayglish iyne tablette
Take a tablet three times a day

Nach dem Essen
naak daym essen
After meals

Abends
aabents
At night

Sie haben eine Entzündung
zee haaben iyne enttsewndoong
You've got an infection

Es ist infiziert
es ist infitseert
It's infected

Ich werde Ihren Blutdruck messen
ish verde eeren blootdrook messen
I'm going to take your blood pressure

Ich muß Ihnen eine Spritze geben
ish mooss eenen iyne shprittse gayben
I have to give you an injection

Das muß genäht werden
das mooss genayt verden
That needs some stitches

Ich muß eine Röntgenaufnahme machen
ish mooss iyne rerntgenowfnaame maaken
I have to take an X-ray

Ich brauche eine Blutprobe
ish browke iyne blootprohbe
I need a blood sample

Ich brauche eine Urinprobe
ish browke iyne ooreen prohbe
I need a urine sample

Sie haben Lebensmittelvergiftung
zee haaben laybenzmittelfergiftoong
You have food poisoning

Es ist ein Infarkt
es ist iyn infarkt
It's a heart attack

Sie müssen sich ausruhen
zee mewssen zish owsroo-en
You must rest

Sie müssen drei Tage im Bett bleiben
zee mewssen driy taage im bett bliyben
You must stay in bed for three days

Sie müssen in fünf Tagen wiederkommen
zee mewssen in fewnf taagen veederkommen
You must come back in five days' time

Ich muß Sie ins Krankenhaus einweisen
ish mooss zee ins krankenhows iynviyzen
I'll have to send you to hospital

Es ist nichts Ernstes
es ist nishts ernstes
It is nothing serious

Sie sind gesund
zee zint gezoont
There is nothing wrong with you

Sie können sich anziehen
zee kernnen zish antsee-en
You can get dressed again

You may want to say

At the dentist's

I need a dentist
Ich brauche einen Zahnarzt
ish browke iynen tsaanartst

I have toothache
Ich habe Zahnschmerzen
ish haabe tsaanshmertsen

This tooth hurts
Dieser Zahn tut weh
deezer tsaan toot vay

I have broken a tooth
Ich habe mir ein Stück vom Zahn abgebrochen
ish haabe meer iyn shtewk fom tsaan apgebroken

I have lost a filling
Ich habe eine Plombe verloren
ish haabe iyne plombe ferloren

I have lost a crown/cap
Ich habe eine Krone verloren
ish haabe iyne krohne ferloren

He/She has toothache
Er/sie hat Zahnschmerzen
er/zee hat tsaanshmertsen

He/She has broken a tooth
Er/sie hat sich ein Stück vom Zahn abgebrochen
er/zee hat zish iyn shtewk vom tsaan apgebroken

He/She has lost a filling
Er/sie hat eine Plombe verloren
er/zee hat iyne plombe ferloren

He/She has lost a crown/cap
Er/sie hat eine Krone verloren
er/zee hat iyne krohne ferloren

Can you fix it temporarily?
Können Sie es provisorisch behandeln?
kernnen zee es provizorish behandeln

How much will it cost?
Was wird es kosten?
vas virt es kosten

Can you give me an injection?
Können Sie mir eine Spritze geben?
kernnen zee meer iyne shprittse gayben

Can you give him/her an injection?
Können Sie ihm/ihr eine Spritze geben?
kernnen zee eem/eer iyne shprittse gayben

This denture is broken
Das Gebiß ist gebrochen
das gebiss ist gebroken

Can you repair it temporarily?
Können Sie es provisorisch reparieren
kernnen zee es provizorish repareeren

You may hear

Machen Sie den Mund auf
maaken zee dayn moont owf
Open your mouth

Sie brauchen eine Plombe
zee browken iyne plombe
You need a filling

Ich muß es rausnehmen
ish moos es rowsnaymen
I'll have to extract it

Ich gebe Ihnen eine Spritze
ish gaybe eenen iyne shprittse
I'm going to give you an injection

Parts of the body

Ankle	**der Knöchel**	*knershel*
Appendix	**der Blinddarm**	*blintdarm*
Arm	**der Arm**	*arm*
Artery	**die Schlagader**	*shlaagaader*
Back	**der Rücken**	*rewken*
Bladder	**die Blase**	*blaaze*
Blood	**das Blut**	*bloot*
Body	**der Körper**	*kerper*
Bone	**der Knochen**	*knoken*
Bottom	**der Hintern**	*hintern*
Bowels	**der Darm**	*darm*
Breast	**die Brust**	*broost*
Buttock	**der Po**	*poh*
Cartilage	**der Knorpel**	*knorpel*
Chest	**der Brustkorb**	*broostkorp*
Chin	**das Kinn**	*kin*
Ear	**das Ohr**	*ohr*
Elbow	**der Ellenbogen**	*ellenbohgen*
Eye	**das Auge**	*owge*
Face	**das Gesicht**	*gezisht*
Finger	**der Finger**	*finger*
Foot	**der Fuß**	*fooss*
Genitals	**die Genitalien**	*genitaalee-en*
Gland	**die Drüse**	*drewze*
Hair	**das Haar**	*haar*
Hand	**die Hand**	*hant*
Head	**der Kopf**	*kopf*
Heart	**das Herz**	*herts*
Heel	**die Ferse**	*fayrze*
Hip	**die Hüfte**	*hewfte*
Jaw	**der Kiefer**	*keefer*
Joint	**das Gelenk**	*gelenk*
Kidney	**die Niere**	*neere*
Knee	**das Knie**	*k-nee*

Leg	**das Bein**	*biyn*
Ligament	**das Ligament**	*ligament*
Lip	**die Lippe**	*lippe*
Liver	**die Leber**	*layber*
Lung	**die Lunge**	*loonge*
Mouth	**der Mund**	*moont*
Muscle	**der Muskel**	*mooskel*
Nail	**der Nagel**	*naagel*
Neck	**der Hals**	*hals*
Nerve	**der Nerv**	*nerf*
Nose	**die Nase**	*naaze*
Penis	**der Penis**	*peenis*
Private parts	**die Geschlechtsteile**	*geshleshtstiyle*
Rib	**die Rippe**	*rippe*
Shoulder	**die Schulter**	*shoolter*
Skin	**die Haut**	*howt*
Spine	**das Rückgrat**	*rewkgraat*
Stomach	**der Magen**	*maagen*
Tendon	**die Sehne**	*zayne*
Testicle	**der Testikel**	*testikel*
Thigh	**der Oberschenkel**	*ohbershenkel*
Throat	**die Kehle**	*kayle*
Thumb	**der Daumen**	*dowmen*
Toe	**der Zeh**	*tsay*
Tongue	**die Zunge**	*tsoonge*
Tonsils	**die Mandeln**	*mandeln*
Tooth	**der Zahn**	*tsaan*
Vagina	**die Vagina**	*vageena*
Vein	**die Ader**	*aader*
Wrist	**das Handgelenk**	*hantgelenk*

PROBLEMS AND COMPLAINTS

● If you lose anything or have anything stolen, you must report it to the police within 24 hours so that you can make a valid insurance claim.

You may see

Außer Betrieb   Out of order

You may want to say

General phrases

Can you mend this (immediately)?
Können Sie das (gleich) reparieren?
kernnen zee das (gliysh) repareeren

When can you mend this?
Wann können Sie das reparieren?
van kernnen zee das repareeren

Can you help me?
Können Sie mir helfen?
kernnen zee meer helfen

Can I speak to the manager?
Kann ich den Geschäftsführer sprechen?
kan ish dayn gesheftsfewrer shpreken

There's a problem with . . .
Es gibt ein Problem mit . . .
es gipt iyn problaym mit

There isn't any . . .
Es gibt kein/keine/keinen . . .
es gipt kiyn/kiyne/kiynen

I need . . .
Ich brauche . . .
ish browke

The . . . doesn't work
Der/die/das . . . funktioniert nicht
der/dee/das . . . foonktsyoneert nisht

The . . . is broken
Der/die/das . . . ist kaputt
der/dee/das . . . ist kapoot

I can't
Ich kann nicht
ish kan nisht

It's not my fault
Ich bin nicht schuldig daran
ish bin nisht shooldig daran

I have forgotten . . .
Ich habe . . . vergessen
ish haabe . . . fergessen

I have lost . . .
Ich habe . . . verloren
ish haabe . . . ferloren

Someone has stolen . . .
Man hat . . . gestohlen
man hat . . . geshtohlen

My . . . has disappeared
Meine/meine . . . ist verschwunden
miyn/miyne . . . ist fershvoonden

My money isn't there
Mein Geld ist nicht da
miyn gelt ist nisht daa

My travellers' cheques aren't there
Meine Reiseschecks sind nicht da
miyne riyzeshecks zint nisht daa

Something is missing
Etwas ist weg
etvas ist vek

The . . . is missing
Der/die/das . . . ist weg
der/dee/das . . . ist vek

This isn't mine
Das gehört mir nicht
das gehert meer nisht

Where you're staying

There isn't any hot water
Es gibt kein heißes Wasser
es gipt kiyn hiysses vasser

There isn't any toilet paper
Es gibt kein Toilettenpapier
es gipt kiyn toylettenpapeer

There isn't any electricity
Es gibt keinen Strom
es gipt kiynen shtrohm

There aren't any towels
Es gibt keine Handtücher
es gipt kiyne hanttewsher

The light doesn't work
Das Licht funktioniert nicht
das lisht foonktsyoneert nisht

The shower doesn't work
Die Dusche funktioniert nicht
dee dooshe foonktsyoneert nisht

I need another pillow
Ich brauche noch ein Kopfkissen
ish browke nok iyn kopfkissen

I need another blanket
Ich brauche noch eine Bettdecke
ish browke nok iyne bettdeke

The lock/the key is broken
Das Schloß/der Schlüssel ist kaputt
das shloss/der shlewssel ist kapoot

The bed is broken
Das Bett ist kaputt
das bett ist kapoot

I can't open the window
Ich kann das Fenster nicht öffnen
ish kan das fenster nisht erffnen

I can't turn the tap off
Ich kann den Hahn nicht zudrehen
ish kan dayn haan nisht tsoodrayen

The drain is blocked
Der Abfluß ist verstopft
der apflooss ist fershtopft

In restaurants and bars

This isn't cooked
Das ist nicht gar
das ist nisht gar

The toilet doesn't flush
Die Toilette spült nicht
dee toylette shpewlt nisht

The wash basin is dirty
Das Waschbecken ist schmutzig
das vashbeken ist shmoottsig

The room is . . .
Das Zimmer ist . . .
das tsimmer ist

The room is too hot/cold
Das Zimmer ist zu heiß/kalt
das tsimmer ist tsoo hiyss/kalt

The room is too dark
Das Zimmer ist zu dunkel
das tsimmer ist tsoo doonkel

The room is too small
Das Zimmer ist zu klein
das tsimmer ist tsoo kliyn

The bed is uncomfortable
Das Bett ist unbequem
das bett ist unbekvaym

There's a lot of noise
Es ist zu laut
es ist tsoo lowt

There's a smell of gas
Es riecht nach Gas
es reesht naak gas

This is burnt
Das ist angebrannt
das ist angebrannt

This is cold
Das ist kalt
das ist kalt

I didn't order this
Ich habe das nicht bestellt
ish haabe das nisht beshtellt

This glass is cracked
Dieses Glas hat einen Sprung
deezes glas hat iynen shproong

This is dirty
Dies ist schmutzig
dees ist shmoottsig

This smells bad
Das riecht schlecht
das reesht shlesht

This tastes strange
Das schmeckt komisch
das shmeckt kohmish

There's a mistake here
Da stimmt etwas nicht
daa shtimmt etvas nisht

My bill is too much
Meine Rechnung ist zu viel
miyne reshnoong ist tsoo feel

In shops

I bought this here (yesterday)
Ich habe das (gestern) hier gekauft
ish haabe das (gestern) heer gekowft

Can I change it?
Kann ich es umtauschen?
kan ish es oomtowshen

I want to return this
Ich möchte das zurückbringen
ish mershte das tsoorewkbringen

Can you give me my money back?
Können Sie mein Geld zurückerstatten?
kernnen zee miyn gelt tsoorewkershtatten

Here is the receipt
Hier ist die Quittung
heer ist dee kvittoong

It's no good
Es funktioniert nicht
es foonktsyoneert nisht

It has a flaw
Es hat einen Fehler
es hat iynen fayler

It has a hole
Es hat ein Loch
es hat iyn lok

There is a stain/mark
Es gibt einen Fleck
es gipt iynen flek

This is off
Das ist schlecht
das ist shlesht

This isn't fresh	The lid is missing
Dies ist nicht frisch	**Der Deckel fehlt**
dees ist nisht frish	*der dekel faylt*

Forgetting and losing things and theft

I have forgotten my ticket
Ich habe meine Fahrkarte vergessen
ish haabe miyne faarkarte fergessen

I have forgotten my key
Ich habe meinen Schlüssel vergessen
ish haabe miynen shlewssel fergessen

I have lost my driving licence
Ich habe meinen Führerschein verloren
ish haabe miynen fewrershiyn ferloren

I have lost my passport
Ich habe meinen Paß verloren
ish haabe miynen pass ferloren

We've lost our rucksacks
Wir haben unsere Rucksäcke verloren
veer haaben oonzere rookzeke ferloren

Where is the lost property office?
Wo ist das Fundbüro?
voh ist das foontbewroh

Where is the police station?
Wo ist die Polizeiwache?
voh ist dee politsiyvake

Someone has stolen my bag
Man hat meine Handtasche gestohlen
man hat miyne hanttashe geshtohlen

Someone has stolen our car
Man hat unser Auto gestohlen
man hat oonzer owto geshtohlen

Someone has stolen my money
Man hat mein Geld gestohlen
man hat miyn gelt geshtohlen

If someone is bothering you

Leave me alone please
Lassen Sie mich bitte allein
lassen zee mish bitte alliyn

Go away or I'll call the police
Gehen Sie weg sonst rufe ich die Polizei
gayen zee vek zonst roofe ish dee politsiy

There's someone annoying me
Jemand belästigt mich
yaymant belestigt mish

You may hear

Helpful and unhelpful replies

Einen Augenblick, bitte
iynen owgenblick bitte
Just a moment, please

Natürlich/Selbstverständlich
natewrlish/zelbstfershtentlish
Of course

Ich werde Ihnen noch einen/eine/ein . . . bringen
ish verde eenen nok iynen/iyne/iyns bringen
I'll bring you another one

Ich werde Ihnen eines sofort bringen
ish verde eenen iynes zohfort bringen
I'll bring you one immediately

Sofort/gleich
zohfort/gliysh
Immediately

Ich werde es für Sie morgen reparieren
ish verde es fewr zee morgen repareeren
I'll fix it for you tomorrow

Es tut mir leid, es ist unmöglich
es toot meer liyt es ist oonmerglish
I'm sorry, it's not possible

Es tut mir leid, ich kann nichts machen
es toot meer liyt ish kan nishts maaken
I'm sorry, there's nothing I can do

Ich bin nicht dafür zuständig
ish bin nisht daafewr tsooshtendig
I'm not responsible for that

Wir sind nicht dafür verantwortlich
veer zint nisht daafewr ferantvortlish
We aren't responsible

Questions you may be asked

Wann haben Sie's gekauft?
van haaben zeez gekowft
When did you buy it?

Haben Sie die Quittung?
haaben zee dee kvittoong
Have you got the receipt?

Wann ist es passiert?
van ist es passeert
When did it happen?

Wie sieht Ihr Auto aus?
vee zeeht eer owto ows
What does your car look like?

Was haben Sie für ein Auto?
vas haaben zee fewr iyn owto
What make of car is it?

Was ist das Kraftfahrzeug-kennzeichen?
vas ist das kraftfaartsoyg-kenntsiyken
What is the registration number of your car?

Wie heißen Sie?
vee hiyssen zee
What's your name?

Wo wohnen Sie?
voh vohnen zee
Where are you staying?

Was ist Ihre Adresse?
vas ist eere adresse
What's your address?

Wo haben Sie's verloren?
voh haaben zeez ferloren
Where did you lose it?

Wo ist es gestohlen worden?
voh ist es geshtohlen vorden
Where was it stolen?

Wie sieht Ihre Tasche aus?
vee zeet eere tashe ows
What does your bag look like?

Was ist Ihre Zimmernummer?
vas ist eere tsimmernoommer
What's your room number?

Welche Nummer hat Ihre Ferienwohnung?
velshe noommer hat eere fayrienvohnoong
What's the number of your apartment?

Ihre Paßnummer, bitte?
Eere passnoommer bitte
What's your passport number?

Sind Sie versichert?
zint zee ferzishert
Are you insured?

Bitte füllen Sie das Formular aus
bitte fewllen zee das formoolar ows
Please fill in this form

BASIC GRAMMAR

Nouns

Nouns in German have one of three genders, masculine, feminine or neuter. There are certain endings which show what gender a noun is. For example **-heit**, **-keit**, **-ung** are always feminine endings and the suffix **-chen** always makes a word neuter, **das Mädchen** – the girl. On the whole though genders have to be learnt from hearing and reading the language.

Nouns in German are always written with a capital letter.

Plurals

Plurals are formed by adding an ending and/or an umlaut on to the noun. Endings vary and although feminine words ending in **-keit**, **-heit** and **-ung** usually add **-en** to make the plural, most plural endings have to be learnt. Dictionaries give the plural endings of words in the German–English section. Some words don't change in the plural, e.g. **der Knochen** – bone.

Definite article – 'the'

The definite article changes according to whether the noun is masculine, feminine, neuter or plural:
der – masculine
die – feminine
das – neuter
die – plural, all genders

e.g. **der Mann** – the man   **die Männer** – the men
     die Frau – the woman   **die Frauen** – the women
     das Haus – the house   **die Häuser** – the houses

The indefinite article – 'a', 'an'

The indefinite articles are:
ein – masculine   **eine** – feminine   **ein** – neuter

The word **kein**, which has the same endings, means 'no', 'not any' and can also be used in the plural.

kein Mann – no man   **keine Männer** – no men
keine Frau – no woman   **keine Frauen** – no women
kein Haus – no house   **keine Häuser** – no houses

Cases

German has four cases: nominative, accusative, genitive and dative. The nominative case is used for the subject of a sentence, the accusative for the direct object, the genitive is the possessive case and the dative goes with the indirect object. There are also certain prepositions (see page 182) which either take the accusative or the dative and verbs which take the dative.

The definite and indefinite articles may change according to what case the noun is in:

Definite article

	Masculine	*Feminine*	*Neuter*	*Plural*
Nom.	**der** Mann	**die** Frau	**das** Haus	**die** Männer
Acc.	**den** Mann	**die** Frau	**das** Haus	**die** Männer
Gen.	**des** Mannes	**der** Frau	**des** Hauses	**der** Männer
Dat.	**dem** Mann	**der** Frau	**dem** Haus	**den** Männern

Indefinite article

	Masculine	*Feminine*	*Neuter*	*Plural*
Nom.	**ein** Mann	**eine** Frau	**ein** Haus	**keine** Männer
Acc.	**einen** Mann	**eine** Frau	**ein** Haus	**keine** Männer
Gen.	**eines** Mannes	**einer** Frau	**eines** Hauses	**keiner** Männer
Dat.	**einem** Mann	**einer** Frau	**einem** Haus	**keinen** Männern

Possessive adjectives

The possessive adjectives add the same endings as the indefinite article:

mein	**mein Vater**	**meine Mutter**
my	my father	my mother

dein	**deine Schwester**	**deine Kinder**
your*	your sister	your children

sein – his, its	**unser** – our	**Ihr** – your*
ihr – her	**euer** – your*	**ihr** – their

* See **'You'** on page 183

Adjectives

Adjectives come before the noun and the ending changes according to the gender of the noun, whether the noun is singular or plural, and whether the noun is with a definite or indefinite article or with no article at all.

Definite article

	Masculine	*Feminine*	*Neuter*
Nom.	**der** arme Mann	**die** arme Frau	**das** arme Mädche⟩
Acc.	**den** armen Mann	**die** arme Frau	**das** arme Mädche⟩
Gen.	**des** armen Mannes	**der** armen Frau	**des** armen Mädch⟩
Dat.	**dem** armen Mann	**der** armen Frau	**dem** armen Mädch⟩

	Plural
Nom.	**die** armen Männer
Acc.	**die** armen Männer
Gen.	**der** armen Männer
Dat.	**den** armen Männern

Indefinite article

	Masculine	*Feminine*	*Neuter*
Nom.	**ein** armer Mann	**eine** arme Frau	**ein** armes Mädchen
Acc.	**einen** armen Mann	**eine** arme Frau	**ein** armes Mädchen
Gen.	**eines** armen Mannes	**einer** armen Frau	**eines** armen Mädchens
Dat.	**einem** armen Mann	**einer** armen Frau	**einem** armen Mädchen

	Plural
Nom.	**keine** armen Männer
Acc.	**keine** armen Männer
Gen.	**keiner** armen Männer
Dat.	**keinen** armen Männern

No article

	Masculine	*Feminine*	*Neuter*
Nom.	**guter** Wein	**gute** Milch	**gutes** Bier
Acc.	**guten** Wein	**gute** Milch	**gutes** Bier
Gen.	**guten** Weins	**guter** Milch	**guten** Bier
Dat.	**gutem** Wein	**guter** Milch	**gutem** Bier

	Plural
Nom.	**gute** Leute
Acc.	**gute** Leute
Gen.	**guter** Leute
Dat.	**guten** Leuten

Comparatives and superlatives

To make an adjective comparative, add **-er** on to the stem and
then add the endings as above.

e.g. **der reiche Mann** – the rich man

    der reichere Mann – the richer man

    ein schnelles Auto – a fast car

    ein schnelleres Auto – a faster car

To make an adjective superlative, add **-st** on to the stem and then the endings.

e.g. **der reichste Mann** – the richest man
    das schnellste Auto – the fastest car

Some common adjectives e.g. **groß** (big), **lang** (long), **alt** (old), add an umlaut as well to make the comparative and superlative.

e.g. **meine ältere Schwester** – my older sister
    das größte Land – the biggest country
    der längste Fluß – the longest river

Prepositions

Aus, bei, mit, seit, nach, von and **zu** always take the dative. **Bis, entlang, durch, ohne, gegen, wider, um** and **für** always take the accusative.

Other prepositions can take either the accusative or the dative. The accusative usually indicates movement, e.g. **in den Garten**, into the garden, while the dative indicates position, e.g. **im (in + dem) Garten**, in the garden.

Subject pronouns ('I', 'you', 'he', 'she', etc.)

I	**ich**
you (informal)	**du**
he	**er**
she	**sie**
it	**es**
we	**wir**
you (informal)	**ihr**
you (formal)	**Sie**
they	**sie**

'You'

There are three words for 'you' in German:

Du is informal and is used when you are talking either to someone you know well, or to a child or someone much younger than yourself. Young people tend to address each other as **du** as well.

Ihr is informal and is used in the same situations as **du** when you are addressing more than one person.

Sie is always written with a capital letter and is the formal word for 'you'. It can be used to address one person or a group of people. Always use it when you don't know the person you are talking to, or if they are much older than you.

If in doubt about which word for 'you' to use, stick to **Sie**.

The possessive adjective 'your' (**dein**, **euer** or **Ihr** in German), follows the same guidelines.

Word order

Normally the main verb of a sentence comes second; however, there are certain words which send the verb to the end of the sentence or clause. The most common of these are:

daß	that
weil	because
wenn	when, if

e.g. **Sie kommt nicht, weil sie krank ist**
She's not coming because she's ill

The present perfect tense (I have been, we have seen etc.) is made up of two parts in German: the auxiliary verb (**haben** or **sein**) and the past participle which always goes to the end of the sentence or clause.

e.g. **Ich habe ihn im Theater gesehen**	I've seen him in the theatre
Wir haben sie für nächsten Dienstag eingeladen	We've invited them/her for next Tuesday

Verbs

Endings change on verbs according to (i) the subject of the verb and (ii) the tense of the verb. Regular verbs are known as 'weak' verbs and the endings in the present tense are as follows:

sagen to say

Ich	sage
du	sagst
er, sie, es	sagt
wir	sagen
ihr	sagt
Sie	sagen
sie	sagen

The endings are added to the stem of the verb. To find the stem, knock **-en** off the infinitive (which is the form of the verb given in a dictionary).

Irregular verbs are known as 'strong' verbs.
Sein to be and **haben** to have, are both strong verbs.

sein		haben	
ich	bin	ich	habe
du	bist	du	hast
er, sie, es	ist	er, sie, es	hat
wir	sind	wir	haben
ihr	seid	ihr	habt
Sie	sind	Sie	haben
sie	sind	sie	haben

Some strong verbs change the vowel in the second person singular (**du**) and the third person singular (**er, sie, es**)
e.g.

fahren to drive, to go

ich	fahre
du	fährst
er, sie, es	fährt
wir	fahren
ihr	fahrt
Sie	fahren
sie	fahren

geben to give

ich	gebe
du	gibst
er, sie, es	gibt
wir	geben
ihr	gebt
Sie	geben
sie	geben

185

Another useful irregular verb is **wissen** to know

ich	weiß
du	weißt
er, sie, es	weiß
wir	wissen
ihr	wißt
Sie	wissen
sie	wissen

Negatives

To make a verb negative, add **nicht**

e.g. **Ich kann nicht** I can't
Wir verstehen nicht We don't understand

Separable verbs

A lot of verbs change or add to their meaning simply by adding a prefix.

e.g. **fahren**	to go, to drive
abfahren	to leave
kommen	to come
ankommen	to arrive

In a sentence the prefix splits from the rest of the verb and goes to the end of the sentence.

e.g. **Er kommt um neun Uhr an** He's arriving at nine o'clock

Some prefixes are inseparable and don't go to the end of the sentence.

Modal verbs

Modals are a group of verbs which are very useful if you want to express attitudes or intentions. Modal verbs include:

dürfen: ich darf – I may, I am allowed to
       darf ich? – may I?
       Sie dürfen – you may, you are allowed to

können: ich kann – I can
       Sie können – you can

mögen: ich mag – I like
       Sie mögen – you like

müssen: ich muß – I must, have to
       Sie müssen – you must, have to

sollen: ich soll – I am supposed to
       Sie sollen – you are supposed to

wollen: ich will – I want
       Sie wollen – you want

They are often used in the 'conditional' form or in the simple past rather than in the present:

e.g.

ich könnte – I could
wir/Sie könnten – we/you could

ich möchte – I'd like
wir/Sie möchten – we'd/you'd like
Was möchten Sie? – what would you like?

ich sollte – I should, I ought to
wir/Sie sollten – we/you should, ought to

Ich mußte – I had to

Ich wollte – I wanted to

Verbs in other tenses you may find useful:

sein	ich war	I was, I used to be
	wir waren	we were, we used to be
	ich bin gewesen	I have been
	wir sind gewesen	we have been
haben	ich hatte	I had, I used to have
	wir hatten	we had, we used to have
gehen	ich ging	I went, I used to go
	wir gingen	we went, we used to go

The future tense is used relatively little in German and the verb tends to stay in the present tense, especially when time is mentioned.

e.g. You'll pick me up tomorrow morning then

Du holst mich also morgen früh ab

We're going there tomorrow

Wir gehen morgen dahin

Questions

To ask a question, use a question word and invert the subject and verb:

e.g. **Was machst du?**	What are you doing?
Was wollen Sie?	What do you want?
Wer bist du?	Who are you?

If there is no question word simply invert the subject and verb:

e.g. **Kommen Sie?**	Are you coming?
Verstehst du?	Do you understand?

DAYS, MONTHS, DATES

Days

Monday	**Montag**	*mohntaag*
Tuesday	**Dienstag**	*deenztaag*
Wednesday	**Mittwoch**	*mittvok*
Thursday	**Donnerstag**	*donnerztaag*
Friday	**Freitag**	*friytaag*
Saturday	**Samstag/Sonnabend**	*zamstaag/zonnaabent*
Sunday	**Sonntag**	*zonntaag*

Months

January	**Januar**	*yanoo-ar*
February	**Februar**	*faybroo-ar*
March	**März**	*merts*
April	**April**	*april*
May	**Mai**	*miy*
June	**Juni**	*yoonee*
July	**Juli**	*yoolee*
August	**August**	*owgoost*
September	**September**	*zeptember*
October	**Oktober**	*oktohber*
November	**November**	*november*
December	**Dezember**	*detsember*

Seasons

Spring	**der Frühling**	*frewling*
Summer	**der Sommer**	*zommer*
Autumn	**der Herbst**	*herpst*
Winter	**der Winter**	*vinter*

General phrases

Day	der Tag	*taag*
Week	die Woche	*voke*
Fortnight	vierzehn Tage	*feertsayn taage*
Month	der Monat	*mohnaat*
Year	das Jahr	*yaar*
Six months	ein halbes Jahr	*iyn halbez yaar*
on Monday	(am) Montag	*am mohntaag*
on Tuesdays	dienstags	*deenztaagz*
every Wednesday	jeden Mittwoch	*yayden mittvok*
in August	im August	*im owgoost*
at the beginning of March	Anfang März	*anfang merts*
in the middle of June	Mitte Juni	*mitte yoonee*
at the end of September	Ende September	*ende zeptember*
in six months' time	in einem halben Jahr	*in iynem halben yaar*
during the summer	während des Sommers	*vayrent des zommerz*
two years ago	vor zwei Jahren	*for tsviy yaaren*
(in) the nineties	in den neunziger Jahren	*in dayn noyntsiger yaaren*
last …	letzten/letzte/letztes	*lettsten/lettste/lettstes*
last Monday	letzten Montag	*lettsten mohntaag*
last week	letzte Woche	*lettste voke*
last month	letzten Monat	*letsten mohnaat*
last year	letztes Jahr	*lettstes yaar*
next …	nächsten/nächste/nächstes	*neksten/nekste/nekstes*
next Tuesday	nächsten Dienstag	*neksten deenztaag*
next week	nächste Woche	*nekste voke*

next month	**nächsten Monat**	*neksten mohnaat*
next year	**nächstes Jahr**	*nekstes yaar*
What day is it today?	**Welchen Tag haben wir heute?**	
		velshen taag haaben veer hoyte
What is the date today?	**Was ist das heutige Datum?**	
		vas ist das hoytige daatoom
When is your birthday?	**Wann hast du Geburstag?**	
		van hast doo geboortstaag
Today	**heute**	*hoyte*
This morning	**heute morgen**	*hoyte morgen*
This afternoon	**heute nachmittag**	*hoyte naakmittaag*
(In the) morning	**am Morgen**	*am morgen*
(In the) afternoon	**am Nachmittag**	*am naakmittaag*
(In the) evening	**am Abend**	*am aabent*
(At) night	**in der Nacht**	*in der naakt*
Yesterday	**gestern**	*gestern*
The day before yesterday	**vorgestern**	*forgestern*
Yesterday morning	**gestern morgen**	*gestern morgen*
Yesterday evening	**gestern abend**	*gestern aabent*
Tomorrow	**morgen**	*morgen*
The day after tomorrow	**übermorgen**	*ewbermorgen*
Tomorrow afternoon	**morgen nachmittag**	*morgen naakmittaag*
Tomorrow morning	**morgen früh**	*morgen frew*
Before Saturday	**vor Samstag**	*for zamztaag*
After Thursday	**nach Donnerstag**	*naak donnerstaag*
Until/by Friday	**bis Freitag**	*bis friytaag*
Two days ago	**vor zwei Tagen**	*for tsviy taagen*

On the first of January	**am ersten Januar**
	am ersten yanoo-ar
On Tuesday 10 May	**am Dienstag den zehnten Mai**
	am deenztaag dayn tsaynten miy
1990	**neunzehnhundertneunzig**
	noyntsaynhoondertnoyntsig
In the 15th century	**im fünfzehnten Jahrhundert**
	im fewnftsaynten yaarhoondert

TIME

● To say that it's 'half past ...' in German you have to say that it's half way round to the next hour, e.g. half past five is **halb sechs**, because it's half way round to six; half past two is **halb drei**, because it's half way to three o'clock.

One o'clock
Ein Uhr
iyn oor

Two o'clock
Zwei Uhr
tsviy oor

Three o'clock etc.
Drei Uhr
driy oor

Quarter past ...
Viertel nach ...
feertel naak

Half past ...
Halb ...
halp

Five past ...
Fünf nach ...
fewnf naak

Twenty-five past ...
Fünfundzwanzig nach ...
fewnfoonttsvantsig naak
Fünf vor halb ...
fewnf for halp

Just after ...
Kurz nach ...
koorts naak

Quarter to ...
Viertel vor ...
feertel for

Ten to ...
Zehn vor ...
tsayn for

Twenty to ...
Zwanzig vor ...
tsvantsig for

Quarter past one
Viertel nach eins
feertel naak iyns

Half past three
Halb vier
halp feer

Half past seven
Halb acht
halp aakt

Five past nine
Fünf nach neun
fewnf naak noyn

Just after four o'clock
Kurz nach vier
koorts naak feer

In the morning (am)
Morgens
morgenz

Quarter to five
Viertel vor fünf
feertel for fewnf

In the afternoon (pm)
Nachmittags
naakmittaags

Ten to eleven
Zehn vor elf
tsayn for elf

In the evening
Abends
aabents

Noon/midday
Zwölf Uhr mittags/Mittag
zwerlf oor mittaags/mittaag

A quarter of an hour
Eine Viertelstunde
iyne feertelshtoonde

Midnight
Mitternacht
mitternaakt

Three quarters of an hour
Eine Dreiviertelstunde
iyne driyfeertelshtoonde

Half an hour
Eine halbe Stunde
iyne halbe shtoonde

24-hour clock

0045
null Uhr fünfundvierzig
nooll oor fewnfoontfeertsig

1430
vierzehn Uhr dreißig
feertsayn oor driyssig

0900
neun Uhr
noyn oor

2149
**einundzwanzig Uhr
neunundvierzig**
*iynoonttsvantsig oor
noynoontfeertsig*

1300
dreizehn Uhr
driytsayn oor

General phrases

What time is it?
Wieviel Uhr ist es?
veefeel oor ist es

It's . . .
Es ist . . .
es ist

It's one o'clock
Es ist ein Uhr
es ist iyn oor

It's six o'clock
Es ist sechs Uhr
es ist zeks oor

It's quarter past eight
Es ist viertel nach acht
es ist veertel naak aakt

What time . . .?
Um wieviel Uhr . . .?
oom veefeel oor

At . . .
Um . . .
oom

At half past one
Um halb zwei
oom halp tsviy

At quarter to seven
Um viertel vor sieben
oom feertel for zeeben

At 2155
**Um einundzwanzig Uhr
fünfundfünfzig**
*oom iynoonttsvantsig oor
fewnfoontfewnftsig*

At exactly/precisely two o'clock
Punkt um zwei Uhr
poonkt oom tsviy oor

Exactly two o'clock
Punkt zwei Uhr
poonkt tsviy oor

About half past six
Ungefähr halb sieben
oongefayr halp zeeben

Nearly quarter to five
Fast viertel vor fünf
fast feertel for fewnf

Soon
Bald
balt

Early
Früh
frew

Late
Spät
shpayt

On time
Pünktlich
pewnktlish

Earlier
Früher
frewer

Later
Später
shpayter

Half an hour ago
Vor einer halben Stunde
for iyner halben shtoonde

In ten minutes' time
In zehn Minuten
in tsayn minooten

In quarter of an hour
In einer Viertelstunde
in iyner feertelshtoonde

COUNTRIES AND NATIONALITIES

● It's usual in German to refer to someone's nationality by saying 'he is a Dane', **Er ist Däner**, or 'She is a Frenchwoman', **Sie ist Französin**, rather than saying 'he is Danish', 'she is French' etc.

● Languages, where appropriate, are the same as the adjective, but written with a capital letter.

Country	Nationality *masculine/feminine*	Adjective
Africa		
Afrika	**Afrikaner(in)**	**afrikanisch**
Asia		
Asien	**Asiat(in)**	**asiatisch**
Austria		
Österreich	**Österreicher(in)**	**österreichisch**
Australia		
Australien	**Australier(in)**	**aus Australien**
Belgium		
Belgien	**Belgier(in)**	**belgisch**
Bulgaria		
Bulgarien	**Bulgare/Bulgarin**	**bulgarisch**
Canada		
Kanada	**Kanadier(in)**	**kanadisch**
Central America		
Mittelamerika	**Mittelamerikaner(in)**	**aus Mittelamerika**
China		
China	**Chinese/Chinesin**	**chinesisch**
Cuba		
Kuba	**Kubaner(in)**	**kubanisch**
Czechoslovakia		
die Tschechoslowakei	**Tscheche/Tschechin**	**tschechisch**

Denmark		
Dänemark	**Däne/Dänin**	**dänisch**
Egypt		
Ägypten	**Ägypter(in)**	**ägyptisch**
Eire		
Eire	**Ire/Irin**	**irisch**
England		
England	**Engländer(in)**	**englisch**
Europe		
Europa	**Europäer**	**europäisch**
Finland		
Finnland	**Finne/Finnin**	**finnisch**
France		
Frankreich	**Franzose/Französin**	**französisch**
Germany		
Deutschland	**Deutscher/Deutsche**	**deutsch**
Great Britain		
Großbritannien	**Brite/Britin**	**britisch**
Greece		
Griechenland	**Grieche/Griechin**	**griechisch**
Hungary		
Ungarn	**Ungar(in)**	**ungarisch**
India		
Indien	**Inder(in)**	**indisch**
Ireland		
Irland	**Ire/Irin**	**irisch**
Israel		
Israel	**Israeli**	**israelisch**
Italy		
Italien	**Italiener(in)**	**italienisch**
Japan		
Japan	**Japaner(in)**	**japanisch**
Luxembourg		
Luxemburg	**Luxemburger(in)**	**aus Luxemburg**
Malta		
Malta	**Malteser(in)**	**aus Malta**

Mexico		
Mexiko	**Mexikaner(in)**	**mexikanisch**
Netherlands		
Holland	**Holländer(in)**	**holländisch**
New Zealand		
Neuseeland	**Neuseeländer(in)**	**neuseeländisch**
Northern Ireland		
Nordirland	**Ire/Irin**	**irisch**
Norway		
Norwegen	**Norweger(in)**	**norwegisch**
Poland		
Polen	**Pole/Polin**	**polnisch**
Portugal		
Portugal	**Portugiese/ Portugiesin**	**portugiesisch**
Rumania		
Rumänien	**Rumäne/Rumänin**	**rumänisch**
Russia		
Rußland	**Russe/Russin**	**russisch**
Scotland		
Schottland	**Schotte/Schottin**	**schottisch**
South America		
Südamerika	**Südamerikaner(in)**	**südamerikanisch**
Soviet Union		
die Sowjetunion	**Sowjetbürger(in)**	**sowjetisch**
Spain		
Spanien	**Spanier(in)**	**spanisch**
Sweden		
Schweden	**Schwede/Schwedin**	**schwedisch**
Switzerland		
die Schweiz	**Schweizer(in)**	**schweizerisch**
Turkey		
die Türkei	**Türke/Türkin**	**türkisch**
United Kingdom		
Vereinigtes Königreich		

United States		
die Vereinigten	**Amerikaner(in)**	**amerikanisch**
Staaten/Amerika/		
USA		
Wales		
Wales	**Waliser(in)**	**walisisch**
West Indies		
Westindische Inseln	**Westinder(in)**	**westindisch**
Yugoslavia		
Jugoslawien	**Jugoslawe/**	**jugoslawisch**
	Jugoslawin	

GENERAL SIGNS AND NOTICES

Achtung	Caution
Aufzug	Lift
. . . Auf eigene Gefahr	At your own risk
Ausgang	Exit
Auskunft	Information
Ausverkauf	Sale
Außer Betrieb	Out of order
Baustelle	Building site
Belegt	Full, no vacancies
Besetzt	Engaged
Betreten verboten	No trespassing
Betriebsferien	Closed for holidays
Bitte klingeln	Please ring
Bitte klopfen	Please knock
Bitte nicht stören	Do not disturb
Damen	Ladies, Women
Drücken	Push
Eingang	Entrance
Eintreten ohne zu klopfen	Enter without knocking
Eintritt frei	Admission free
Entwerter	Ticket stamping machine
Erdgeschoß	Ground floor
Erste Hilfe	First Aid
Fahrstuhl	Lift
Feiertags geschlossen	Closed on public holidays
Feuermelder	Fire alarm
Frei	Free, vacant
Frisch gestrichen	Wet paint
Für Unbefugte verboten	Trespassers will be prosecuted
Gefahr	Danger
Geldeinwurf	Insert money

Geöffnet	Open
Geschlossen	Closed
Heiß	Hot
Herren	Men, Gentlemen
Kalt	Cold
Kasse	Cashier
Kein Durchgang für Fußgänger	No thoroughfare for pedestrians
Kein Trinkwasser	Not drinking water
Kein Zutritt	No entrance
Kundendienst	Customer service
Lebensgefahr	Danger of death
Mehrwertsteuer	VAT
Münzrückgabe	Coin return button
Nicht berühren	Do not touch
Notausgang	Emergency exit
Polizei	Police
Privatweg	Private road
Radweg	Cycle path
Rauchen verboten	No smoking
Reserviert	Reserved
Rolltreppe	Escalator
Ruhetag	Closed all day
Schlussverkauf	Sale
Sonderangebot	Special offer
Spätvorstellung	Late performance
Stehplätze	Standing room
Trinkwasser	Drinking water
Verboten	Forbidden, prohibited
Vorsicht	Caution
Vorsicht, bissiger Hund	Beware of the dog
Werktags geöffnet	Open on workdays
Ziehen	Pull
Zimmer frei	Rooms to let
Zu verkaufen	For sale
Zu vermieten	To let, for hire

CONVERSION TABLES
(approximate equivalents)

Linear measurements

centimetres   **Zentimeter (cm)**
metres   **Meter (m)**
kilometres   **Kilometer (km)**

10 cm = 4 inches	1 inch = 2.45 cm
50 cm = 19.6 inches	1 foot = 30 cm
1 metre = 39.37 inches	1 yard = 0.91 m
(just over 1 yard)	
110 metres = 100 yards	
1 km = 0.62 miles	1 mile = 1.61 km

To convert
km to miles: divide by 8 and multiply by 5
miles to km: divide by 5 and multiply by 8

Miles		Kilometres
0.6	1	1.6
1.2	2	3.2
1.9	3	4.8
2.5	4	6.4
3	5	8
6	10	16
12	20	32
19	30	48
25	40	64
31	50	80
62	100	161
68	110	177
75	120	193
81	130	209

Liquid measures

litre	**Liter (l)**
1 litre = 1.8 pints	1 pint = 0.57 litre
5 litres = 1.1 gallons	1 gallon = 4.55 litres

'A litre of water's a pint and three quarters'

Gallons   Litres

Gallons		Litres
0.2	1	4.5
0.4	2	9
0.7	3	13.6
0.9	4	18
1.1	5	23
2.2	10	45.5

Weights

gram	**Gramm (g)**
100 grams	**Hundert Gramm**
200 grams	**Zweihundert Gramm**
pound	**Pfund (pfd)**
kilo	**Kilo (kg)**

100 g = 3.5 oz	1 oz = 28 g
200 g = 7 oz	¼ lb = 113 g
½ kilo = 1.1 lb	½ lb = 225 g
1 kilo = 2.2 lb	1 lb = 450 g

Pounds   Kilos (Grams)

Pounds		Kilos (Grams)
2.2	1	0.45 (450)
4.4	2	0.9 (900)
6.6	3	1.4 (1400)
8.8	4	1.8 (1800)
11	5	2.3 (2300)
22	10	4.5 (4500)

Area

hectare   **Hektar**
1 hectare = 2.5 acres   1 acre = 0.4 hectares

To convert
hectares to acres: divide by 2 and multiply by 5
acres to hectares: divide by 5 and multiply by 2

Hectares		Acres
0.4	1	2.5
2.0	5	12
4	10	25
10	50	124
40.5	100	247

Clothing and shoe sizes

Women's dresses and suits

UK	10	12	14	16	18	20
Continent	36	38	40	42	44	46

Men's suits and coats

UK	36	38	40	42	44	46
Continent	46	48	50	52	54	56

Men's shirts

UK	14	14½	15	15½	16	16½	17
Continent	36	37	38	39	41	42	43

Shoes

UK	2	3	4	5	6	7	8	9	10	11
Continent	35	36	37	38	39	41	42	43	44	45

Waist and chest measurements

inches	28	30	32	34	36	38	40	42	44	46	48	50
centimetres	71	76	80	87	91	97	102	107	112	117	122	127

Tyre pressures

lb/sq in	15	18	20	22	24	26	28	30	33	35
kg/sq cm	1.1	1.3	1.4	1.5	1.7	1.8	2.0	2.1	2.3	2.5

NATIONAL HOLIDAYS

G = Germany, S = Switzerland, A = Austria

Neujahrstag	New Year's Day	1 January *(GSA)*
		2 January *(S)*
Dreikönigsfest	Epiphany	6 January *(A)*
Faschingsdienstag	Shrove Tuesday *(afternoon)*	*(GSA)*
Karfreitag	Good Friday	*(GS)*
Ostermontag	Easter Monday	*(GSA)*
Tag der Arbeit	Labour Day	1 May *(GA)*
Himmelfahrt	Ascension	*(GSA)*
Pfingstmontag	Whit Monday	*(GSA)*
Fronleichnam	Corpus Christi	*(A, and parts G)*
Siebzehnter Juni	Day of Unity	17 June *(G)*
Maria Himmelfahrt	Assumption	15 August *(A)*
Nationalfeiertag	National Day	26 October *(A)*
Allerheiligen	All Saints Day	1 November *(A, and parts G)*
Buß- und Bettag	Day of Prayer and Repentance	*(G)*
Die unbefleckte Empfängnis	Immaculate Conception	8 November *(A)*
Heiligabend	Christmas Eve	24 December *(Half day) (GSA)*
Erster Weihnachtstag	Christmas Day	25 December *(GSA)*
Zweiter Weihnachtstag	Boxing Day	26 December *(G)*
Stephanstag	St Stephen's Day	26 December *(SA)*

USEFUL ADDRESSES

Tourist offices in the UK

German National Tourist Office
Nightingale House
65 Curzon Street
London W1Y 7PE
Tel: 071-495 3990/91

Swiss National Tourist Office
Swiss Centre
New Coventry Street
London W1V 8EE
Tel: 071-734 1921

Austrian National Tourist Office
30 St George Street
London W1R 0AL
Tel: 071-629 0461

Embassies in UK

Embassy of the Federal Republic of Germany
23 Belgrave Square
Chesham Place
London SW1X 8PZ
Tel: 071-235 5033

Embassy of Switzerland
16/18 Montagu Place
London W1H 2BQ
Tel: 071-723 0701

Austrian Embassy
18 Belgrave Mews West
London SW1X 8HU
Tel: 071-235 3731

Embassies in Ireland

Embassy of the Federal Republic of Germany
31 Trimleston Avenue
Booterstown
Blackrock
County Dublin
Tel: Dublin 69 30 11

Austrian Embassy
15 Ailesbury Court
93 Ailesbury Road
Dublin 4
Tel: Dublin 69 45 77

Embassy of Switzerland
6 Ailesbury Road
Ballsbridge
Dublin 4
Tel: Dublin 69 25 15

Other organisations

Goethe Institute
(for information about
cultural events and
language courses)
50/51 Prince's Gate
Exhibition Road
London SW77 2PH
Tel: 071-581 3344/7

Goethe Institute
37 Merrion Square
Dublin 2
Tel: Dublin 76 64 51

German Chamber of Industry and Commerce
12–13 Suffolk Street
London SW1Y 4HG
Tel: 071-930 7251

DER Travel Service
(Deutsches Reisebüro GmbH)
18 Conduit Street
London W1
Tel: 071-408 0111

British embassies abroad

Germany
Friedrich-Ebert Allee 77
5300 Bonn 1
Tel: 23 40 61
There are also consulates in:
Berlin, Bremen, Düsseldorf, Frankfurt, Freiburg, Hamburg,
Hanover, Kiel, Munich, Nuremberg and Stuttgart

Austria
Jauresgaße 12
1030 Wien
Tel: 713 15 75/9
There are also consulates in:
Bregenz, Graz, Innsbruck and Salzburg

Switzerland
Thunstraße 50
3005 Berne
Tel: 44 50 21/6
There are also consulates in:
Geneva, Lugano, Montreux and Zurich

Irish embassies abroad

Germany
Godesberger Allee 119
5300 Bonn 2
Tel: 37 69 37

Switzerland
Eigerstraße 71
3007 Berne
Tel: 46 23 53

Austria
Hilton Centre
1030 Wien
Tel: 75 42 46

NUMBERS

0	null	*nooll*
1	eins	*iyns*
2	zwei	*tsviy*
3	drei	*driy*
4	vier	*feer*
5	fünf	*fewnf*
6	sechs	*zeks*
7	sieben	*zeeben*
8	acht	*aakt*
9	neun	*noyn*
10	zehn	*tsayn*
11	elf	*elf*
12	zwölf	*zwerlf*
13	dreizehn	*driytsayn*
14	vierzehn	*feertsayn*
15	fünfzehn	*fewnftsayn*
16	sechzehn	*zektsayn*
17	siebzehn	*zeebtsayn*
18	achtzehn	*aakttsayn*
19	neunzehn	*noyntsayn*
20	zwanzig	*tsvantsig*
21	einundzwanzig	*iynoonttsvantsig*
22	zweiundzwanzig	*tsviyoonttsvantsig*
23	dreiundzwanzig	*driyoonttsvantsig*
24	vierundzwanzig	*feeroonttsvantsig*
25	fünfundzwanzig	*fewnfoonttsvantsig*
26	sechsundzwanzig	*zeksoonttsvantsig*
27	siebenundzwanzig	*zeebenoonttsvantsig*
28	achtundzwanzig	*aaktoonttsvantsig*
29	neunundzwanzig	*noynoonttsvantsig*
30	dreißig	*driyssig*
31	einunddreißig	*iynoontdriyssig*

32 etc.	**zweiunddreißig**	*tsviyoontdriyssig*
40	**vierzig**	*feertsig*
50	**fünfzig**	*fewnftsig*
60	**sechzig**	*zektsig*
70	**siebzig**	*zeebtsig*
80	**achtzig**	*aakttsig*
90	**neunzig**	*noyntsig*
100	**hundert**	*hoondert*
101	**hunderteins**	*hoondertiyns*
102 etc.	**hundertzwei**	*hoonderttsviy*
150	**hundertfünfzig**	*hoondertfewnftsig*
200	**zweihundert**	*tsviyhoondert*
300	**dreihundert**	*driyhoondert*
400	**vierhundert**	*feerhoondert*
500	**fünfhundert**	*fewnfhoondert*
600	**sechshundert**	*zekshoondert*
700	**siebenhundert**	*zeebenhoondert*
800	**achthundert**	*aakthoondert*
900	**neunhundert**	*noynhoondert*
1000	**tausend**	*towzent*
1100 etc.	**tausendeinhundert**	*towzentiynhoondert*
2000 etc.	**zweitausend**	*tsviytowzent*
100 000	**hunderttausend**	*hoonderttowzent*
1 000 000	**eine Million**	*iyne millyohn*
2 000 000 etc.	**zwei Millionen**	*tsviy millyohnen*

● One: use **ein** or **eine** with a noun to mean 'one' or 'a', e.g. **ein Bier** (one/a beer), **eine heiße Schokolade** (a/one hot chocolate).

● The word for a hundred, **hundert**, doesn't change in the plural – **zweihundert**, **dreihundert** etc. The same applies to **tausend**, a thousand.

● Years:
| **1990** | **neunzehnhundertneunzig** |
| **1815** | **achtzehnhundertfünfzehn** |

DICTIONARY

Words for food and drink are given in the Menu reader, page 113.

See also General signs and notices, page 201, and the lists of Signs you may see in the individual sections.

German nouns are given with the definite article ('the') to show their gender: **der** for masculine, **die** for feminine, **das** for neuter (**die** in the plural).

Adjective endings change according to the case, gender and number of the noun the adjective is describing. A full table of adjective endings is given in the Basic grammar section, page 178.

Other abbreviations: acc. – accusative case; dat. – dative case (see page 179); adj. – adjective.

German-English

A

abbiegen to turn off
der **Abend** evening
das **Abendbrot** supper
das **Abendessen** dinner (*evening meal*)
    aber but
    abfahren to depart (*bus, car*)
die **Abfahrt** departure (*bus, car*)
der **Abfahrtslauf** downhill skiing
der **Abfall** rubbish, litter
der **Abfertigungsschalter** check-in desk
    abfliegen to depart (*plane*)
der **Abflug** departure (*plane*)
das **Abflußrohr** drain
das **Abführmittel** laxative
die **Abholung** collection (*post, rubbish*)

der **Absatz** heel (*shoe*)
    abschicken to post, send off
    abschleppen to tow
das **Abschleppseil** tow rope
der **Abschleppwagen** breakdown truck
    abschließen to lock
das **Abteil** compartment
die **Abteilung** department
die **Agentur** agency
    ähnlich similar
der **Alkohol** alcohol
    alkoholfrei non-alcoholic
der **Alkoholiker** alcoholic (*person*)
    alkoholisch alcoholic (*content*)

alle all
die Allee avenue
allein alone
alles everything
allgemein general
  im allgemeinen in general
als as, when (*with past tense*); than
also so, well, therefore
alt old
altmodisch old fashioned
das Amtzeichen dialling tone
an at, on
andere other
die anderen the others
anders different(ly)
der Anfang beginning
anfangen to begin
der Anfänger beginner, learner
das Angebot offer

angebrannt burnt (*food*)
angeln to fish, go fishing
die Angelrute fishing rod
angenehm pleasant
der Anhänger fan (*supporter*); trailer (*car*)
ankommen to arrive
die Anlegestelle jetty, pier
anprobieren to try on
der Anruf call (*phone*)
anrufen to telephone
ansehen to look at
  sich ansehen to look at each other
ansteckend infectious
das Antibiotikum antibiotic
die Antiquität antique
antiseptisch antiseptic
die Antwort answer
antworten to answer
die Anzahlung deposit

anziehen to put on
  sich anziehen to dress, get dressed
der Anzug suit
anzünden to light (*fire*)
die Arbeit job, work
arbeiten to work
arbeitslos unemployed
arm poor
der Arm arm
die Armbanduhr watch
die Art kind (*sort of*)
der Artikel article
der Arzt, die Ärztin doctor
der Assistent, die Assistentin assistant
atmen to breathe
die Atmosphäre atmosphere
auch also
auf on, on top of, up
aufgeregt excited
auf jeden Fall in any case
auflegen to hang up (*telephone*)
aufstehen to stand up, get up
Auf Wiedersehen goodbye
Auf Wiederschauen goodbye (*Austria*)
das Auge eye
der Augenblick moment
aus out, from, off (*light etc.*)
die Auseinandersetzung argument
der Ausflug trip, excursion
ausgeben to spend (*money*)
ausgebucht full up (*booked up*)
ausgehen to go out
ausgezeichnet excellent
die Auskunft information

das **Ausland** abroad
    im Ausland sein to be abroad
    ins Ausland fahren to go abroad
der **Ausländer, die Ausländerin** foreigner
    ausländisch foreign
    auspacken to unpack
    sich ausruhen to rest, relax
    ausschalten to turn out, switch off
    außer except
    außerdem besides
die **Aussicht** view
    aussprechen to pronounce
die **Ausstattung** equipment
    aussteigen to get off (*bus*)
die **Ausstellung** exhibition
der **Ausverkauf** sale (*bargains*)
    ausziehen to move out (*house*)
    sich ausziehen to get undressed
das **Auto** car
    mit dem Auto by car
die **Autobahn** motorway
    automatisch automatic
die **Autovermietung** car hire

B

das **Baby** baby
die **Babynahrung** baby food
die **Babywischtücher** baby wipes
das **Bad** bath
    ein Bad nehmen to have a bath
der **Badeanzug** bathing costume
die **Badehose** swimming trunks

der **Bademeister** attendant (*bathing*), lifeguard
    baden to bathe
das **Badezimmer** bathroom
die **Bahn** track, way
der **Bahnhof** station
der **Bahnhofsvorsteher** stationmaster
der **Bahnsteig** platform
    bald soon
    so bald wie möglich as soon as possible
der **Ball** ball (*tennis, football etc.*)
das **Ballet** ballet
die **Banane** banana
der **Bankier** banker
das **Bargeld** cash
    bar bezahlen to pay cash
die **Batterie** battery
der **Bauarbeiter** builder
    bauen to build
der **Bauer** farmer
der **Bauernhof** farm
der **Baum** tree
die **Baumwolle** cotton
die **Baustelle** building site
der **Becher** mug
    bedeuten to mean, signify
    was bedeutet das? what does this mean?
    bedienen to serve
    begeistert enthusiastic
    beginnen to begin
    behalten to keep
die **Behandlung** treatment
    behindert disabled, handicapped
die **Beilage** side dish, side salad
das **Bein** leg
das **Beispiel** example
    zum Beispiel for example

bekannt famous
bekommen to get
beleidigt insulted
beliebt popular
benutzen to use
das **Benzin** petrol
bequem comfortable
der **Berg** mountain
bergauf up the hill
berichten to report
der **Beruf** career, profession
    was sind Sie vom Beruf?
    what do you do?
das **Beruhigungsmittel** sedative
berühren to touch
beschäftigt busy
beschränkt limited
beschreiben to describe
besetzt taken, engaged,
    occupied
besichtigen to visit (*tourist sites*)
der **Besitzer, die Besitzerin**
    owner
besondere special, particular
besonders especially
besorgt worried
besser better
das **Beste** the best
bestehen to insist
bestellen to order
bestimmt definitely
besuchen to go round, visit
der **Besucher, die Besucherin**
    visitor
der **Betrag** amount (*money*)
betrunken drunk
das **Bett** bed, berth
die **Bettdecke** blanket
das **Bettuch** sheet
bevor before

bewegen to move
bezahlen to pay
beziehungsweise (bzw)
    respectively
die **Bibel** the Bible
die **Bibliothek** library
das **Bier vom Faß** draught beer
das **Bild** picture
der **Bildschirm** screen
billig cheap
bis until
ein bißchen a little
bitte please; not at all
blaß pale
blau blue
das **Blei** lead
bleiben to remain
das **Bleichmittel** bleach
bleifrei lead free
der **Bleistift** pencil
blind blind
der **Blitz** lightning
die **Blume** flower
das **Blut** blood
bluten to bleed
blutig rare (*steak*)
der **Boden** ground, floor
der **Bogen** arch
die **Bordkarte** boarding card
die **Börse** stock exchange
die **Botschaft** embassy
brauchen to need
die **Braut** bride
der **Bräutigam** bridegroom
brechen to break
breit broad, wide
brennen to burn
der **Brennstoff** fuel
der **Brief** letter
der **Brieffreund, die Brieffreundin**
    penfriend
der **Briefkasten** letterbox

die Briefmarke stamp (*postage*)
das Briefpapier writing paper
die Brieftasche wallet
der Briefträger, die Briefträgerin postman, postwoman
der Briefumschlag envelope
die Brille glasses
bringen to bring
das Brot bread
das Brötchen bread roll
die Brücke bridge
der Bruder brother
der Brunnen fountain, well
das Buch book
buchen to book, reserve
die Bucht bay
das Bügeleisen iron (*for clothes*)
die Burg castle, fortress
das Büro office
die Bürste brush
der Bus bus
  mit dem Bus by bus
der Busbahnhof bus station
der Busfahrer bus driver
das Butangas butane gas

C

der Chef head (*boss*)
die Chips potato crisps
der Cousin cousin (*male*)
die Creme lotion, cream

D

da there
das Dach roof
Damen Ladies (*toilets*)
die Damenbinden sanitary towels
der Dampf steam
der Dampfer steamer

dankbar grateful
danke thank you
dann then
das the, this, that, which (*neuter*)
das Datum date (*date*)
dauern to last, take time
der Daumen thumb
dein/e your (*adj.*) (*familiar*)
dein/e/r yours (*familiar*)
denken to think
das Denkmal monument
denn for, as
der the, who, which (*masculine*)
der-/die-/dasselbe the same
deshalb therefore, for that reason
das destillierte Wasser distilled water
das Detail detail
deutsch German
  die deutsche Frage the German question
Deutschland (das) Germany
dich you (*familiar*)
dick thick, fat
die the, who, which (*feminine*)
der Dieb thief
dies this
diese these
dir (to) you
der Direktor, die Direktorin director
das Dokument document
der Dom cathedral
der Donner thunder
das Doppelbett double bed
doppelt double
das Dorf village
dort there

die **Dose** can, tin
die **Dosenmilch** tinned milk
der **Dosenöffner** can opener
der **Dozent, die Dozentin** lecturer
die **Drahtseilbahn** cable car
   draußen outside
   drehen to turn
   dringend urgent
   drinnen indoors
   dritte/r/s third
die **Droge** drug
   drucken to print
   drücken to press, push
   du you (*familiar*)
   dumm stupid
   dunkel dark
   dünn thin
   durch through; cooked, well
     done (*steak*)
der **Durchfall** diarrhoea
   durchgehend direct (*train*)
   durchkommen to get through
   durstig thirsty
die **Dusche** shower

E

   echt genuine, real
die **Ecke** corner
   egal: es ist mir egal I don't
     mind
   ehrlich honest
     ehrlich gesagt frankly
das **Ei, die Eier** egg(s)
     das gekochte Ei boiled egg
   eigentlich in fact
   in Eile sein hurry; to be in a
     hurry
der **Eimer** bucket
   ein one, a

   eindrucksvoll impressive
   eine one, a (*feminine*)
   einfach simple, plain
   einige some
   einkaufen gehen to go
     shopping
das **Einkaufszentrum** shopping
     centre
das **Einkommen** income
   einladen to invite
die **Einladung** invitation
   einmal once
     auf einmal all of a sudden
   eins one (*number*)
   einsam lonely
   einschalten to switch on
   einschiffen to embark (*boat*)
   einsteigen to enter, get on
     (*bus, train*)
der **Eintritt** admission
    das **Eintrittsgeld**
     admission charge
    die **Eintrittskarte** ticket
     (*theatre etc.*)
   einzel single
das **Einzelbett** single bed
das **Eis** ice
das **Eisen** iron (*metal*)
die **Eisenbahn** railway
der **Elektriker** electrician
die **Elektrizität** electricity
der **Empfang** reception
   empfehlen to recommend
das **Ende** end
die **Endstation** last stop,
    terminus
die **Energie** energy
   eng narrow, tight
   englisch English
der **Enkel** grandson

die **Enkelin** granddaughter
die **Enkelkinder** grandchildren
die **Ente** duck
  entlang along
  sich entschließen to decide
  entschuldigen Sie mich
    excuse me
  enttäuscht disappointed
  entweder either
    entweder . . . oder either
    . . . or
  entwickeln to develop
die **Entzündung** inflammation
  er he
das **Erdbeben** earthquake
die **Erde** earth
das **Erdgeschoß** ground floor
die **Erdnuß** peanut
die **Erfahrung** experience
der **Erfolg** success
  sich erholen to recover
  sich erinnern an to remember
  erkennen to recognise
  erklären to declare, explain
  erlauben to let (*allow*)
die **Ermäßigung** reduction,
  discount
  ernst serious
  erreichen to reach
der **Ersatzreifen** spare tyre
  erste/r/s first
die **Erste Hilfe** first aid
der/die **Erwachsene** adult
  erwarten expect
  erzählen to tell
  es it
  es sei denn unless
  es tut mir leid I'm sorry
der **Esel** donkey
  essen to eat
das **Essen** food, meal

der **Essig** vinegar
das **Eßzimmer** dining-room
das **Etikett** label
  etwas something
    etwas gern tun to like
    doing something
  euch (to) you (*familiar*)
  euer/e your (*adj.*) (*familiar*)
  eure/r/s yours (*familiar*)
  eventuell perhaps
das **Examen** examination
der **Export** export
  expreß express

F

die **Fabrik** factory
die **Fähre** ferry
  fahren to drive
der **Fahrer** driver
das **Fahrgeld** fare

die **Fahrkarte** ticket (*travel*)
der **Fahrkartenschalter** ticket
  office
der **Fahrplan** timetable (*travel*)
das **Fahrrad** bicycle
die **Fahrt** trip, journey, tour
das **Fahrzeug** vehicle
  falls in case
  falsch false, wrong
die **Familie** family
  fantastisch fantastic
die **Farbe** colour
  farbecht colour fast
  fast nearly
  faul lazy; rotten
das **Federbett** duvet
der **Fehler** fault, flaw, mistake
    einen Fehler machen to
    make a mistake
  fehlerhaft faulty

das **Feld** field
das **Fenster** window
die **Ferien** holidays (*school*)
   das **Ferienhaus** holiday house
   die **Ferienwohnung** holiday flat
   Fern- long-distance
   das **Ferngespräch** long-distance call
das **Fernsehen** television
   fernsehen to watch television
die **Ferse** heel (*foot*)
   fertig ready
das **Fest** festival, party
   fest firm, solid
das **Fett** fat
   fettarm low-fat
   fettig greasy
   feucht damp
das **Feuer** fire
das **Feuerwerk** firework
das **Feuerzeug** lighter (*cigarette*)
das **Fieber** fever, temperature
   finden to find
der **Finger** finger
die **Firma** firm (*company*)
der **Fisch** fish
   flach level (*flat*)
die **Flasche** bottle
der **Flaschenöffner** bottle opener
das **Fleisch** meat
die **Fliege** fly
   fliegen to fly
   fließend fluent (*languages*)
die **Flitterwochen** honeymoon
der **Flohmarkt** flea market
der **Flügel** wing
der **Flug** flight
die **Fluggesellschaft** airline
der **Flughafen** airport

das **Flugzeug** aeroplane, aircraft
der **Fluß** river
die **Flüssigkeit** liquid
   folgen to follow
der **Fön** hairdrier
   fönen to blow-dry (*hair*)
   formell formal
   nicht formell informal
   fortgeschritten advanced
der **Fortschritt** progress
die **Frage** question
   fragen to ask
   Frau Mrs
die **Frau** woman
   Fräulein Miss
   frech cheeky
   frei free (*available, unoccupied*)
die **Freiheit** freedom
der/die **Fremde** stranger
der **Freund** friend, boyfriend
die **Freundin** friend, girlfriend
der **Frieden** peace
der **Friedhof** cemetery
   frieren to freeze
   frisch fresh
der **Frostschutz** antifreeze
die **Frucht** fruit
   früh early
   früher earlier
der **Frühling** spring
das **Frühstück** breakfast
   sich fühlen to feel
   sich unwohl/wohl fühlen to feel ill/well
der **Führerschein** driving licence
die **Führung** guided tour
   füllen to fill
   funktionieren to work (*function*)
   für for

furchtbar dreadful
der **Fuß** foot
  zu Fuß on foot
der **Fußball** football
der **Fußweg** footpath
füttern to feed (*inc. baby*)

G

die **Gabel** fork
die **Galerie** gallery
der **Gang** corridor, gangway
ganz bestimmt yes, absolutely
die **Garantie** guarantee
der **Garten** garden
die **Gartenbohnen** kidney beans, haricot beans
die **Gaskartusche** gas refill
der **Gast** guest
der **Gastgeber, die Gastgeberin** host, hostess
das **Gebäude** building
geben to give
das **Gebiet** district, region
das **Gebiß** denture
die **Gebühr** charge, fee
der **Geburtstag** birthday
die **Gefahr** danger
gefährlich dangerous
das **Gefängnis** prison
gefroren frozen
der **Gegenstand** object (*thing*)
gegenüber opposite
das **Geheimnis** secret
gehen to go
das **Gehirn** brain
das **Gehör** hearing
gehören to belong (to)
der **Gehsteig** pavement

der **Geistliche** priest
gelähmt paralysed
gelb yellow
das **Geld** money
der **Geldbeutel** purse
das **Gelee** jelly
das **Gemälde** painting
gemeinsam common (*shared*)
genau exact(ly)
genießen to enjoy
genug enough
das **Gepäck** luggage
gerade straight, even (*not odd*)
der **Geruch** smell
das **Geschäft** shop, business
  geschäftlich on business
der **Geschäftsführer, die Geschäftsführerin** managing director
die **Geschäftsreise** business trip
das **Geschenk** gift, present
die **Geschichte** history
geschieden divorced
das **Geschirrtuch** drying-up cloth
geschlossen closed
der **Geschmack** flavour, taste
geschnitten cut, sliced
die **Geschwindigkeit** speed
die **Geschwindigkeitsbegrenzung** speed limit
die **Geschwister** brothers and sisters
die **Gesellschaft** society, company (*business*)
das **Gesicht** face
  die **Gesichtscreme** face cream
  der **Gesichtspuder** face powder

gesperrt closed (*road*)
gestern yesterday
gestohlen stolen
gestreift striped
gesund fit (*healthy*)
die **Gesundheit** health
das **Getränk** drink
getrennt separated
die **Gewerkschaft** trade union
das **Gewicht** weight
gewöhnlich usual, common
das **Gewürz** spice
gibt es . . . ? is there . . . ?
gießen to pour
das **Gift** poison
giftig poisonous
der **Gipfel** summit, top
das **Glas** glass
glatt smooth
glauben to believe, think
gleich equal
der/die/das **Gleiche** the same
der **Gleisanschluß** junction (*rail*)
die **Glocke** bell
das **Glück** luck
  Glück haben to be lucky
glücklich happy
die **Glühbirne** light bulb
gnädige Frau madam
der **Golfplatz** golf course
die **Golfschläger** golf clubs
Gott God
der **Gottesdienst** church service
grau grey
die **Grenze** frontier, border
der **Griff** handle
die **Grippe** flu
groß big, tall
die **Größe** size
die **Großeltern** grandparents
größer bigger

die **Großmutter** grandmother
der **Großvater** grandfather
großzügig generous
grün green
der **Grund** reason
die **Gruppe** group
gültig valid
der **Gummi** rubber
günstig convenient
die **Gurke** cucumber
der **Gürtel** belt
gut good, well
  guten Abend good evening
  gute Nacht good night
  guten Morgen good
    morning
  guten Tag good day

H

das **Haar, die Haare** hair
die **Haarschnellkur** conditioner
der **Haarschnitt** haircut
haben to have
  er/sie hat he/she has
das **Hackfleisch** mince (*meat*)
der **Hafen** harbour
  die **Hafenrundfahrt**
    harbour trip
der **Hahn** tap
halb half (*adj.*)
  eine halbe Stunde half-
    hour, half an hour
die **Hälfte** half
die **Halspastillen** throat lozenges
halt! stop!
halten to hold, stop
die **Hand** hand
die **Handelsmesse** trade fair
handgearbeitet hand made
das **Handgepäck** hand luggage

der **Händler** dealer
der **Handschuh, die Handschuhe** glove, gloves
die **Handtasche** handbag
das **Handtuch** towel
hart hard
häßlich ugly
häufig frequent
haupt main
die **Hauptstadt** capital city
die **Hauptstraße** high (main) street
das **Haus** house
    nach Hause gehen to go home
    zu Hause at home
die **Hausarbeit** housework
die **Hausfrau** housewife
die **Haut** skin
das **Heftpflaster** sticking plaster
heilig holy
    Heiligabend Christmas Eve
die **Heimat** home
    Heimweh haben to be homesick
heiß hot
heißen to be called
    ich heiße . . . my name is . . .
    wie heißen Sie? what's your name?
    was heißt das? what does this mean?
helfen to help
hell light (*coloured*)
    das helle Bier lager
das **Hemd** shirt
herausnehmen to take out, remove
der **Herbst** autumn
der **Herd** stove, cooker

herein! come in!
hereinkommen to come in
Herr Mr
der **Herr** man, gentleman
herum around
das **Herz** heart
    der **Herzanfall** heart attack
heute today
    heute abend this evening, tonight
hier here
    hier ist . . . here is . . .
die **Hilfe** help
    Hilfe! help!
der **Himmel** sky, heaven
hinauslehnen to lean out
hineingehen to enter
sich hinlegen to lie down
hinstellen to put down
hinten at the back
hinter behind
hin und wieder occasionally
hin und zurück return (*ticket*)
hinunter down (*movement*)
die **Hitze** heat
hoch high
das **Hochwasser** high tide
die **Hochzeit** wedding
hoffen to hope
höflich polite
die **Höhle** cave
holen to fetch
das **Holz** wood
homeopatisch homeopathic
homosexuell homosexual
hören to hear
der **Hörer** receiver (*telephone*)
die **Hose** trousers
hübsch pretty
der **Hubschrauber** helicopter

der **Hügel** hill
der **Hund** dog
Hunger haben to be hungry
hungrig hungry
husten to cough
der **Hut** hat

I

ich I
die **Idee** idea
ihm (to) him
ihn him
ihnen (to) them
Ihnen (to) you (*polite*)
ihr (to) her
ihr/e her, their (*adj.*)
ihre/r/s hers, theirs
Ihr/e your (*adj.*) (*polite*)
Ihre/r/s yours (*polite*)
immer always
  immer geradeaus straight on
  immer wieder again and again
in in
inbegriffen included
die **Infektion** infection
der **Ingenieur, die Ingenieurin** engineer
innere inner
innerhalb within
das **Insekt** insect
  das **Insektenbekämpfungs-mittel** insect repellent
die **Insel** island
insgesamt altogether
das **Institut** college, institute
interessant interesting
irgendwie somehow
irgendwo somewhere

sich irren to make a mistake
  Sie haben sich geirrt you've made a mistake

J

die **Jacke** jacket
das **Jahr** year
die **Jahreszeit** season
der **Jahrmarkt** fair
der **Jeansstoff** denim
jede/r/s each, every
jemand someone
jene those
jenseits beyond
jetzt now
das **Jod** iodine
jüdisch Jewish
die **Jugend** youth
die **Jugendherberge** youth hostel
jung young
der **Junge** boy
Jura law (*study subject*)

K

die **Kabine** cabin
der **Kaffee** coffee
kalt cold
der **Kamm** comb
kämpfen to fight
das **Kaninchen** rabbit
der **Kanister** petrol can
die **Kanne** jug
die **Kapelle** chapel
kaputt broken
Karfreitag (der) Good Friday
die **Karte** map
der **Käse** cheese
der **Kater** cat; hangover
die **Katze** cat

kaufen to buy
keine/r/s no, none
der Keks biscuit
der Keller cellar
der Kellner waiter
die Kellnerin waitress
kennen to know (*someone*)
die Kernkraft nuclear power
die Kerze candle
die Kette chain
der Kiefer jaw
das Kind child
die Kinder children
das Kinderbett cot
der Kinderwagen pram
das Kino cinema
die Kirche church
das Kissen cushion, pillow
klar clear
die Klasse class
das Klavier piano
klebrig sticky
das Kleid dress
die Kleider clothes
klein little
der Kleinbus minibus
das Kleingeld change
klemmt: es klemmt it's stuck
der Klempner plumber
das Klima climate
die Klimaanlage air conditioning
klopfen to knock
das Kloster monastery
klug clever
das Knäckebrot crispbread
der Kochtopf saucepan
der koffeinfreie Kaffee
    decaffeinated coffee
der Koffer suitcase
die Kohlensäure carbon dioxide
    mit Kohlensäure fizzy
    ohne Kohlensäure still

komisch funny (*peculiar*)
kommen to come
kommerziell commercial
kompliziert complicated
die Konferenz conference
die Konfitüre jam
der König king
die Königin queen
können to be able (*see grammar, p. 186-7*)
könnte could (*see grammar, p. 186-7*)
das Konto bank account
die Kontaktlinsen contact lenses
der Kontrolleur, die Kontrolleurin inspector
das Konzert concert, concerto
der Kopf head
    die Kopfschmerzen headache
der Kopfsalat lettuce
der Korb basket
der Korken cork
der Korkenzieher corkscrew
der Körper body
kosten to cost
    was kostet das? how much does it cost?
    was kosten sie? how much do they cost?
das Kostüm suit (*lady's*)
das Kraftfahrzeugkennzeichen registration number
krank ill
das Krankenhaus hospital
der Krankenpfleger, die Krankenschwester nurse
der Krankenwagen ambulance
die Krankheit illness
das Kraut herb
der Krebs cancer
der Kreis circle

der **Kreisverkehr** roundabout
das **Kreuz** cross
die **Kreuzfahrt** cruise
der **Krieg** war
der **Kuchen** cake
die **Kuh** cow
die **Küche** kitchen
   kühl cool
der **Kühlschrank** fridge
die **Kunst** art
   die schönen Künste the
     fine arts
der **Künstler** artist
   künstlich artificial
die **Kurve** curve, bend
der **Kurs** course
die **Kusine** cousin (*female*)
die **Küste** coast
der **Kuß** kiss

die **Lebensmittelvergiftung** food
   poisoning
   lecker delicious
das **Leder** leather
   ledig single (*unmarried*)
   leer empty
   legal legal
der **Lehrer, die Lehrerin**
   instructor, teacher
   leicht easy, light (*weight*)
   leider unfortunately
die **Leiter** ladder
   lernen to learn
   lesen to read
   letzte/r/s last
die **Leukämie** leukaemia
die **Leute** people
das **Licht** light
   lieben to love
   Lieblings- favourite
das **Lied** song
die **Lieferung** delivery
der **Lieferwagen** delivery van
der **Liegestuhl** deckchair
der **Liegewagen** couchette
die **Linie** line
   links left
die **Linse** lens (*camera*)
die **Lippe** lip
die **Liste** list
der **Liter** litre
die **Lizenz** licence (*fishing etc.*)
der **LKW (Lastkraftwagen)** lorry
der **Löffel** spoon
der **Lohn** wage
   lohnen: es lohnt sich nicht it's
     not worth it
   los:was ist los? what's the
     matter?
der **Löwe** lion
die **Lotion** lotion

L

   lachen to laugh
   lächeln to smile
der **Laden** shop
die **Lampe** lamp
das **Land** country, land
die **Landschaft** countryside,
   scenery
   lang long (*inc. hair*)
der **Langlauf** cross-country
   skiing
   langsam slow(ly)
   langweilig boring
der **Lärm** noise
   lassen to leave
   laut loud, noisy
die **Lawine** avalanche
   leben to live
das **Leben** life

die Lungenentzündung
pneumonia
lustig funny (*amusing*)

M

machen to do, make
  es macht nichts it doesn't
  matter
  **macht das Ihnen etwas aus,
  wenn . . . ?** do you mind
  if . . . ?
das Mädchen girl
der Magen stomach
  die Magenschmerzen
  stomach ache
  die Magenverstimmung
  indigestion
die Magermilch skimmed milk
der Maler, die Malerin painter
man one (*pronoun*)
manchmal sometimes
der Mann man, husband
  männlich male, masculine
der Mantel coat
die Marine navy
der Markt market
die Maschine machine
die Masern measles
die Maske mask (*diving*)
das Maß measurement
der Matrose sailor
die Mauer wall
das Medikament medicine (*drug*)
  medizinisch medical
das Meer sea
das Mehl flour
mehr more
  nicht mehr no more
mehrere several

der Mehrfachstecker adaptor
(*electrical*)
die Mehrwertsteuer VAT
mein/e my (*adj.*)
mein/e/s mine (*of me*)
die Meinung opinion
  meiner Meinung nach in
  my opinion
die meisten (von) most (of)
der Mensch human being
merkwürdig odd
die Messe mass (*church*); trade
fair
messen to measure
das Messer knife
das Metall metal
mich me
mieten to hire, rent
die Milch milk
mild mild
mindestens at least
der Minister minister
**der Ministerpräsident, die
  Ministerpräsidentin** prime
  minister
die Minute minute (*time*)
mir (to) me
mit with
das Mitglied member
der Mittag midday
das Mittagessen lunch
die Mitte middle
  **mittel: das kontrazeptive
  Mittel** contraceptive
  mittelalterlich medieval
das Mittelmeer mediterranean
die Mitternacht midnight
die Mode fashion
  möchte (he, she) would like
  (*see grammar, p. 186–7*)
  mögen to like

möglich possible
möglicherweise possibly
die **Möglichkeiten** facilities
der **Monat** month
monatlich monthly
der **Mond** moon
morgen tomorrow
   morgen früh tomorrow
   morning
der **Morgen** morning
der **Motor** engine
das **Motorboot** motorboat
das **Motorrad** motorbike
der **Mülleimer** dustbin
müde tired
der **Mund** mouth
die **Münze** coin
das **Museum** museum
die **Musik** music
der **Musiker, die Musikerin** musician

   Sie müssen . . . must; you must . . .
das **Muster** pattern, sample
mutig brave
die **Mutter** mother

N

nach to, towards, after
der **Nachbar, die Nachbarin** neighbour
nachfüllen to refill
der **Nachmittag** afternoon
der **Nachname** surname
die **Nachrichten** news
nächste/r/s next
die **Nacht** night
das **Nachthemd** nightdress
der **Nachtklub** nightclub
die **Nadel** needle

der **Nagel** nail
nah near
nähe: in der Nähe nearby
der **Name** name
die **Nase** nose
   die Nase voll haben to be fed up
das **Nasenbluten** nosebleed
naß wet
die **Nässe** wet(ness)
national national
die **Nationalität** nationality
natürlich natural(ly)
der **Naturschutz** conservation
der **Nebel** fog
   nebelig foggy
neben next to
der **Neffe** nephew
das **Negativ** negative
nehmen to take, catch (*train etc.*)
   ich nehm' es wohl an I suppose so
nein no
nervös nervous
nett kind (*generous*), nice
das **Netz** net
die **Netzkarte** all zone travel card
neu new
   der Neujahrstag New Year's Day
nicht not
die **Nichte** niece
nichts nothing
nie never
niedrig low
das **Niedrigwasser** low tide
niemand nobody
die **Niere** kidney
niesen to sneeze
nirgendwo nowhere

das **Niveau** level
noch still, yet
der **Norden** north
der **Notfall** emergency
nötig necessary
die **Notrufsäule** emergency telephone (*on motorway*)
nüchtern sober
die **Nummer** number
nur just, only
die **Nuß** nut
nützlich useful
nutzlos useless

O

ob whether, if
oben on top of, above, upstairs
der **Ober** waiter
Obst fruit
obwohl although
offensichtlich obviously
öffentlich public (*adj.*)
die **Öffentlichkeit** public
öffnen to open
oft often
ohne without
das **Ohr** ear
der **Ohrring** earring
das **Öl** oil
die **Oma** granny
der **Onkel** uncle
der **Opa** grandpa
die **Oper** opera
ordentlich tidy
Ordnung: in Ordnung all right, OK, fine
der **Ort** place
örtlich local
der **Osten** east

P

das **Paar** pair, couple
ein **paar** (a) few
das **Paket** packet, parcel
das **Papier** paper
die **Papiertaschentücher** tissues
der **Paprika** pepper (*vegetable*)
der **Papst** pope
die **Parkscheibe** parking disc
die **Partei** party (*political*)
der **Paß** passport
passen to fit
das paßt dir gut it fits you well, it suits you
passieren to happen
die **Pastille** lozenge
die **Pauschalreise** package tour
die **Pause** interval (*theatre etc.*)
peinlich embarrassing
pensioniert retired
persönlich personal(ly)
der **Pfeffer** pepper (*spice*)
die **Pfeife** pipe
das **Pferd** horse
die **Pflanze** plant
das **Pflaster** (sticking) plaster
der **Photoapparat** camera
der **Pier** jetty
die **Plastiktüte** plastic bag
die **Platte** puncture
der **Plattenspieler** record-player
der **Platz** place, seat (*in theatre etc.*), space, square (*in town*)
die **Plombe** filling (*dental*)
plötzlich suddenly
die **Polizei** police
die **Polizeiwache** police station
die **Pommes frites** chips
die **Post** mail
die **Postkarte** post card
die **Postleitzahl** post code

prima! great!
pro per
der **Produzent, die Produzentin**
　　producer (*radio, televsion*)
der **Prospekt** brochure, leaflet
Prost! cheers!
provisorisch temporarily
prüfen to check
das **Pulver** powder
purpur purple
die **Putzfrau** cleaning lady

Q

die **Qualität** quality
die **Qualle** jellyfish
die **Quittung** receipt

R

der **Rabbiner** rabbi
das **Rad** wheel
das **Radfahren** cycling
der **Rasierer** razor
das **Rathaus** town hall
rauchen to smoke
rauh rough
der **Raum** room, space
die **Rechnung** bill
rechts right
der **Rechtsanwalt, die**
　　Rechtsanwältin lawyer
die **Reformkost** health foods
die **Regelschmerzen** period pains
der **Regen** rain
　　es regnet it's raining
der **Regenschirm** umbrella
die **Regierung** government
reich rich
reif mature

rein clean, pure
die **Reise** journey
das **Reisebüro** travel agent
der **Reiseführer** guidebook
reisekrank travel sick
das **Reiseziel** destination
reiten to ride
rennen to run
der **Rentner, die Rentnerin**
　　pensioner
reparieren fix (*mend*)
retten to save, rescue
das **Rettungsboot** lifeboat
der **Rettungsgürtel** lifebelt
das **Rezept** recipe, prescription
der **Richter** judge
richtig right, correct
die **Richtung** direction
riechen to smell
der **Rock** skirt
roh raw
das **Rohr** pipe
der **Rollstuhl** wheel chair
die **Rolltreppe** escalator
rosa pink
rot red
die **Röteln** German measles
der **Rowdy** yob
die **Rückerstattung** refund
die **Rückseite** the back (*reverse side*)
rückwärts backwards
rufen to call
ruhig calm, quiet
rund round
die **Rundfunkstation** radio station
rutschig slippery

die **Sache** thing
die **Sahne** cream
das **Salz** salt
sammeln to collect
sauber clean
saubermachen to clean
sauer acid, sour
der **Sauerregen** acid rain
das **Schaf** sheep
schaffen to manage (*cope*)
die **Schallplatte** record (*disc*)
der **Schalter** counter (*post office, ticket office etc.*)
die **Schaltiere** shellfish
scharf sharp, hot (*spicy*)
der **Schatten** shade, shadow
das **Schaufenster** shop window
der **Scheck** cheque
die **Scheibe** slice, disc (*parking*)
der **Schein** note (*bank*)
scheinen to seem, appear
die **Schere** scissors
scheußlich horrible
schicken to send
das **Schiff** ship, boat
das **Schild** sign
der **Schinken** ham
schlafen to sleep
der **Schlafsack** sleeping bag
das **Schlafzimmer** bedroom
schlagen to hit
die **Schlange** queue, snake
schlecht bad
schließen to close, shut
das **Schließfach** locker
schlimm bad, serious
schlimmer worse
das **Schlimmste** the worst
der **Schlips** tie
der **Schlitten** toboggan

die **Schlittschuhbahn** ice rink
die **Schlittschuhe** skates (*ice*)
das **Schloß** castle, palace; lock
der **Schlüssel** key
der **Schlüsselring** key ring
der **Schluß** finish
schmecken to taste
   schmeckt es Ihnen? does it
   taste all right?
der **Schmerz** pain
schmerzhaft painful
das **Schmerzmittel** pain killer
der **Schminkstoff** make-up
schmutzig dirty
der **Schnee** snow
schneiden to cut
schneien to snow
schnell fast
der **Schnurrbart** moustache
die **Schokolade** chocolate
schon already
schön pretty, nice, fine
   (*weather*)
der **Schrank** cupboard
schrecklich awful, dreadful
schreiben to write
die **Schreibmaschine** typewriter
der **Schriftsteller** writer
der **Schritt** (foot)step
die **Schublade** drawer
die **Schuld** debt
schuldig guilty
die **Schule** school
die **Schüssel** bowl, dish
der **Schuster** shoe mender
der **Schutz** shelter, protection
die **Schutzbrille** goggles
der **Schwager** brother-in-law
die **Schwägerin** sister-in-law
der **Schwamm** sponge
schwanger pregnant

schwarz black
schwarzweiß black and white
schwarzfahren to travel without a ticket
das Schwein pig
schwer difficult, hard, heavy
schwerhörig deaf
die Schwester sister
die Schwiegermutter mother-in-law
der Schwiegersohn son-in-law
die Schwiegertochter daughter-in-law
der Schwiegervater father-in-law
das Schwimmbad swimming bath
das Schwimmbecken swimming pool
schwimmen to swim
die Schwimmflossen flippers
die Schwimmweste lifejacket
schwindelig dizzy
schwitzen to sweat
der See lake
die See sea
seekrank seasick
segeln to sail
sehen to see
die Sehenswürdigkeit tourist site
sehr very
die Seife soap
das Seil rope
sein to be (see grammar, p. 184)
sein/e his (adj. and pronoun)
seit since
die Seite side, page
der Sekt German equivalent of Champagne
die Selbstbedienung self-service

Selbstversorger: für Selbstversorger self catering
selten seldom, rare
seltsam strange
die Semmel bread roll (Austria)
der Senf mustard
sicher certain, sure, positive, safe
der Sicherheitsgurt seat belt
sicherlich certainly
die Sicherung fuse
der Sicherungskasten fusebox
sie she, her, they, them (pronoun)
Sie you (polite)
das Silvester New Year's Eve
sind are (see grammar, p. 18)
der Sitz seat
Ski laufen to ski
die Skischuhe ski boots
der Slip knickers
sofort immediately
sogar even (including)
der Sohn son
solche/r/s such
der Sommer summer
die Sonne sun
der Sonnenbrand sunburn
die Sonnenbrille sunglasses
der Sonnenschirm sunshade
der Sonnenstich sunstroke
sonst otherwise
sowieso anyway
der Sozialarbeiter, die Sozialarbeiterin social worker
sparen to save (money)
Spaß machen to be fun
das hat Spaß gemacht that was fun
spät late

später later
der Spaziergang walk
die Speisekarte menu (*à la carte*)
der Speisewagen dining car
sperren to block
der Spiegel mirror
das Spiel game
das Spielen gambling
spielen to play
das Spielzeug toy
der Sportwagen push-chair
die Sprache language
der Sprachführer phrase book
sprechen to speak
springen to jump
das Spülbecken sink
der Staat state
das Stadion stadium
die Stadt town, city
der Stadtplan town plan
das Stadtzentrum town centre
die Starthilfekabel jump leads
statt instead of
der Staub dust
stechen to sting (*insect*)
die Stechmücke mosquito
die Steckdose socket
der Stecker plug (*electrical*)
stehen to stand
steil steep
der Stein stone
sterben to die
der Stern star
die Steuer tax, duty
Stief- step-
  die Stiefmutter stepmother
die Stiefel boots
der Stift pen
der Stil style
  still quiet, silent
die Stimme voice

stimmen: das stimmt that's true
der Stock stick
das Stockwerk floor, storey
  im ersten Stock on the first floor
der Stoff fabric, material
die Stoßzeit rush hour
der Strand beach
die Straße street
  die Straße hoch up the road
die Straßenbahn tram
die Straßenbauarbeiten roadworks
der Streifen stripe
streuen to scatter
der Strom current (*electricity*)
der Stromanschluß electricity (*wiring etc.*)
die Stromsperre power cut
die Strümpfe stockings
das Stück piece, bit
das Stückchen little bit
der Stuhl chair
die Stunde hour
  eine halbe Stunde half-hour
suchen to look for
das Surfbrett surfboard
  süß sweet
die Süßigkeiten sweets
  synchronisiert dubbed
die Szene scene

T

der Tabak tobacco
der Tag day
die Tage days, period
  täglich daily

das **Tal** valley
tanken to fill up with petrol
die **Tankstelle** garage (*for petrol*)
die **Tante** aunt
der **Tanz** dance
die **Tasche** bag, pocket
das **Taschenmesser** penknife
das **Taschentuch** handkerchief
die **Tasse** cup
die **Tatsache** fact
tatsächlich really, actually, indeed
tauchen to dive
der **Tee** tea
der **Teebeutel** tea bag
der **Teelöffel** teaspoon
der **Teil** part, piece
  zum Teil partly
teilweise partly
die **Telefonkarte** telephone card
die **Telefonzelle** telephone box
der **Teller** plate
der **Teppich** carpet
der **Termin** date, appointment
teuer dear (*expensive*)
das **Theater** theatre
das **Theaterstück** play (*theatre*)
tief deep
das **Tier** animal
der **Tierarzt, die Tierärztin** vet
der **Tiergarten** zoo
tippen to type
der **Tisch** table
die **Tochter** daughter
toll lovely, wonderful
das **Tonbandgerät** tape recorder
der **Topf** pot
das **Tor** gate; goal (*football*)
tot dead
tragbar portable
tragen to carry

das **Tragflächenboot** hydrofoil
trampen to hitchhike
traurig sad
die **Treppe** stairs
trinken to drink
das **Trinkgeld** tip
trocken dry
tropfen to drip
Tschüß goodbye (*casual*)
das **Tuch** cloth
tun to do, make
die **Tür** door
der **Turm** tower
die **Turnschuhe** plimsolls, trainers
die **Tüte** bag

U

über over, above, via
überall everywhere
die **Überfahrt** crossing (*sea*)
überfallen to attack, mug
das **Übergewicht** excess luggage
überholen to overtake
übermorgen day after tomorrow
überrascht surprised
übersetzen to translate
das **Überzelt** fly sheet
die **Übung** exercise
die **Uhr** clock, time
  wieviel Uhr ist es? what time is it?
die **Umleitung** diversion
umsonst free
umsteigen to change (*trains*)
die **Umwelt** environment
  umweltfreundlich environmentally friendly

umziehen to change (*clothes*); to move house
unabhängig independent
unangenehm unpleasant
unbeleuchtet unlit
unbequem uncomfortable
und and
der **Unfall** accident
ungeduldig impatient
ungefähr roughly, about
ungerade odd (*number*)
ungewöhnlich unusual
unglücklich unhappy, unlucky
unhöflich rude
unmöglich impossible
uns us, to us
unschuldig innocent
unser our
unsere/r/s ours
unten downstairs, below
unter under, underneath
die **Unterführung** underpass
das **Untergeschoß** basement
die **Unterhaltung** entertainment
das **Unterhemd** vest
die **Unterhose** underpants
die **Unterkunft** accommodation
der **Unterricht** lesson (*instruction*)
unterrichten to teach, instruct
unterschreiben to sign
die **Unterschrift** signature
die **Untertasse** saucer
die **Untertitel** subtitles
die **Unterwäsche** underclothes
unvorsichtig careless
unwohl unwell
der **Urlaub** holiday (*period of time*)
   im Urlaub on holiday
ursprünglich original(ly)

V

der **Vater** father
verantwortlich responsible
verärgert annoyed
der **Verbandskasten** first aid kit
die **Verbindung** connection (*travel*)
verboten forbidden, prohibited
verderben to spoil, ruin
verdienen to earn
vereinbaren to agree
die **Vergangenheit** past
vergessen to forget
vergewaltigen to rape
vergleichen to compare
der **Vergnügungspark** amusement park
verhaftet: Sie sind verhaftet you're under arrest
sich verheiraten to get married
verheiratet married
verkaufen to sell
der **Verkäufer, die Verkäuferin** shop assistant
der **Verkehr** traffic
die **Verkehrsampel** traffic light
der **Verkehrsstau** traffic jam
verleihen to lend
verletzen to injure
verletzt injured
verlieren to lose
verlobt engaged (*to be married*)
der/die **Verlobte** fiancé(e)
vermeiden to avoid
vermieten to let (*rent*)
vermissen to miss (*nostalgia*)
vernünftig sensible, reasonable

verpacken to wrap (up)
verpassen to miss (*bus etc.*)
verrenkt twisted
verrückt mad, crazy
verschieden different
die **Verschmutzung** pollution
versichert insured
die **Versicherung** insurance
die **Versicherungskarte** insurance document
die **Verspätung** delay
versprechen to promise
verstauchen to sprain
verstehen to understand
verstopft blocked
die **Verstopfung** constipation
der/die **Verwandte** relation
das **Verzeichnis** directory (*index*)
viel (von) a lot (of), much
   nicht viel not much
viele many
   nicht viele not many
vielen Dank thank you very much
vielleicht perhaps
ein Viertel quarter
vierzehn Tage fortnight
das **Visum** visa
der **Vogel** bird
das **Volk** people, nation
voll full
das **Vollkornbrot** wholemeal bread
von from, by
vor before, in front of
   vor allem above all, especially
vorbereiten to prepare
vorgestern day before yesterday
der **Vorname** first name

236

vorne in front (of)
der **Vorort** suburb
die **Vorsicht** caution
vorsichtig careful
vorstellen to introduce
sich vorstellen to imagine
die **Vorstellung** performance
die **Vorverkaufsstelle** booking office (*theatre*)
die **Vorwahl** dialling code
vorwärts forward
vorziehen to prefer

W

der **Wagen** carriage (*on train*)
die **Wahl** election
wählen to choose, vote; dial (*telephone*)
wahr true
während during, while
wahrscheinlich probably, likely
der **Wald** forest
die **Wand** wall (*inside*)
wann? when?
das **Warenhaus** department store
warten (auf) to wait (for)
der **Warteraum** waiting room
waschbar washable
das **Waschbecken** sink, wash basin
die **Wäsche** laundry
waschen to wash
das **Wasser** water
wasserdicht waterproof
wechseln to change, exchange (*money*)
der **Wecker** alarm clock
weder . . . noch . . . neither . . . nor . . .

weg away
der Weg path
wegen because of
weggehen to go away
wegnehmen to take away
wegwerfbar disposable
weh tun to hurt
  es tut mir weh it hurts
weiblich female, feminine
weich soft
Weihnachten (das) Christmas
  der Weihnachtsabend Christmas Eve
  der erste Weihnachtstag Christmas Day
weil because
der Weinberg vineyard
weinen to cry
die Weintraube grape
weiß white
weit far (*away*)
  wie weit . . . ? how far . . . ?
  ist es weit? is it far?
weiter further
welche/r/s which
die Welle wave
die Welt world
  der erste/zweite Weltkrieg the First/Second World War
weniger less
wenigstens at least
wenn if, when, whenever
wer? who?
werfen to throw
der Werktag weekday
die Wertsachen valuables
wertvoll valuable
wesentlich essential
das Wetter weather

die Wettervorhersage weather forecast
wichtig important, serious
wie like, as, how
  wie bitte? pardon?
  wie immer as usual
  wie ist . . . ? what is . . . like?
  wie lange? how long?
  wie sind . . . ? what are . . . like?
  wieviel? how much?
  wie viele? how many?
  wie weit? how far?
wieder again
wiederholen to repeat
wiederkommen to return
der Winter winter
wir we
wirklich really
der Wirt, die Wirtin landlord, landlady

die Wirtschaft economy
  das Wirtschaftswunder the economic miracle
wissen to know (*something*)
die Wissenschaft science
die Witwe widow
der Witwer widower
der Witz joke
wo where
die Woche week
wöchentlich weekly
wohnen to live (*dwell*)
die Wohnung flat (*apartment*)
der Wohnwagen caravan
das Wohnzimmer living-room, lounge
die Wolke cloud
die Wolle wool
wollen to want (to)

das **Wort** word
das **Wörterbuch** dictionary
wünschen to wish
würzig spicy

Z

zäh tough (*meat*)
zählen to count
der **Zähler** meter
der **Zahn** tooth
der **Zahnarzt, die Zahnärztin** dentist
die **Zahnbürste** toothbrush
die **Zahnpasta** toothpaste
die **Zahnschmerzen** toothache
der **Zahnstocher** toothpick
zart tender
das **Zeichen** signal
zeichnen to draw
die **Zeichnung** drawing
zeigen to show
die **Zeit** time
die **Zeitkarte** season ticket
die **Zeitschrift** magazine
die **Zeitung** newspaper
das **Zelt** tent
der **Zeltboden** groundsheet
zelten to camp
die **Zeltschnur** guy rope
zentral central
die **Zentralheizung** central heating
das **Zentrum** centre
ziehen to pull
das **Ziel** goal
ziemlich fairly
die **Zigarette** cigarette
der **Zirkus** circus
die **Zitrone** lemon

zu to, too
der **Zucker** sugar
der **Zug** train
   mit dem Zug by train
   zum Beispiel for example
   zum Wohl! cheers!
die **Zunge** tongue
zurück back
zurückerstatten to refund
zurückgeben to give back
zurücklegen to put by
zusätzlich extra
der **Zuschlag** supplement
die **Zweigstelle** branch (*of bank etc.*)
zweimal twice
zweite/r/s second
die **Zwillinge** twins
zwischen between

English-German

There is a list of car and bicycle parts on page 43, and parts of the body on page 168. See also the menu reader on page 113, numbers on page 211 and pages 189–202.

A

a, an **ein, eine**
abbey **die Klosterkirche**
about (*relating to*) **über + acc.** (*see grammar, p. 182*)
(*approximately*) **ungefähr**
above **über + acc./dat.** (*see grammar, p. 182*)
abroad **im Ausland**
abscess **der Abszeß**
to accept (*take*) **nehmen**
accident **der Unfall**
accommodation **die Unterkunft**
account (*bank*) **das Konto**
accountant **der Buchhalter**
ache **der Schmerz**
acid (*adj.*) **sauer**
across **über + acc.**
(*opposite*) **gegenüber + dat.** (*see grammar, p. 182*)
acrylic (*noun/adj.*) **das Akryl, aus Akryl**
to act **spielen**
actor **der Schauspieler**
actress **die Schauspielerin**
adaptor (*electrical*) **der Mehrfachstecker**
to add **hinzufügen**
addicted **süchtig**
address **die Adresse**
adhesive tape **der Klebstreifen**

admission **der Eintritt**
admission charge **das Eintrittsgeld**
adopted **adoptiert**
adult **der/die Erwachsene**
advance: in advance **im voraus**
advanced (*level*) **fortgeschritten**
advertisement, advertising **die Werbung**
aerial **die Antenne**
aeroplane **das Flugzeug**
afford: I can't afford it **das kann ich mir nicht leisten**
afraid: I'm afraid **Ich habe Angst**
after **nach + dat.** (*see grammar, p. 182*)
afterwards **nachher**
afternoon **der Nachmittag**
aftershave **das After-Shave**
again **wieder**
against **gegen + acc.** (*see grammar, p. 182*)
age **das Alter**
agency **die Agentur**
ago **vor + dat.** (*see grammar, p. 182*)
to agree **vereinbaren**
AIDS **AIDS**
air **die Luft**
by air **per Flugzeug**
(by) air mail **per Luftpost**

air conditioning **die Klimaanlage**
air force **die Luftwaffe**
airline **die Fluggesellschaft**
airport **der Flughafen**
aisle **der Gang**
alarm **der Alarm**
   alarm clock **der Wecker**
alcohol **der Alkohol**
alcoholic (*content*) **alkoholisch**
   (*person*) **der Alkoholiker**
alive **lebendig**
all **alle**
allergic to **allergisch gegen**
   + acc. (*see grammar, p.182*)
alley **die Gasse**
to allow **erlauben**
   allowed **erlaubt**
all right (*OK*) **in Ordnung**
almond **die Mandel**
alone **allein**
along **entlang** + acc. (*see grammar, p.182*)
already **schon**
also **auch**
although **obwohl**
always **immer**
am (*see 'to be'*) **bin**
ambassador **der Botschafter**
ambition **die Ambition**
ambitious **ehrgeizig**
ambulance **der Krankenwagen, die Ambulanz**
among **unter** + acc./dat. (*see grammar, p. 182*)
amount (*money*) **der Betrag**
amusement park **der Vergnügungspark**
anaesthetic (*local*) **die örtliche Betäubung**
   (*general*) **die volle Narkose**

and **und**
angry **zornig**
animal **das Tier**
anniversary **der Jahrestag**
annoyed **verärgert**
anorak **der Anorak**
another (one) **noch ein/eine**
answer **die Antwort**
to answer **antworten**
antibiotic **das Antibiotikum**
antifreeze **der Frostschutz**
antique **die Antiquität**
antiseptic **antiseptisch**
anxious **ängstlich**
any **irgendein(e)**
anyone **jemand**
anything **(irgend)etwas**
   anything else **noch etwas**
anyway **auf jeden Fall**
anywhere **irgendwo**
apart (from) **außer** + dat. (*see grammar, p. 182*)
apartment **das Appartement**
appendicitis **die Blinddarmentzündung**
apple **der Apfel**
appointment **der Termin**
approximate(ly) **ungefähr**
apricot **die Aprikose /die Marille** (*Austria*)
arch **der Bogen**
archaeology **die Archäologie**
architect **der Architekt**
are (*see 'to be'*) **sind**
area **die Gegend**
argument **die Auseinandersetzung**
arm **der Arm**
armbands (*swimming*) **die Schwimmflügel**

army **die Armee**
around **herum**
to arrange (*fix*) **vereinbaren**
arrest: under arrest **verhaftet**
arrival **die Ankunft**
to arrive **ankommen**
  he's arriving at 5.00 pm **er kommt um fünf an**
art **die Kunst**
  art gallery **die Kunsthalle**
  fine arts **die schönen Künste**
arthritis **die Arthritis**
artichoke **die Artischocke**
article **der Artikel**
artificial **künstlich**
artist **der Künstler**
as (*like*) **wie**
as far as **soviel**
  as far as I know **soviel ich weiß**
ash **die Asche**
ashtray **der Aschenbecher**
to ask **fragen**
asparagus **der Spargel**
aspirin **das Aspirin**
assistant **der Assistent/die Assistentin**
asthma **das Asthma**
at **an + dat. or acc.** (*see grammar, p. 182*)
athletics **die Leichtathletik**
atmosphere **die Atmosphäre**
to attack **angreifen**
  (*mug*) **überfallen**
attendant (*bathing*) **der Bademeister**
attractive **attraktiv**
aubergine **die Aubergine**
auction **die Auktion**
aunt **die Tante**

author **der Schriftsteller**
automatic **automatisch**
autumn **der Herbst**
avalanche **die Lawine**
avenue **die Allee**
avocado **die Avocatobirne**
to avoid **vermeiden**
away **entfernt**
awful **schrecklich**

B

baby **das Baby**
  baby food **die Babynahrung**
  baby wipes **die Babywischtücher**
baby's bottle **die (Knockel)flasche**
babysitter **der Babysitter/die Babysitterin**
back (*reverse side*) **die Rückseite**
back: at the back **hinten**
backwards **rückwärts**
bacon **der Speck**
bad **schlecht**
bag **die Tüte, die Tasche**
baggage **das Gepäck**
baker **der Bäcker/die Bäckerin**
baker's **die Bäckerei**
balcony (*theatre etc.*) **der Balkon**
bald **kahl**
ball (*tennis, football etc.*) **der Ball**
ballet **das Ballett**
ballpoint pen **der Kugelschreiber**
banana **die Banane**
band (*music*) **die Band**
bandage **die Binde**
bank (*money*) **die Bank**
banker **der Bankier**
bar **die Bar**
barber's **der (Herren)friseur**
bargain **das Sonderangebot**

baseball **der Baseball**
basement **das Untergeschoß**
basin (*bowl*) **die Schüssel**
  (*sink*) **das Waschbecken**
basket **der Korb**
basketball **der Basketball**
bath **das Bad**
  to have a bath **ein Bad nehmen**
  to bathe **baden**
bathing costume **der Badeanzug**
bathroom **das Badezimmer**
battery **die Batterie**
bay **die Bucht**
to be **sein** (*see grammar, p. 184*)
beach **der Strand**
beans **die Bohnen**
  French/green **grüne Bohnen**
  kidney/haricot **die Gartenbohnen**
  red/white/black **rote/weiße/schwarze Bohnen**
beard **der Bart**
beautiful **schön**
because **weil**
bed **das Bett**
bedroom **das Schlafzimmer**
bee **die Biene**
beef **das Rindfleisch**
beer **das Bier**
beetroot **die rote Bete**
before **bevor, vor** + dat. (*see grammar, p. 182*)
to begin **beginnen, anfangen**
  it begins at 8.00 pm **es fängt um acht Uhr abends an**
beginner **der Anfänger**
beginning **der Anfang**
behind **hinter** + dat. or acc. (*see grammar, p. 182*)

beige **beige**
to believe **glauben**
bell **die Glocke**
to belong to **gehören** + dat. (*see grammar, p. 179*)
below **unten**
belt **der Gürtel**
bend **die Kurve**
bent **gebogen**
berry **die Beere**
berth **das Bett**
  (*on ship*) **die Koje**
besides **außerdem**
best **beste/r/s**
better **besser**
between **zwischen** + dat. (*see grammar, p. 182*)
beyond **jenseits** + gen. (*see grammar, p. 182*)
bib **das Lätzchen**
Bible **die Bibel**
bicycle **das Fahrrad**
big **groß**
bigger **größer**
bill **die Rechnung**
bin (*rubbish*) **der Mülleimer**
  bin liners **die Abfallbeutel**
binding (*ski*) **die Bindung**
binoculars **das Fernglas**
biochemistry **die Biochemie**
biology **die Biologie**
bird **der Vogel**
birthday **der Geburtstag**
biscuit **der Keks**
bishop **der Bischof**
a bit **ein bißchen**
to bite **beißen**
bitter **bitter**
black **schwarz**
  black and white (*film*) **schwarzweiß**

black coffee **schwarzer Kaffee**
blackberry **die Brombeere**
blackcurrant **die Johannisbeere**
blanket **die Bettdecke**
bleach **das Bleichmittel**
to bleed **bluten**
blind **blind**
blister **die Blase**
to block (*road*) **sperren**
blocked **verstopft** (*road*) **gesperrt**
blond(e) **blond**
blood **das Blut**
blouse **die Bluse**
to blow **blasen**
to blow-dry **fönen**
blue **blau**
blusher **das Rouge**
to board **an Bord gehen**
boarding card **die Bordkarte**
boat **das Schiff**
boat trip **die Schiffahrt**
body **der Körper**
to boil **kochen**
boiled egg **das gekochte Ei**
boiler **der Boiler**
bomb **die Bombe**
bone **der Knochen**
book **das Buch**
to book **buchen**
booking **die Buchung**
booking office (*rail*) **der Fahrkartenschalter** (*theatre*) **die Vorverkaufsstelle**
booklet (*bus tickets*) **das Fahrscheinheft**
bookshop **die Buchhandlung**
boot (*shoe*) **der Stiefel**

border (*edge*) **der Rand** (*frontier*) **die Grenze**
boring **langweilig**
both **beide**
bottle **die Flasche**
bottle opener **der Flaschenöffner**
bottom **der Boden**
bow (*ship*) **der Bug**
bow (*knot*) **die Schleife**
bowl **die Schüssel**
box **die Kiste** (*theatre*) **die Loge**
box office **die Kasse**
boy **der Junge**
boyfriend **der Freund**
bra **der Büstenhalter (BH)**
bracelet **das Armband**
braces **die Hosenträger**
brain **das Gehirn**
branch (*bank etc.*) **die Zweigstelle**
brand **die Marke**
brandy **der Weinbrand**
brass **das Messing**
brave **mutig**
bread **das Brot**
    bread roll **das Brötchen, die Semmel** (*Austria*)
    wholemeal bread **das Vollkornbrot**
to break (*inc. limb*) **brechen**
to break down **eine Panne haben**
breakdown truck **der Abschleppwagen**
breakfast **das Frühstück**
breast **die Brust**
to breathe **atmen**
bricklayer **der Maurer**

bride **die Braut**
bridegroom **der Bräutigam**
bridge **die Brücke**
briefcase **die Aktentasche**
bright (*colour*) **leuchtend**
  (*light*) **strahlend**
to bring **bringen**
British **britisch**
broad **breit**
brochure **der Prospekt**
broken **kaputt**
bronchitis **die Bronchitis**
bronze **die Bronze**
brooch **die Brosche**
broom **der Besen**
brother **der Bruder**
brother-in-law **der Schwager**
brown **braun**
  brown sugar **der braune Zucker**

bruise **der blaue Fleck**
brush **die Bürste**
bucket **der Eimer**
budgerigar **der Wellensittich**
buffet **das Büffet**
to build **bauen**
  builder **der Bauarbeiter**
building **das Gebäude**
building site **die Baustelle**
bulb (*light*) **die Glühbirne**
bull **der Stier**
bumper (*car*) **die Stoßstange**
burn (*on skin*) **die Brandwunde**
to burn **brennen**
  burnt (*food*) **angebrannt**
bus **der Bus**
  by bus **mit dem Bus**
bus-driver **der Busfahrer**
bush **der Busch**

business **das Geschäft**
business trip **die Geschäftsreise**
  on business **geschäftlich**
businessman/woman **der Geschäftsmann/die Geschäftsfrau**
business studies **die Wirtschaftslehre**
bus station **der Busbahnhof**
bus stop **die Bushaltestelle**
busy **beschäftigt**
but **aber**
butane gas **das Butangas**
butcher's **die Metzgerei/die Fleischerei**
butter **die Butter**
butterfly **der Schmetterling**
button **der Knopf**
to buy **kaufen**
by (*author etc.*) **von + dat.** (*see grammar, p. 182*)

C

cabbage **der Kohl**
cabin **die Kabine**
cable car **die Drahtseilbahn**
café **das Café**
cake **der Kuchen**
cake shop **die Konditorei**
calculator **der Taschenrechner**
call (*phone*) **der Anruf**
to call **rufen**
  to be called **heißen**
calm **ruhig**
camera **der Photoapparat**
camomile tea **der Kamillentee**
to camp **zelten**
  campbed **die Campingliege**

camping **das Camping**
  camping gas **das Campinggas**
campsite **der Campingplatz**
can (*to be able*) **können**
  could **könnte**
can (*tin*) **die Dose**
  (*petrol*) **der Kanister**
can opener **der Dosenöffner**
to cancel **stornieren**
  an appointment **absagen**
cancer **der Krebs**
candle **die Kerze**
canoe **das Kanu**
capital (*city*) **die Hauptstadt**
captain (*boat*) **der Kapitän**
car **das Auto**
  by car **mit dem Auto**
  car hire **die Autovermietung**
car park **der Parkplatz**
carafe **die Karaffe**
caravan **der Wohnwagen**
  caravan site **der Campingplatz für Wohnwagen**
cardigan **die Strickjacke**
care: I don't care **das macht mir nichts aus**
careful **vorsichtig**
careless (*driver*) **unvorsichtig**
carpenter **der Tischler**
carpet **der Teppich**
carriage (*rail*) **der Wagen**
carrier bag **die Tragetasche**
carrot **die Mohrrübe, die Karotte, die Möhre**
to carry **tragen**
to carry on (*walking/driving*) **weitergehen**
car wash **die Autowäsche**
case: in case **falls**

cash **das Bargeld**
  to pay cash **bar bezahlen**
to cash **einlösen**
cash desk, cashier **die Kasse**
cassette **die Kassette**
castle (*palace*) **das Schloß**
  (*fortress*) **die Burg**
cat **die Katze**
catalogue **der Katalog**
to catch (*train/bus*) **nehmen**
cathedral **die Kathedrale, der Dom**
Catholic **katholisch**
cauliflower **der Blumenkohl, der Karfiol** (*Austria*)
to cause **verursachen**
caution **die Vorsicht**
cave **die Höhle**
ceiling **die Decke**
celery **die Stangensellerie**
cellar **der Keller**
cemetery **der Friedhof**
centimetre **der Zentimeter**
central **zentral**
central heating **die Zentralheizung**
centre **das Zentrum**
century **das Jahrhundert**
cereal (*food*) **die Getreideflocken**
certain **sicher**
certainly **sicherlich**
certificate **die Bescheinigung**
CFCs **FKWs**
chain **die Kette**
chair **der Stuhl**
  chair lift **der Sessellift**
chalet **das Chalet**
champagne **der Sekt**
change (*small coins*) **das Kleingeld**

to change (clothes) **umziehen**
  (money) **wechseln**
  (trains) **umsteigen**
changing room **die Umkleidekabine**
chapel **die Kapelle**
charcoal **die Holzkohle**
charge (money) **die Gebühr**
charter flight **der Charterflug**
cheap **billig**
to check **prüfen**
checked (pattern) **kariert**
check-in (desk) **der Abfertigungsschalter**
to check in **einchecken**
cheek **die Backe**
cheeky **frech**
cheers! **Prost!/zum Wohl!**
cheese **der Käse**
cheesecake **der Käsekuchen, die Käsesahne**

chef **der Chefkoch**
chemist **der Chemiker**
chemistry **die Chemie**
cheque **der Scheck**
cherry **die Kirsche**
chess **das Schachspiel**
chestnut **die Kastanie**
chewing gum **das Kaugummi**
chicken **das Hähnchen**
chickenpox **die Windpocken**
child **das Kind**
children **die Kinder**
chimney (exterior) **der Schornstein**
  (hearth) **der Kamin**
chin **das Kinn**
china **das Porzellan**
chips **die Pommes frites**
chocolate **die Schokolade**
chocolates **die Pralinen**
to choose **wählen**

chop (lamb/pork) **das Kotelett**
Christian **christlich**
  Christian name **der Vorname**
Christmas **das Weihnachten**
Christmas Day **der erste Weihnachstag**
Christmas Eve **der Heiligabend**
church **die Kirche**
cigar **die Zigarre**
cigarette **die Zigarette**
  cigarette paper **das Zigarettenpapier**
cinema **das Kino**
circle **der Kreis**
  (theatre) **der erste Rang**
city **die Stadt**
civil servant **der Staatsbeamte, die Staatsbeamtin**
class **die Klasse**
classical music **die klassische Musik**
claustrophobia **die Klaustrophobie**
to clean **saubermachen**
clean **sauber**
cleaner **die Putzfrau/der Putzmann**
cleansing lotion **die Reinigungsmilch**
clear **klar**
clerk **der/die Büroangestellte**
clever **klug**
cliff **der Felsen**
climate **das Klima**
to climb **klettern**
climber **der Bergsteiger/die Bergsteigerin**
clinic **die Klinik**
cloakroom **die Garderobe**

clock **die Uhr**
close (*by*) **in der Nähe**
to close **schließen**
closed **geschlossen**
cloth **das Tuch**
clothes **die Kleider**
clothes pegs **die Wäscheklammern**
cloud **die Wolke**
cloudy **bewölkt**
club **der Klub**
coach **der Bus**
    (*railway*) **der Wagen**
coal **die Kohle**
coarse **grob**
    (*food*) **einfach**
coast **die Küste**
coat **der Mantel**
coat-hanger **der Kleiderbügel**
cocktail **der Cocktail**
coffee **der Kaffee**
coin **die Münze**
cold: to have a cold **erkältet sein**
collar **der Kragen**
colleague **der Kollege/die Kollegin**
to collect **sammeln**
collection (*e.g. stamps*) **die Sammlung**
    (*postal/rubbish*) **die Abholung**
college **das Institut**
colour **die Farbe**
    colour-blind **farbenblind**
    colour-fast **farbecht**
comb **der Kamm**
to come **kommen**
    to come back **zurückkommen**
    to come in **hereinkommen**
    come in! **herein!**
    to come off (*e.g. button*) **herunterfallen**

comedy **die Komödie**
comfortable **bequem**
comic (*magazine*) **das Comic-Heft**
commercial **kommerziell**
common (*usual*) **gewöhnlich**
    (*shared*) **gemeinsam**
communion **das Abendmahl**
communism **der Kommunismus**
compact disc **die CD**
company **die Gesellschaft**
compared with **verglichen mit + dat.** (*see grammar, p. 182*)
compartment **das Abteil**
to complain **klagen**
complaint **die Klage**
complete (*finished*) **fertig**
    (*whole*) **komplett**
complicated **kompliziert**
compulsory **obligatorisch**
composer **der Komponist**
computer **der Computer**
    operator **der EDV Arbeiter/ die EDV Arbeiterin**
    programmer **der Programmierer/die Programmiererin**
    science **die Informatik**
concert **das Konzert**
concert hall **die Konzerthalle**
concussion **die Gehirnerschütterung**
condition (*state*) **der Zustand**
conditioner **die Pflegespülung**
condom **der Kondom**
conference **die Konferenz**
confirm **bestätigen**
conjunctivitis **die Konjunktivitis**
connection (*travel*) **die Verbindung**

conscious **bei Bewußtsein**
conservation **der Naturschutz**
conservative **konservativ**
constipation **die Verstopfung**
consulate **das Konsulat**
consultant **der Berater/die Beraterin**
contact lens **die Kontaktlinse**
contact lens cleaner **der Kontaktlinsenreiniger**
continent **der Kontinent**
contraceptive **das kontrazeptive Mittel**
contract **der Vertrag**
control (*passport*) **die Kontrolle**
convent **das Frauenkloster**
convenient **günstig**
cook **der Koch**
to cook **kochen**
   cooked **gekocht**
cooker **der Herd**
cool **kühl**
cool box **die Kühlbox**
copper **das Kupfer**
copy **die Kopie**
cork **der Korken**
corkscrew **der Korkenzieher**
corner (*outside*) **die Ecke**
correct **richtig**
corridor **der Gang**
cosmetics **das Kosmetikum**
to cost **kosten**
cot **das Kinderbett**
cottage **das Häuschen**
cotton (*material*) **die Baumwolle**
   (*thread*) **das Nähgarn**
cotton wool **die Watte**
couchette **der Liegewagen**
cough **der Husten**
to cough **husten**
(I, he, she, it) could (*see 'can'*) **könnte**

to count **zählen**
counter (*post office*) **der Schalter**
country (*nation*) **das Land**
country(side) **die Landschaft**
   in the country **auf dem Lande**
couple (*pair*) **das Paar**
courgettes **die Zucchini**
course (*lessons*) **der Kurs**
court (*law*) **der Gerichtshof**
   (*tennis*) **der Platz**
cousin **der Cousin/die Kusine**
cover (*lid*) **der Deckel**
cow **die Kuh**
crab **der Krebs**
cramp **der Muskelkater**
crayon **der Buntstift**
crazy **verrückt**
cream **die Sahne**
   (*lotion*) **die Creme**
   (*colour*) **creme**
credit card **die Kreditkarte**
cricket **das Kricket**
crispbread **das Knäckebrot**
crisps **die Chips**
cross **das Kreuz**
   Red Cross **das rote Kreuz**
to cross (*border*) **hinüberfahren**
cross-country (*skiing*) **der Langlauf**
crossing (*sea*) **die Überfahrt**
crossroads **die Kreuzung**
crowd **die Menschenmenge**
crowded **überfüllt, voll**
crown **die Krone**
cruise **die Kreuzfahrt**
crutch **die Krücke**
to cry **weinen**
crystal **kristall**
cucumber **die Gurke**
cuff **die Manschette**

cup die Tasse
cupboard der Schrank
cure (*remedy*) das Heilmittel
to cure heilen
curler (*hair*) der Lockenwickler
curly lockig
curry der Curry
current (*electricity*) der Strom
curtain die Gardine
curve die Kurve
cushion das Kissen
custard die Vanillesoße
customs der Zoll
cut der Schnitt
to cut schneiden
   to cut oneself sich schneiden
cutlery das Besteck
cycling das Radfahren
cylinder (*car*) der Zylinder
cyclist der Radfahrer
cystitis die Blasenentzündung

D

daily täglich
damage der Schaden
to damage schaden + dat. (*see grammar, p. 179*)
damp feucht
dance der Tanz
to dance tanzen
danger die Gefahr
dangerous gefährlich
dark dunkel
darling der Liebling
darts das Dartspiel
data (*information*) die Daten
date (*day*) das Datum
   (*fruit*) die Dattel
daughter die Tochter
daughter-in-law die Schwiegertochter

day der Tag
day after tomorrow übermorgen
day before yesterday vorgestern
day after/before der Tag danach/davor
dead tot
deaf schwerhörig
dealer der Händler
dear (*loved*) liebe
   (*expensive*) teuer
death der Tod
debt die Schuld
decaffeinated coffee der koffeinfreie Kaffee
deck das Deck
deckchair der Liegestuhl
to decide sich entschließen
to declare erklären
deep tief

deer der Hirsch
defect der Fehler
defective fehlerhaft
definitely bestimmt
defrost (*food*) auftauen
degree (*temperature*) der Grad
   (*university*) der Universitätsabschluß
delay die Verspätung
delicate fein
delicious lecker
to deliver liefern
delivery die Lieferung
demonstration die Demonstration
denim der Jeansstoff
dentist der Zahnarzt
denture das Gebiß
deodorant das Deo(dorant)

to depart (*bus, car*) **abfahren**
(*plane*) **abfliegen**
department **die Abteilung**
department store **das Kaufhaus**
departure (*bus, car*) **die Abfahrt**
(*plane*) **der Abflug**
departure lounge **die Abflughalle**
deposit **die Anzahlung**
desert **die Wüste**
to describe **beschreiben**
description **die Beschreibung**
design **der Entwurf**
(*dress*) **das Design**
to design **entwerfen**
designer **der Designer**
dessert **die Nachspeise**
destination **das Reiseziel**
detail **das Detail**
detergent **das Reinigungsmittel**
to develop **entwickeln**
diabetes **der Diabetes**
diabetic (*adj.*) **diabetisch**
to dial **wählen**
dialling code **die Vorwahl**
dialling tone **das Amtzeichen**
diamond **der Diamant**
diarrhoea **der Durchfall**
diary **das Tagebuch**
dice **der Würfel**
dictator **der Diktator**
dictionary **das Wörterbuch**
to die **sterben**
. . . died **gestorben**
diesel **das Dieselöl**
diet **die Diät**
different(ly) **verschieden, anders**
difficult **schwer**

dining room **das Eßzimmer**
dinner **das Abendessen**
dinner jacket **der Smoking**
diplomat **der Diplomat**
direct (*train*) **durchgehend**
direction **die Richtung**
director **der Direktor/die Direktorin**
directory (index) **das Verzeichnis**
dirty **schmutzig**
disabled **behindert**
disappointed **enttäuscht**
disc **die Scheibe**
(*computer*) **die Platte**
(*record*) **die Schallplatte**
disc film **der Discfilm**
disc jockey **der Discjockey**
disco(thèque) **die Diskothek**
discount **der Rabatt**
dish **die Schüssel**
dishwasher **die Geschirrspülmaschine**
disinfectant **das Desinfektionsmittel**
dislocated **verrenkt**
disposable **wegwerfbar**
disposable nappies **die Papierwindeln**
distance **die Entfernung**
distilled water **das destillierte Wasser**
district **das Gebiet**
to dive **tauchen**
diversion **die Umleitung**
diving **das Tauchen**
diving-board **das Springbrett**
divorced **geschieden**
dizzy **schwindelig**
to do **machen, tun**
dock **das Dock**

doctor **der Arzt/die Ärztin**
document **das Dokument**
dog **der Hund**
doll **die Puppe**
dollar **der Dollar**
dome **die Kuppel**
dominoes **das Dominospiel**
donkey **der Esel**
door **die Tür**
double **doppelt**
double bed **das Doppelbett**
dough **der Teig**
down (*movement*) **hinunter**
downstairs **unten**
drain **das Abflußrohr**
drama **das Drama**
draught (*air*) **der Luftzug**
draught beer **das Bier vom Faß**
to draw **zeichnen**
drawer **die Schublade**
drawing **die Zeichnung**
drawing-pin **die Reißzwecke**
dreadful **furchtbar**
dress **das Kleid**
to dress, get dressed **sich anziehen**
dressing (*medical*) **der Verband**
  (*salad*) **die Soße, die Beilage**
drink **das Getränk**
to drink **trinken**
to drip **tropfen**
to drive **fahren**
driver **der Fahrer**
  (*bus/train*) **der Busfahrer/der Zugfahrer**
driving licence **der Führerschein**
to drown **ertrinken**
drug **die Droge**
  drug addict **der/die Drogensüchtige**
drum **die Trommel**

drunk **betrunken**
dry **trocken**
  (*wine*) **herb/trocken**
dry-cleaner's **die chemische Reinigung**
dubbed **synchronisiert**
duck **die Ente**
dull (*weather*) **trüb**
dumb **taub**
dummy (*baby's*) **der Schnuller**
during **während + gen.** (*see grammar, p. 182*)
dust **der Staub**
dustbin **der Mülleimer**
dusty **staubig**
duty (*tax*) **die Steuer**
duty-free **anmeldefrei**
duvet **das Federbett**

E

each **jede/r/s**
ear **das Ohr**
earache **die Ohrenschmerzen**
eardrops **die Ohrentropfen**
earlier **früher**
early **früh**
to earn **verdienen**
earring **der Ohrring**
earth **die Erde**
earthquake **das Erdbeben**
east **der Osten**
  eastern **östlich**
Easter **das Ostern**
easy **leicht**
to eat **essen**
economical **ökonomisch**
economics **die Volkswirtschaft**
economy **die Wirtschaft**
  the economic miracle **das Wirtschaftswunder**

edible **eßbar**

egg **Ei**

either **entweder**

either . . . or **entweder . . . oder**

elastic band **das Gummiband**

election **die Wahl**

electric **elektrisch**

electrician **der Elektriker**

electricity **die Elektrizität** (*wiring etc.*) **der Stromanschluß**

electronic **elektronisch**

to embark (*boat*) **einschiffen**

embarrassing **peinlich**

embassy **die Botschaft**

emergency **der Notfall**

emergency telephone (*on motorway*) **die Notrufsäule**

empty **leer**

to empty **leeren**

enamel **das Email**

end **das Ende**

to end **enden**

energy **die Energie**

engaged (*to be married*) **verlobt** (*occupied*) **besetzt**

engine **der Motor**

engineer **der Ingenieur/die Ingenieurin**

England **England (das)**

English **englisch**

to enjoy **genießen**

enough **genug**

to enter **hineingehen** (*bus, train*) **einsteigen**

entertainment **die Unterhaltung**

enthusiastic **begeistert**

entrance **der Eingang**

envelope **der Briefumschlag**

environment **die Umwelt**

environmentally friendly **umweltfreundlich**

equal **gleich**

equipment **die Ausstattung**

escalator **die Rolltreppe**

especially **besonders**

essential **wesentlich**

estate agent **der Hausmakler**

evaporated milk **die Dosenmilch**

even (*including*) **sogar** (*not odd*) **gerade**

evening **der Abend**

every **jede/r/s**

everyone **alle**

everything **alles**

everywhere **überall**

exact(ly) **genau**

examination **das Examen**

example **das Beispiel**

for example **zum Beispiel**

excellent **ausgezeichnet**

except **außer + dat.** (*see grammar, p. 182*)

excess luggage **das Übergewicht**

to exchange **tauschen** (*money*) **wechseln**

exchange rate **der Wechselkurs**

excited **aufgeregt**

exciting **aufregend**

excursion **der Ausflug**

excuse me **Entschuldigen Sie**

executive (*adj.*) **exekutiv**

exercise **die Übung**

exhibition **die Ausstellung**

exit **der Ausgang**

to expect **erwarten**

expensive **teuer**

experience **die Erfahrung**

experiment **der Versuch**
expert **der Experte/die Expertin**
to explain **erklären**
explosion **die Explosion**
export **der Export**
to export **exportieren**
express **expreß**
extension cable **das Verlängerungskabel**
external **äußere**
extra **zusätzlich**
eye **das Auge**
eyebrow **die Augenbraue**
eyebrow pencil **der Augenbrauenstift**
eyelash **die Augenwimper**
eyeliner **der Eyeliner**
eyeshadow **der Lidschatten**

F

fabric **der Stoff**
face **das Gesicht**
 face cream **die Gesichtscreme**
 face powder **der Gesichtspuder**
facilities **die Möglichkeiten**
fact **die Tatsache**
 in fact **eigentlich**
factory **die Fabrik**
to fail (*exam/test*) **durchfallen**
failure **der Mißerfolg**
to faint **ohnmächtig werden**
fair (*haired*) **blond**
fair **der Jahrmarkt**
 trade fair **die Handelsmesse**
fairly **ziemlich**
faith **der Glaube**
fake **die Imitation**

to fall (*down/over*) **hinfallen**
false **falsch**
familiar **vertraut**
family **die Familie**
famous **bekannt**
fan (*air*) **der Ventilator**
 (*supporter*) **der Anhänger**
fantastic **fantastisch**
far (*away*) **weit weg**
 how far . . . ? **wie weit . . . ?**
 is it far? **ist es weit?**
fare **das Fahrgeld**
farm **der Bauernhof**
farmer **der Bauer**
fashion **die Mode**
fashionable/in fashion **modisch**
fast **schnell**
fat (*adj./noun*) **dick/das Fett**
fatal **tödlich**
father **der Vater**
father-in-law **der Schwiegervater**
fault **der Fehler**
faulty **fehlerhaft**
favourite **Lieblings-**
 (*e.g. favourite film*) **der Lieblingsfilm**
fax **der Telefax**
feather **die Feder**
to be fed up **die Nase voll haben**
fee **die Gebühr**
to feed (*inc. baby*) **füttern**
to feel **sich fühlen**
 (*ill/well*) **sich unwohl/wohl fühlen**
felt-tip pen **der Filzstift**
female, feminine **weiblich**
feminist **der Feminist/die Feministin**

fence **der Zaun**
ferry **die Fähre**
festival **das Fest**
to fetch **holen**
fever **das Fieber**
(a) few **ein paar**
fiancé(e) **der/die Verlobte**
fibre **die Faser**
field **das Feld**
fig **die Feige**
to fight **kämpfen**
file (*documents*) **der Aktenordner**
(*nail/DIY*) **die Feile**
to fill **füllen**
filling (*dental*) **die Plombe**
film (*cinema/for camera*) **der Film**
film star **der/die Filmstar**
filter **der Filter**
finance **die Finanzen**
to find **finden**
fine (*OK*) **in Ordnung**
(*penalty*) **die Geldstrafe**
(*weather*) **schön**
finger **der Finger**
finish **der Schluß**
fire **das Feuer**
fire brigade **die Feuerwehr**
fire extinguisher **der Feuerlöscher**
firewood **das Brennholz**
firework **das Feuerwerk**
firm **fest**
firm (*company*) **die Firma**
first **erste/r/s**
first aid **die Erste Hilfe**
first aid kit **der Verbandskasten**
fish **der Fisch**
to fish/go fishing **angeln**

fishing **das Angeln**
fishing rod **die Angelrute**
fishmonger's **das Fischgeschäft**
fit (*healthy*) **gesund**
to fit **passen**
that fits you well **das paßt dir gut**
fitting room **die Umkleidekabine**
to fix (*mend*) **reparieren**
fizzy **mit Kohlensäure**
flag **die Fahne**
flash (*camera*) **das Blitzlicht**
flat (*apartment*) **die Wohnung**
flat (*level*) **platt**
(*battery*) **leer**
flavour **der Geschmack**
flaw **der Fehler**
flea market **der Flohmarkt**
flight **der Flug**
flight bag **die Schultertasche**
flippers **die Schwimmflossen**
flood **die Flut**
floor **der Boden**
(*storey*) on the first floor **im ersten Stock**
ground floor **das Erdgeschoß**
flour **das Mehl**
flower **die Blume**
flu **die Grippe**
fluent (*language*) **fließend**
fluid **flüssig**
fly **die Fliege**
fly sheet **das Überzelt**
fly spray **der Fliegenspray**
to fly **fliegen**
fog **der Nebel**
foggy **nebelig**
foil **die Folie**

folding (*e.g. chair*) **Klapp- (der Klappstuhl)**
folk music **die Volksmusik**
to follow **folgen**
following (*next*) **folgend**
food **das Essen**
food poisoning **die Lebensmittelvergiftung**
foot **der Fuß**
on foot **zu Fuß**
football **der Fußball**
footpath **Fußweg**
for **für**
forbidden **verboten**
foreign **ausländisch**
foreigner **der Ausländer/die Ausländerin**
forest **der Wald**
to forget **vergessen**
to forgive **vergeben**
fork **die Gabel**
form **die Form**
fortnight **vierzehn Tage**
forward **vorwärts**
forwarding address **die Nachsendeadresse**
foundation (*make-up*) **die Grundierungscreme**
fountain **der Brunnen**
fox **der Fuchs**
foyer **das Foyer**
fracture **der Bruch**
fragile **zerbrechlich**
frankly **ehrlich gesagt**
freckles **die Sommersprossen**
free **frei/umsonst**
(*available, unoccupied*) **frei**
freedom **die Freiheit**
to freeze **frieren**
freezer **die Tiefkühltruhe**
frequent **häufig**

fresh **frisch**
fridge **der Kühlschrank**
fried **Brat-**
friend **der Freund/die Freundin**
friends **die Freunde**
frightened **erschrocken**
fringe **die Fransen**
frog **der Frosch**
from **von + dat.** (*see grammar, p. 182*)
front **die Vorderseite**
in front of **vorne, vor**
front door **die Haupttür**
frontier **die Grenze**
frost **der Frost**
frozen **gefroren**
fruit **das Obst, die Frucht**
fruit shop **die Obst- und Gemüsehandlung**
to fry **braten**
frying pan **die Bratpfanne**
fuel **der Brennstoff**
full **voll**
full board **die Vollpension**
full up (*booked up*) **ausgebucht**
to have fun **Spaß haben**
it was fun **es hat Spaß gemacht**
funeral **die Beerdigung**
funfair **der Jahrmarkt**
funny (*amusing*) **lustig**
(*peculiar*) **komisch**
fur **der Pelz**
furniture **die Möbel**
further on **weiter**
fuse **die Sicherung**
fusebox **der Sicherungskasten**

G

gallery die Galerie
gambling das Spielen
game (*match*) das Spiel
  (*hunting*) das Wild
gangway der Gang
garage (*for parking*) die Garage
  (*for petrol*) die Tankstelle
garden der Garten
gardener der Gärtner/die
  Gärtnerin
garlic der Knoblauch
gas das Gas
  gas bottle/cylinder die
    Gasflasche
  gas refill die Gaskartusche
gastritis die Gastritis
gate das Tor
  (*airport*) der Flugsteig
gel (*hair*) das Haargel
general allgemein
  in general im allgemeinen
generous großzügig
gentle sanft
gentleman/men der Herr, die
  Herren
  (*gents*) Herren
genuine echt
geography die Geographie
Germany Deutschland (das)
to get bekommen
  to get off (*bus*) aussteigen
  to get on (*bus*) einsteigen
  to get through (*phone*)
    durchkommen
gift das Geschenk
gin der Gin
  and tonic der Gin-Tonic
girl das Mädchen
girlfriend die Freundin

to give geben
  to give back zurückgeben
glass das Glas
glasses die Brille
gloves die Handschuhe
glue der Klebstoff
to go gehen
  to go away weggehen
  to go down hinuntergehen
  to go in eingehen
  to go out ausgehen
  to go round (*visit*) besuchen
  let's go! gehen wir!
goal das Ziel
  (*football*) das Tor
goat die Ziege
God Gott
goggles die Schutzbrille
gold das Gold
golf das Golf
  golf clubs die Golfschläger
  golf course der Golfplatz
good gut
  good day guten Tag
  good evening guten Abend
  good morning guten
    Morgen
  goodnight gute Nacht
goodbye Auf Wiedersehen/
  Auf Wiederschauen (*Austria*)
  (*casual*) Tschüß
goods die Waren
Good Friday Karfreitag (der)
government die Regierung
gram das Gramm
grammar die Grammatik
grandchildren die Enkelkinder
granddaughter die Enkelin
grandfather der Großvater
grandmother die Großmutter
grandparents die Großeltern

instant coffee **der Pulverkaffee**
instead of **statt + dat.** (*see grammar, p. 182*)
instructor **der Lehrer/die Lehrerin**
insulin **das Insulin**
insult **die Beleidigung**
insurance **die Versicherung**
  insurance document **die Versicherungskarte**
to insure **versichern**
  insured **versichert**
intelligent **intelligent**
interested **interessiert**
interesting **interessant**
international **international**
to interpret **dolmetschen**
interpreter **der Dolmetscher/die Dolmetscherin**
interval (*theatre etc.*) **die Pause**
interview **das Interview**

into **in + acc.** (*see grammar p. 182*)
to introduce **vorstellen**
invitation **die Einladung**
invite **einladen**
iodine **das Jod**
Ireland **Irland (das)**
Irish **irisch**
iron (*metal*) **das Eisen**
  (*for clothes*) **das Bügeleisen**
to iron **bügeln**
ironmonger's **die Eisen- und Haushaltswarenhandlung**
is (*see 'to be'*) **ist**
  is there . . . ? **gibt es . . . ?**
island **die Insel**
it **es**
itch **das Jucken**

J

jacket **die Jacke**
jam **die Konfitüre**
jar **das Gefäß**
jaw **der Kiefer**
jazz **der Jazz**
jeans **die Jeans**
jelly **das Gelee**
  (*pudding*) **die Götterspeise**
jellyfish **die Qualle**
Jesus Christ **Jesus Christus**
jetty **der Pier, die Anlegestelle**
jeweller's **der Juwelier**
Jewish **jüdisch**
job **die Arbeit**
to jog **joggen**
jogging **das Joggen**
joke **der Witz**
journalist **der Journalist/die Journalistin**
journey **die Reise**
judge **der Richter**
jug **die Kanne**
juice **der Saft**
to jump **springen**
jump leads **die Starthilfekabel**
jumper **der Pullover**
junction (*rail*) **der Gleisanschluß**
  (*road*) **die Kreuzung**
just (*only*) **nur**

K

kaolin mixture **der Kaolin**
to keep **behalten**
  (*to put by*) **zurücklegen**
kettle **der Kessel**
key **der Schlüssel**
  key ring **der Schlüsselring**

grandson **der Enkel**
grandstand **die Haupttribüne**
grape **die Weintraube**
grapefruit **die Pampelmuse**
grass **das Gras**
grateful **dankbar**
greasy **fettig**
great! **prima!**
green **grün**
  green card **die grüne Karte**
  (*environmentally aware*) **grün**
greengrocer's **die Obst- und Gemüsehandlung**
to greet **grüßen**
grey **grau**
grilled **gegrillt**
grocer's **der Lebensmittelhändler**
ground **der Boden**
groundsheet **der Zeltboden**
ground floor **das Erdgeschoß**
group **die Gruppe**
guarantee **die Garantie**
guest **der Gast**
guest house **die Pension**
guide **der Führer**
  guided tour **die Führung**
guidebook **der Reiseführer**
guilty **schuldig**
guitar **die Gitarre**
gun **das Gewehr**
guy rope **die Zeltschnur**
gymnastics **die Gymnastik**

H

habit **die Gewohnheit**
hail **der Hagel**
hair **das Haar, die Haare**
hairbrush **die Haarbürste**
haircut **der Haarschnitt**

hairdresser **der Friseur**
hairdrier **der Fön**
hairgrip **die Haarklemme**
hairspray **der Haarspray**
half **die Hälfte**
half (*adj.*) **halb**
  half board **die Halbpension**
  half price/fare **zum halben Preis**
  half-hour/half an hour **eine halbe Stunde**
  half past . . . (*see Time p. 193*) **halb . . .**
hall (*in house*) **die Diele**
ham **der Schinken**
  cured ham **geräucherter Schinken**
hamburger **der Hamburger**
hammer **der Hammer**
hand **die Hand**
  hand cream **die Handcreme**
  hand luggage **das Handgepäck**

  hand made **handgearbeitet**
handbag **die Handtasche**
handicapped **behindert**
handkerchief **das Taschentuch**
handle **der Griff**
hangover **der Kater**
to hang up **auflegen**
to happen **passieren**
happy **glücklich**
harbour **der Hafen**
  harbour trip **die Hafenrundfahrt**
hard **hart**
  (*difficult*) **schwer**
hard shoulder **der Seitenstreifen**
hat **der Hut**
to hate **hassen**
to have **haben**

hay **das Heu**
hay fever **der Heuschnupfen**
hazelnut **die Haselnuß**
he **er**
head **der Kopf**
  (*boss*) **der Chef**
headache **die Kopfschmerzen**
headphones **die Kopfhörer**
to heal **heilen**
health **die Gesundheit**
healthy **gesund**
health foods **die Reformkost**
to hear **hören**
hearing **das Gehör**
  hearing aid **das Hörgerät**
heart **das Herz**
  heart attack **der Herzanfall**
heat **die Hitze**
heater **das Heizgerät**
heating **die Heizung**
heaven **der Himmel**
heavy **schwer**
hedge **die Hecke**
heel **die Ferse**
  (*shoe*) **der Absatz**
height **die Höhe**
helicopter **der Hubschrauber**
hell **die Hölle**
hello **Hallo**
helmet (*motorbike*) **der Helm**
help **die Hilfe**
  help! **Hilfe!**
to help **helfen**
her (*adj. and pronoun*) **ihr/sie**
  (to) her **ihr**
herb **das Kraut**
herbal tea **der Kräutertee**
here **hier**
  here is ... **hier ist ...**
hers **ihre/r/s**
hiccups: to have hiccups
  (den) Schluckauf haben

258

high **hoch**
  high chair **der Hochstuhl**
to hijack **entführen**
hill **der Hügel**
him **ihn**
  (to) him **ihm**
to hire **mieten**
his (*adj. and pronoun*) **sein**
history **die Geschichte**
to hit **schlagen**
to hitchhike **trampen**
hobby **das Hobby**
to hold **halten**
hole **das Loch**
holiday (*period of time*) **der Urlaub**
holidays (*school*) **die Ferien**
  on holiday **im Urlaub**
holy **heilig**
  Holy Week **die Passionswoche**
home **die Heimat**
  at home **zu Hause**
to go home **nach Hause gehen**
homeopathic **homeopathisch**
to be homesick **Heimweh haben**
homosexual **homosexuell**
honest **ehrlich**
honeymoon **die Flitterwoche**
to hope **hoffen**
  I hope so **ich hoffe schon**
horrible **scheußlich**
horse **das Pferd**
hose **der Schlauch**
hospital **das Krankenhaus**
host **der Gastgeber/die Gastgeberin**
hot **heiß**
  (*spicy*) **scharf**
hotel **das Hotel**
hour **die Stunde**

half-hour **eine halbe Stunde**
house **das Haus**
housewife **die Hausfrau**
housework **die Hausarbeit**
hovercraft **das Hovercraft**
how **wie**
  how far? **wie weit?**
  how long? **wie lange?**
  how many? **wie viele?**
  how much? **wieviel?**
  how much does it cost? **was kostet das?**
  how much do they cost? **was kosten sie?**
human **menschlich**
  human being **der Mensch**
hungry **hungrig**
to be hungry **Hunger haben**
to hunt **jagen**
hunting **die Jagd**
hurry: to be in a hurry **in Eile sein**
to hurt **weh tun**
  it hurts **es tut weh**
husband **der Mann**
hut **die Hütte**
hydrofoil **das Tragflächenboot**

I

I **ich**
ice **das Eis**
  (*on roads*) **das Glatteis**
ice cream **das Eis**
ice rink **die Schlittschuhbahn**
icy **eisig**
idea **die Idee**
if **wenn**
ill **krank**
illness **die Krankheit**
to imagine **sich vorstellen**
imagination **die Phantasie**

immediately **sofort**
immersion heater **der Boile**
impatient **ungeduldig**
important **wichtig**
impossible **unmöglich**
impressive **eindrucksvoll**
in **in + acc. or dat** (*see grammar, p. 182*)
included **inbegriffen**
income **das Einkommen**
indeed **tatsächlich**
independent **unabhängig**
indigestion **die Magenverstimmung**
indoors **drinnen**
industry **die Industrie**
infected **infiziert**
infection **die Infektion**
infectious **ansteckend**
inflamed **entzündet**
inflammation **die Entzündung**
influenza **die Grippe**
informal **nicht formell**
information **die Auskunft**
  information desk/office **das Auskunftsbüro**
injection **die Spritze**
to injure **verletzen**
  injured **verletzt**
injury **die Verletzung**
ink **die Tinte**
inner **innere**
innocent **unschuldig**
insect **das Insekt**
  insect bite **der Insektenstich**
  insect repellent **das Insektenbekämpfungsmitte**
inside **das Innere**
to insist **bestehen**
inspector **der Kontrolleur/di Kontrolleurin**

259

kidney **die Niere**
to kill **töten**
kilo(gram) **das Kilogramm**
kilometre **der Kilometer**
kind (*sort*) **die Art**
  (*generous*) **nett**
king **der König**
kiss **der Kuß**
to kiss **küssen**
kitchen **die Küche**
knee **das Knie**
knickers **der Slip**
knife **das Messer**
to knit **stricken**
knitting **das Stricken**
  knitting needle **die Stricknadel**
to knock **klopfen**
knot **der Knoten**
to know (*someone*) **kennen**
  (*something*) **wissen**
  I don't know **Ich weiß nicht**

L

label **das Etikett**
lace **die Spitze**
ladder **die Leiter**
lady **die Dame**
  ladies **Damen**
lager **das helle Bier**
lake **der See**
lamb (*meat*) **das Lammfleisch**
lamp **die Lampe**
lamp post **der Laternenpfahl**
land **das Land**
to land **landen**
landing (*aeroplane*) **die Landung**
  (*house*) **der Flur**
  (*ship*) **das Anlegen**

landlady **die Wirtin**
landlord **der Wirt**
language **die Sprache**
large **groß**
last **letzte/r/s**
to last **dauern**
late **spät**
later **später**
laugh **das Lachen**
to laugh **lachen**
launderette **der Waschsalon**
laundry **die Wäsche**
law (*study subject*) **die Jura**
lawyer **der Rechtsanwalt/die Rechtsanwältin**
laxative **das Abführmittel**
lazy **faul**
lead **das Blei**
  lead-free **bleifrei**
leaf **das Blatt**
leaflet **der Prospekt**
to lean out **hinauslehnen**
to learn **lernen**
learner **der Anfänger**
least: at least **wenigstens, mindestens**
leather **das Leder**
to leave **lassen**
  (*to go away*) **verlassen, weggehen**
lecturer **der Dozent/die Dozentin**
left **links**
left luggage (*office*) **die Gepäckaufbewahrung**
left-handed **linkshändig**
leg **das Bein**
legal **legal**
lemon **die Zitrone**
lemonade **die Limonade**

to lend **verleihen**
length **die Länge**
lens (*camera*) **die Linse**
less **weniger**
lesson (*instruction*) **der Unterricht**
to let (*allow*) **erlauben**
　(*rent*) **vermieten**
letter **der Brief**
　(*of alphabet*) **der Buchstabe**
letterbox **der Briefkasten**
lettuce **der Kopfsalat**
leukemia **die Leukämie**
level (*height, standard*) **das Niveau**
level (*flat*) **flach**
level crossing **der Bahnübergang**
library **die Bibliothek**
licence (*driving*) **der Führerschein**
　(*fishing etc.*) **die Lizenz**
lid **der Deckel**
to lie down **sich hinlegen**
life **das Leben**
lifebelt **der Rettungsgürtel**
lifeboat **das Rettungsboot**
lifeguard (*swimming pool*) **der Bademeister**
lifejacket **die Schwimmweste**
lift **der Fahrstuhl**
light **das Licht**
　light bulb **die Glühbirne**
light (*coloured*) **hell**
　(*weight*) **leicht**
to light (*fire*) **anzünden**
lighter (*cigarette*) **das Feuerzeug**
lighter fuel **das Gas für's Feuerzeug**
lightning **der Blitz**

like (*similar to*) **wie**
　like this/that **wie das**
　what is . . like? **wie ist . ?**
　what are . . like? **wie sind . ?**
to like (*food, people*) **mögen**
　I like **ich mag**
to like doing something **etwas gern tun**
　I like doing that **ich tue das gern**
likely **wahrscheinlich**
limited **beschränkt**
line **die Linie**
lion **der Löwe**
lip **die Lippe**
lipstick **der Lippenstift**
liqueur **der Likör**
liquid **die Flüssigkeit**
list **die Liste**
to listen (*to*) **zuhören + dat.**
　(*see grammar, p. 179*)
litre **der Liter**
litter **der Abfall**
little **klein**
　a little **ein bißchen**
to live **leben**
　(*dwell*) **wohnen**
liver **die Leber**
living-room **das Wohnzimmer**
local **örtlich**
lock **das Schloß**
to lock **abschließen**
locker **das Schließfach**
London **London**
lonely **einsam**
long (*ing. hair*) **lang**
long-distance **Fern-**
　long-distance call **das Ferngespräch**
look **der Blick**
to look (*at*) **sich ansehen**

262

to look for **suchen**
loose **los**
lorry **der LKW
(Lastkraftwagen)**
lorry-driver **der LKW-Fahrer**
to lose **verlieren**
lost property (*office*) **das
Fundbüro**
a lot (*of*) **viel (von)**
lotion **die Lotion**
lottery **die Lotterie**
loud **laut**
lounge **das Wohnzimmer**
(*in ship etc.*) **der Salon**
love **die Liebe**
to love **lieben**
low **niedrig**
low-fat **fettarm**
lower **niedriger**
lozenge **die Pastille**
LP **die LP**
lucky: to be lucky **Glück haben**
luggage **das Gepäck**
lump (*swelling*) **die Beule**
lunch **das Mittagessen**

M

machine **die Maschine**
machinist **der Machinist**
mad **verrückt**
madam **gnädige Frau**
magazine **die Zeitschrift**
mail **die Post**
main **Haupt-**
to make **machen**
make-up **der Schminkstoff**
male **männlich**
man **der Mann**
to manage (*cope*) **schaffen**
manager **der Manager**

managing director **der
Geschäftsführer/die
Geschäftsführerin**
many **viele**
not many **nicht viele**
map **die Karte**
marble **der Marmor**
margarine **die Margarine**
market **der Markt**
married **verheiratet**
to get married **heiraten**
mascara **die Maskara**
masculine **männlich**
mask (*diving*) **die Maske**
mass (*church*) **die Messe**
match **das Streichholz**
(*game*) **das Spiel**
material **der Stoff**
mathematics **die Mathematik**
matter: it doesn't matter **es
macht nichts**
what's the matter? **was ist <u>263</u>
los?**
mattress **die Matratze**
air mattress **die Luftmatratze**
mature (*cheese*) **reif**
mayonnaise **die Mayonnaise**
me **mich**
meadow **die Wiese**
meal **das Essen**
mean: what does this mean?
**was bedeutet das?
was heißt das?**
meanwhile **in der Zwischenzeit**
measles **die Masern**
German measles **die Röteln**
to measure **messen**
measurement **das Maß**
meat **das Fleisch**
cold meats **der Aufschnitt**
mechanic **der Mechaniker**

medical **medizinisch**
medicine (*subject*) **die Medizin**
(*drug*) **das Medikament**
medieval **mittelalterlich**
Mediterranean **das Mittelmeer**
medium (*size*) **mittelgroß**
(*steak*) **medium**
(*wine*) **halbtrocken**
meeting **das Treffen**
melon **die Melone**
member **das Mitglied**
men **die Männer**
to mend **reparieren**
menu (*à la carte*) **die
Speisekarte**
(*set*) **das Menü**
message **die Mitteilung**
metal **das Metall**
meter **der Zähler**
metre **der Meter**

microwave oven **der
Mikrowellenherd**
midday **der Mittag**
middle **die Mitte**
middle-aged **in den mittleren
Jahren**
midnight **die Mitternacht**
migraine **die Migräne**
mild **mild**
mile **die Meile**
milk **die Milch**
milkshake **das
Milchmixgetränk**
mill **die Mühle**
mince **das Hackfleisch**
mind: do you mind if . . . ?
**macht das Ihnen etwas aus,
wenn . . . ?**
I don't mind **es ist mir egal**
mine (*of me*) **mein/e/s**
minibus **der Kleinbus**
minister **der Minister**

minute (*time*) **der Augenblick/
die Minute**
mirror **der Spiegel**
Miss **Fräulein**
to miss (*bus etc.*) **verpassen**
(*nostalgia*) **vermissen**
mist **der Nebel**
mistake **der Fehler**
to make a mistake **einen
Fehler machen**
mixed **gemischt**
mixture **die Mischung**
model **das Modell**
modern **modern**
moisturiser **die
Feuchtigkeitscreme**
monastery **das Kloster**
money **das Geld**
month **der Monat**
monthly **monatlich**
monument **das Denkmal**
moon **der Mond**
moped **das Moped**
more **mehr**
no more **nicht mehr**
morning **der Morgen**
mortgage **die Hypothek**
mosquito **die Stechmücke**
mosquito net **das Moskitonetz**
most (of) **die meisten (von)**
mother **die Mutter**
mother-in-law **die
Schwiegermutter**
motor **der Motor**
motorbike **das Motorrad**
motorboat **das Motorboot**
motor racing **der Rennsport**
motorway **die Autobahn**
mountain **der Berg**
mountaineering **das
Bergsteigen**
moustache **der Schnurrbart**

mouth **der Mund**
to move **bewegen**
  to move house **umziehen**
Mr **Herr**
Mrs, Ms **Frau**
much **viel**
  not much **nicht viel**
mug **der Becher**
to murder **ermorden**
museum **das Museum**
mushroom **der Pilz**
  (*button*) **der Champignon**
music **die Musik**
musical **das Musical**
musician **der Musiker/die Musikerin**
must: you must ... **Sie müssen ...**
mustard **der Senf**
my **mein**
mystery **das Rätsel**

N

nail **der Nagel**
nail clippers/scissors **der Nagelzwicker**
nail file **die Nagelfeile**
nail polish **der Nagellack**
nail polish remover **der Nagellackentferner**
naked **nackt**
name **der Name**
  my name is ... **ich heiße ...**
  what is your name? **wie heißen Sie?**
napkin **die Serviette**
nappy **die Windel**
  disposable nappy **die Papierwindel**
  nappy liner **die Einlegewindel**
national **national**

nationality **die Nationalität**
natural(ly) **natürlich**
naughty **bös**
navy **die Marine**
navy blue **marineblau**
near **nah**
  nearby **in der Nähe**
nearest **der/die/das nächste**
nearly **fast**
necessary **nötig**
necklace **die Halskette**
to need **brauchen**
needle **die Nadel**
negative (*photo*) **das Negativ**
neighbour **der Nachbar/die Nachbarin**
neither ... nor ... **weder ... noch ...**
nephew **der Neffe**
nervous **nervös**
net **das Netz**
never **nie**
new **neu**
  New Year's Day **der Neujahrstag**
  New Year's Eve **das Silvester**
news **die Nachrichten**
newspaper **die Zeitung**
newspaper kiosk **der Kiosk**
next **nächste/r/s**
  week/month/year (*see page 191*)
next to **neben + dat. or acc.** (*see grammar, p. 182*)
nice **nett**
niece **die Nichte**
night **die Nacht**
nightclub **der Nachtklub**
nightdress **das Nachthemd**
no **nein**
nobody **niemand**
noise **der Lärm**

noisy **laut**
non-alcoholic **alkoholfrei**
none **kein/e/r**
non-smoking **Nichtraucher**
normal **normal**
  normally **normalerweise**
north **der Norden**
nose **die Nase**
nosebleed **das Nasenbluten**
nostril **das Nasenloch**
not **nicht**
note (*bank*) **der Schein**
notepad **der Notizblock**
nothing **nichts**
  nothing else **sonst nichts**
now **jetzt**
nowhere **nirgendwo**
nuclear power **die Kernkraft**
number **die Nummer**
nurse **der Krankenpfleger/die Krankenschwester**

nursery slope **der Anfängerhügel**
nut **die Nuß**
  (*DIY*) **die Schraubenmutter**
nylon **das Nylon**

O

oar **das Ruder**
object (*thing*) **der Gegenstand**
obvious **offensichtlich**
occasionally **hin und wieder**
occupied (*seat*) **besetzt**
odd **merkwürdig**
  (*not even*) **ungerade**
of **von + dat.** (*see grammar, p. 182*)
of course **natürlich**
off (*TV, light*) **aus**
  (*milk*) **alt**
offended **beleidigt**

offer **das Angebot**
  special offer **das Sonderangebot**
office **das Büro**
officer **der Offizier**
official **der Beamte/die Beamtin**
often **oft**
  how often? **wie oft?**
oil **das Öl**
OK **OK**
old **alt**
  how old are you? **wie alt sind Sie?/wie alt bist du?**
  how old is he/she? **wie alt ist er/sie?**
  I am . . . years old **Ich bin . . . Jahre alt**
old-fashioned **altmodisch**
olive **die Olive**
olive oil **das Olivenöl**
on **auf + acc. or dat.** (*see grammar, p. 182*)
once **einmal**
onion **die Zwiebel**
only **nur**
open **geöffnet**
to open **öffnen**
opera **die Oper**
operation **die Operation**
opinion **die Meinung**
  in my opinion **meiner Meinung nach**
opposite **gegenüber + dat.** (*see grammar, p. 182*)
optician **der Optiker/die Optikerin**
or **oder**
orange (*fruit*) **die Orange, die Apfelsine**
  (*colour*) **orange**
order **die Bestellung**

to order **bestellen**
ordinary **gewöhnlich**
to organise **organisieren**
original **ursprünglich**
other **andere**
others **die anderen**
our **unser**
ours **unsere/r/s**
out (of) **aus + dat.** (*see grammar, p. 182*)
outdoor(s), outside **draußen**
over **über + acc. or dat.** (*see grammar, p. 182*)
overcast **bedeckt**
to overtake **überholen**
to owe **schuldig sein**
how much do I owe? **was bin ich schuldig?**
owner **der Besitzer/die Besitzerin**
ozone-friendly **ozonfreundlich**

P

package tour **die Pauschalreise**
packet **das Paket**
paddle (*canoeing*) **das Paddel**
padlock **das Vorhängeschloß**
page **die Seite**
pain **der Schmerz**
painful **schmerzhaft**
painkiller **das Schmerzmittel**
paint **die Farbe**
to paint **streichen**
(*picture*) **malen**
painter **der Maler/die Malerin**
painting **das Gemälde**
pair **das Paar**
palace **der Palast**
pale **blaß**
panties, pants **der Slip**
paper **das Papier**

paper clip **die Büroklammer**
paraffin **das Paraffin**
paralysed **gelähmt**
parcel **das Paket**
pardon? **wie bitte?**
parents **die Eltern**
park **der Park**
to park **parken**
parking **das Parken**
parking disc **die Parkscheibe**
parking meter **die Parkuhr**
parliament **das Parlament**
part **der Teil**
parting (*hair*) **der Scheitel**
partly **zum Teil, teilweise**
partner **der Partner/die Partnerin**
party **die Party**
(*political*) **die Partei**
to pass (*on road*) **überholen**
(*salt etc.*) **geben**
(*exam/test*) **bestehen**

passenger **der Passagier**
(*bus, taxi*) **der Fahrgast**
passion **die Leidenschaft**
passport **der Paß**
passport control **die Paßkontrolle**
past **die Vergangenheit**
in the past **in der Vergangenheit**
(*see Time, p. 193*) **nach . . .**
pasta **die Teigwaren, die Nudeln**
pastille **die Pastille**
pastry **der Teig**
path **der Weg**
patient (*hospital*) **der Pazient/die Pazientin**
pattern **das Muster**
pavement **der Gehsteig**
to pay **bezahlen**
to pay cash **bar bezahlen**

peas die Erbsen
peace der Frieden
peach der Pfirsich
peanut die Erdnuß
pear die Birne
pedal das Pedal
pedal-boat (*pedalo*) das **Tretboot**
pedestrian der Fußgänger
pedestrian crossing der **Zebrastreifen, der Fußgängerüberweg**
to peel schälen
peg die Wäscheklammer
pen der Stift
pencil der Bleistift
pencil sharpener der Spitzer
penfriend der Brieffreund/die **Brieffreundin**
penknife das Taschenmesser
penicillin das Penizillin
pension die Rente
pensioner der Rentner/die **Rentnerin**
people die Leute
pepper der Pfeffer (*sweet/green/red*) der Paprika
peppermint der Pfefferminz
per pro
perfect perfekt
performance die Vorstellung
perfume das Parfüm
perhaps vielleicht
period (*menstrual*) die Tage
  period pains die **Regelschmerzen**
perm die Dauerwelle
permit die Erlaubnis
to permit erlauben
person die Person
personal persönlich

personal stereo der Walkman
petrol das Benzin
petrol can der Kanister
petrol station die Tankstelle
petticoat der Unterrock
philosophy die Philosophie
photocopy die Fotokopie
to photocopy fotokopieren
photo(graph) die Foto(grafie)
photographer der Fotograf/ die Fotografin
photography die Fotografie
phrase book der Sprachführer
physics die Physik
piano das Klavier
to pick (*choose*) wählen (*flowers etc.*) pflücken
picnic das Picknick
picture das Bild
piece das Stück
pier die Anlegestelle
pig das Schwein
pill die Tablette
  the pill die Pille
pillow das Kissen
pillowcase der Kopfkissenbezug
pilot der Pilot/die Pilotin
pilot light die Zündflamme
pin die Stecknadel
pineapple die Ananas
pink rosa
pipe (*smoking*) die Pfeife (*drain*) das Rohr
place der Ort (*seat*) der Platz
plain einfach
plan (*of town*) der Stadtplan
plane das Flugzeug
plant die Pflanze
plaster (*sticking*) das Pflaster

plastic **plastik**
plastic bag **die Plastiktüte**
plate **der Teller**
platform **der Bahnsteig**
play (*theatre*) **das Theaterstück**
to play **spielen**
pleasant **angenehm**
please **bitte**
pleased **erfreut**
plenty (of) **eine Menge (von) + dat.** (*see grammar, p. 182*)
pliers **die Zange**
plimsolls **die Turnschuhe**
plug (*bath*) **der Stöpsel**
(*electrical*) **der Stecker**
plumber **der Klempner**
pneumonia **die Lungenentzündung**
pocket **die Tasche**
point **der Punkt**
(*needle, pin*) **die Spitze**
poison **das Gift**
poisonous **giftig**
pole **der Pfahl**
police **die Polizei**
police car **das Polizeiauto**
police station **die Polizeiwache**
polish **die Politur**
polite **höflich**
politician **der Politker/die Politikerin**
political **politisch**
politics **die Politik**
polluted **verschmutzt**
pollution **die Verschmutzung**
pool (*swimming*) **das Schwimmbecken**
poor **arm**
pop (*music*) **die Popmusik**
Pope **der Papst**
popular **beliebt**

pork **das Schweinefleisch**
port (*harbour*) **der Hafen**
(*wine*) **der Portwein**
portable **tragbar**
porter **der Gepäckträger**
porthole **das Bullauge**
portion **die Portion**
portrait **das Porträt**
positive (*sure*) **sicher**
possible **möglich**
as . . . as possible **so . . . wie möglich**
possibly **möglicherweise**
post (*mail*) **die Post**
to post **abschicken**
postbox **der Briefkasten**
postcard **die Postkarte**
postcode **die Postleitzahl**
poster **das Poster**
(*billboard*) **das Plakat**
postman **der Briefträger**
post office **das Postamt**
to postpone **aufschieben**
pot **der Topf**
potato **die Kartoffel**
pottery **die Töpferei**
potty (*child's*) **das Töpfchen**
pound (*sterling*) **das Pfund Sterling**
to pour **gießen**
powder **das Pulver**
(*talcum*) **der Puder**
powdered milk **das Milchpulver**
powdery **pulvrig**
power **die Macht**
(*physical strength*) **die Kraft**
power cut **die Stromsperre**
pram **der Kinderwagen**
to prefer **vorziehen**
pregnant **schwanger**
to prepare **vorbereiten**

269

prescription **das Rezept**
present (*gift*) **das Geschenk**
press (newspapers) **die Presse**
to press **drücken**
pretty **hübsch**
price **der Preis**
priest **der Geistliche**
prime minister **der Ministerpräsident/die Ministerpräsidentin**
prince **der Prinz**
princess **die Prinzessin**
print (*photo*) **der Abzug**
to print **drucken**
prison **das Gefängnis**
private **privat**
prize **der Preis**
probably **wahrscheinlich**
problem **das Problem**
producer (*radio/TV/film*) **der Produzent/die Produzentin**
profession **der Beruf**
professor **der Professor/die Professorin**
profit **der Gewinn**
programme **das Programm**
prohibited **verboten**
to promise **versprechen**
to pronounce **aussprechen**
properly **richtig**
property **das Eigentum**
protestant **protestantisch**
public (*noun*) **die Öffentlichkeit** (*adj.*) **öffentlich**
public holiday **der gesetzliche Feiertag**
public relations officer **der Pressesprecher/die Pressesprecherin**
to pull **ziehen**
to pump up **aufpumpen**

puncture **die Platte**
pure **rein**
purple **purpur**
purse **der Geldbeutel**
to push **schieben**
push-chair **der Sportwagen**
to put down **hinstellen**
to put on (*clothes*) **anziehen**
pyjamas **der Pyjama**

Q

quality **die Qualität**
quarter **das Viertel**
quay **der Kai**
queen **die Königin**
question **die Frage**
queue **die Schlange**
quick(ly) **schnell**
quiet **still**
quite **ziemlich**

R

rabbi **der Rabbiner**
rabbit **das Kaninchen**
rabies **die Tollwut**
racecourse **die Rennbahn**
racing (*horse*) **der Pferderennsport** (*motor*) **das Motorrennen**
racket (*tennis*) **der Schläger**
radiator (*heating*) **der Radiator**
radio **das Radio**
radioactive **radioaktiv**
radio station **die Rundfunkstation**
raft **das Floß**
railway **die Eisenbahn**
railway station **der Bahnhof**

rain **der Regen**
   it's raining **es regnet**
raincoat **der Regenmantel**
to rape **vergewaltigen**
rare **selten**
   (steak) **blutig**
rash *(spots)* **der Ausschlag**
raspberries **die Himbeeren**
rate *(speed)* **das Tempo**
   (tariff) **der Satz**
rather *(quite)* **ziemlich**
raw **roh**
razor **der Rasierer**
razor blade **die Rasierklinge**
to reach **erreichen**
to read **lesen**
   reading **das Lesen**
ready **fertig**
real *(authentic)* **echt**
really **wirklich**
rear **der hintere Teil**
reason **der Grund**
receipt **die Quittung**
receiver *(telephone)* **der Hörer**
reception **der Empfang**
receptionist **die Rezeptionistin**
recipe **das Rezept**
to recognise **erkennen**
to recommend **empfehlen**
record **die Schallplatte**
to record **aufnehmen**
record-player **der Plattenspieler**
to recover *(from an illness)*
   sich erholen
red **rot**
   Red Cross **das Rote Kreuz**
reduction **die Ermäßigung**
to refill **nachfüllen**
refrigerator **der Kühlschrank**
refugee **der Flüchtling**

refund **die Rückerstattung**
to refund **zurückerstatten**
region **das Gebiet**
to register *(luggage etc.)*
   einschreiben
registered *(letter)*
   eingeschrieben
registration number **das Kraftfahrzeugkennzeichen**
registration document *(car)*
   der Kraftfahrzeugbrief
relation **der/die Verwandte**
relatively **einigermaßen**
religion **die Religion**
to remain **bleiben**
to remember **sich erinnern an +**
   acc. *(see grammar, p. 182)*
to remove **wegnehmen**
   (tooth) **herausnehmen**
rent **die Miete**
to rent **mieten**
to repair **reparieren**
to repeat **wiederholen**
reply **die Antwort**
to reply **antworten**
report **der Bericht**
to report **berichten**
to rescue **retten**
reservation *(hotel etc.)* **die Reservierung**
to reserve **buchen**
reserved **reserviert**
responsible **verantwortlich**
to rest **sich ausruhen**
restaurant **das Restaurant**
restaurant-car **der Speisewagen**
result **das Ergebnis**
retired **pensioniert**
return **die Rückkehr**
   (ticket) **hin und zurück**

to return **wiederkommen**
to reverse (*car*) **rückwärts fahren**
reverse-charge call **das Rückgespräch**
rheumatism **das Rheuma**
ribbon **das Band**
  (*typewriter*) **das Farbband**
rice **der Reis**
rich **reich**
to ride (*horse/bike*) **reiten, fahren**
right **rechts**
  (*correct*) **richtig**
  to be right **recht haben**
  you're right **Sie haben recht**
right-hand **die rechte Seite**
ring (*jewellery*) **der Ring**
ripe **reif**
river **der Fluß**
road **die Straße**
  (*main*) **die Hauptstraße**
roadworks **die Straßenbauarbeiten**
roast **der Braten**
to rob **berauben**
robbery **der Raub**
roof **das Dach**
roll (*bread*) **das Brötchen, die Semmel** (*Austria*)
roller (*hair*) **der Lockenwickler**
room **das Zimmer**
  (*space*) **der Raum**
rope **das Seil**
rose **die Rose**
rosé **der Rosé**
rotten **faul**
rough (*surface*) **rauh**
  (*sea*) **stürmisch**
round **rund**
roundabout **der Kreisverkehr**

row (*theatre etc.*) **die Reihe**
to row **rudern**
  rowing boat **das Ruderboot**
royal **königlich**
rubber **der Gummi**
rubbish **der Abfall**
rucksack **der Rucksack**
rude **unhöflich**
ruins **die Ruinen**
ruler (*for measuring*) **das Lineal**
rum **der Rum**
to run **rennen**
rush hour **die Stoßzeit**
rusty **rostig**

S

sad **traurig**
safe (*strongbox*) **der Safe**
safe **sicher**
safety pin **die Sicherheitsnadel**
sail **das Segel**
to sail **segeln**
sailboard **das Surfbrett**
sailing **das Segeln**
sailing boat **das Segelboot**
sailor **der Matrose**
saint **der/die Heilige**
salad **der Salat**
sale (*bargains*) **der Ausverkauf**
sales representative **der Verkaufsvertreter/die Verkaufsvertreterin**
salmon **der Lachs**
salt **das Salz**
salty **salzig**
same **der-/die-/dasselbe**
sample **das Muster**
sand **der Sand**
sandals **die Sandalen**

sandwich **das Sandwich**
  open sandwich **das belegte Brot**
sandy **sandig**
sanitary towel **die Damenbinde**
sauce **die Soße**
saucepan **der Kochtopf**
saucer **die Untertasse**
sauna **die Sauna**
sausage **die Wurst**
to save (*money*) **sparen**
to say **sagen**
  scald **verbrühen**
scales **die Waage**
scarf **das Halstuch**
  (*head*) **das Kopftuch**
scene **die Szene**
scenery **die Landschaft**
scent **der Duft**
school **die Schule**
science **die Wissenschaft**
scientist **der Wissenschaftler**
scissors **die Schere**
scooter **der Motorroller**
score: what's the score? **wie steht es?**
Scotland **Schottland (das)**
Scottish **schottisch**
scratch **der Kratzer**
to scratch **kratzen**
screen **der Bildschirm**
screw **die Schraube**
screwdriver **der Schraubenzieher**
sculpture **die Skulptur**
sea **das Meer, die See**
seafood **die Meeresfrüchte**
seasick **seekrank**
season **die Jahreszeit**
season ticket **die Zeitkarte**
seat **der Sitz**
seatbelt **der Sicherheitsgurt**

second **der/die/das zweite**
  (*adj.*) **zweite/r/s**
second (*time period*) **die Sekunde**
secret **das Geheimnis**
secretary **die Sekretärin**
section **der Teil**
sedative **das Beruhigungsmittel**
to see **sehen**
to seem **scheinen**
self-catering **für Selbstversorger**
self-service **die Selbstbedienung**
to sell **verkaufen**
to send **schicken, senden**
senior citizen **der Rentner/die Rentnerin**
sensible **vernünftig**
sentence **der Satz**
separate(d) **getrennt**
septic tank **die Sickergrube**
serious **ernst(haft)**
  (*grave*) **schlimm**
  (*important*) **wichtig**
to serve **bedienen**
service (*charge*) **die Bedienung**
  (*church*) **der Gottesdienst**
set (*collection*) **der Satz**
setting lotion **der Haarfestiger**
several **mehrere**
to sew **nähen**
sewing **das Nähen**
sex (*gender*) **das Geschlecht**
  (*intercourse*) **der Sex**
shade (*not sunny*), shadow **der Schatten**
shampoo **das Shampoo**
shampoo and set **das Waschen und Legen**
sharp **scharf**
shave **die Rasur**
to shave **rasieren**

273

shaving cream/foam **die Rasiercreme**
she **sie**
sheep **das Schaf**
sheet **das Bettuch**
shelf **das Regal**
shell (*egg, nut*) **die Schale**
shellfish **die Schaltiere**
shelter **der Schutz**
sherry **der Sherry**
shiny **glänzend**
ship **das Schiff**
shirt **das Hemd**
shock (*electrical*) **der Schlag**
(*emotional*) **der Schock**
shocked **geschockt**
shoe(s) **der Schuh. die Schuhe**
shoelace **der Schnursenkel**
shoe polish **die Schuhcreme**
shoe repairer's **der Schuster**
shoe shop **das Schuhgeschäft**
shop **der Laden, das Geschäft**
shop assistant **der Verkäufer/ die Verkäuferin**
shopping: to go shopping **einkaufen gehen**
shopping centre **das Einkaufszentrum**
short **kurz**
shorts **die Shorts**
shout **der Ruf**
show **die Aufführung**
to show **zeigen**
shower **die Dusche**
to shrink **einlaufen**
shrunk **eingelaufen**
shut **geschlossen**
shutter **der Fensterladen**
sick **krank**
to be sick **sich übergeben**
to feel sick **sich schlecht fühlen**

sick bag **die Spucktüte**
side **die Seite**
sieve **das Sieb**
sight (*vision*) **das Sehvermögen**
(*tourist*) **die Sehenswürdigkeit**
sightseeing **die Besichtigungen**
sign **das Schild**
to sign **unterschreiben**
signal **das Zeichen**
signature **die Unterschrift**
silent **still**
silk **die Seide**
silver **das Silber**
similar **ähnlich**
simple **einfach**
since **seit + dat.** (*see grammar, p. 182*)
to sing **singen**
single (*room, ticket*) **Einzel-** (*unmarried*) **ledig**
sink **das Spülbecken**
sir **mein Herr**
sister **die Schwester**
sister-in-law **die Schwägerin**
to sit (*down*) **sich hinsetzen**
size (*clothes, shoes*) **die Größe**
skates (*ice*) **die Schlittschuhe** (*roller*) **die Rollschuhe**
to skate **Schlittschuh laufen**
ski **der Ski**
to ski **Ski laufen**
ski boots **die Skistiefel, die Skischuhe**
skiing **das Skilaufen**
downhill skiing **der Abfahrtslauf**
cross-country skiing **der Langlauf**
ski-lift **der Skilift**
skimmed milk **die Magermilch**
skin **die Haut**

skindiving **das Tauchen**	social worker
ski pole **der Skistock**	**der Sozialarbeiter/die**
skirt **der Rock**	**Sozialarbeiterin**
ski-run/slope **die Piste**	sociology **die Soziologie**
sky **der Himmel**	sock **die Socke**
to sleep **schlafen**	socket **die Steckdose**
sleeper/sleeping-car **der**	soda (*water*) **das Soda**
Schlafwagen	soft **weich**
sleeping bag **der Schlafsack**	soft drink **das alkoholfreie**
sleeve **der Ärmel**	**Getränk**
slice **die Scheibe**	sold out **ausverkauft**
sliced **geschnitten**	soldier **der Soldat**
slide film **der Diafilm**	solicitor **der Rechtsanwalt/die**
slim **schlank**	**Rechtsanwältin**
slip (*petticoat*) **der Unterrock**	solid **fest**
slippery **rutschig**	some **einige**
slow(ly) **langsam**	somehow **irgendwie**
small **klein**	someone **jemand**
smell **der Geruch**	something **etwas**
to smell **riechen**	sometimes **manchmal**
(*of . . .*) **nach + dat.** (*see*	somewhere **irgendwo**
grammar, p. 182)	son **der Sohn**
(*bad/good*) **schlecht/gut**	song **das Lied**
smile **das Lächeln**	son-in-law **der**
to smile **lächeln**	**Schwiegersohn**
smoke **der Rauch**	soon **bald**
to smoke **rauchen**	as soon as possible **so bald**
smooth **glatt**	**wie möglich**
to sneeze **niesen**	sore (*inc. throat*) **weh**
snorkel **der Schnorchel**	sorry: I'm sorry **es tut mir leid**
snow **der Schnee**	sort **die Sorte**
snow chains **die Schneeketten**	sound **der Ton**
to snow **schneien**	soup **die Suppe**
it's snowing **es schneit**	sour **sauer**
so **so**	south **der Süden**
(*therefore*) **also**	souvenir **das Souvenir**
so much **so viel**	space **der Raum**
soap **die Seife**	spade **der Spaten**
sober **nüchtern**	spanner **der**
socialism **der Sozialismus**	**Schraubenschlüssel**
socialist **sozialistisch**	spare **übrig**

spare time **die Freizeit**

spare tyre **der Ersatzreifen**

sparkling wine **der Schaumwein**

to speak **sprechen**

special **besondere**

special offer **das Sonderangebot**

specialist **der Spezialist/die Spezialistin**

speciality **die Spezialität**

spectacles **die Brille**

speed **die Geschwindigkeit**

speed limit **die Geschwindigkeitsbegrenzung**

to spend (money) **ausgeben** (time) **verbringen**

spice **das Gewürz**

spicy **würzig**

spinach **der Spinat**

spirits **die Spirituosen**

splinter **der Splitter**

to spoil **verderben**

sponge (bath) **der Schwamm**

spoon **der Löffel**

sport **der Sport**

spot **der Punkt** (place) **die Stelle**

to sprain **verstauchen**

sprained **verstaucht**

spray **der Spray**

spring (season) **der Frühling**

square **der Platz** (shape) **das Quadrat**

stadium **das Stadion**

stain **der Fleck**

stainless steel **der rostfreie Edelstahl**

stairs **die Treppe**

stalls (theatre) **das Parkett**

stamp (postage) **die Briefmarke**

stand (stadium) **die Tribüne**

to stand **stehen**

to stand up **aufstehen**

stapler **die Heftmaschine**

star **der Stern**

start **der Beginn**

to start **anfangen**

starter (food) **die Vorspeise**

state **der Staat**

station **der Bahnhof**

station master **der Bahnhofsvorsteher**

stationer's **die Schreibwarenhandlung**

statue **die Statue**

to stay (live) **wohnen** (remain) **bleiben**

steak **das Steak**

to steal **stehlen**

steam **der Dampf**

steamer **der Dampfer**

steel **der Stahl**

steep **steil**

step (footstep) **der Schritt**

step-brother **der Stiefbruder**

step-children **die Stiefkinder**

step-father **der Stiefvater**

step-mother **die Stiefmutter**

step-sister **die Stiefschwester**

stereo **das Stereo**

sterling: pound sterling **das Pfund Sterling**

steward (air) **der Steward**

stewardess (air) **die Stewardeß**

stick **der Stock**

sticking plaster **das Heftpflaster**

sticky **klebrig**

sticky tape **das Klebeband**

stiff **steif**

still (yet) **noch**

still (*non-fizzy*) **ohne Kohlensäure**
sting **der Stich**
to sting **stechen**
stock cube **der Suppenwürfel**
stock exchange **die Börse**
stockings **die Strümpfe**
stolen **gestohlen**
stomach **der Magen**
stomach ache **die Magenschmerzen**
stomach upset **der verdorbene Magen**
stone **der Stein**
stop (*bus*) **die Haltestelle**
to stop **halten**
stop! **halt!**
stopcock **der Abstellhahn**
story **die Geschichte**
stove **der Herd**
straight **gerade**
straight on **immer geradeaus**
strange **seltsam**
stranger **der/die Fremde**
strap **der Riemen**
straw (*drinking*) **der Strohhalm**
strawberries **die Erdbeeren**
stream **der Fluß**
street **die Straße**
streetlight **die Straßenlampe**
stretcher **die Bahre**
strike **der Streik**
string **die Schnur**
stripe **der Streifen**
striped **gestreift**
strong **stark**
to stick: it's stuck **es klemmt**
student **der Student/die Studentin**
studio (*radio/TV*) **das Studio**
to study **studieren**

stupid **dumm**
style **der Stil**
styling mousse **der Schaumfestiger**
subtitles **die Untertitel**
suburb **der Vorort**
to succeed **Erfolg haben**
success **der Erfolg**
such **solche/r/s**
suddenly **plötzlich**
sugar **der Zucker**
sugar lump **der Zuckerwürfel**
suit (*man's*) **der Anzug** (*woman's*) **das Kostüm**
suitcase **der Koffer**
summer **der Sommer**
sun **die Sonne**
to sunbathe **sonnenbaden**
sunburn **der Sonnenbrand**
sunglasses **die Sonnenbrille**
sunny **sonnig**
sunshade **der Sonnenschirm**
sunstroke **der Sonnenstich**
suntan cream **die Sonnencreme**
suntan oil **das Sonnenöl**
supermarket **der Supermarkt**
supper **das Abendbrot**
supplement **der Zuschlag**
suppose: I suppose so **ich nehme es wohl an**
suppository **das Zäpfchen**
sure **sicher**
surface **die Oberfläche**
surname **der Nachname**
surprise **die Überraschung**
surprised **überrascht**
surrounded by **umgeben von + dat.** (*see grammar, p. 182*)
to sweat **schwitzen**
sweater **der Pullover**
sweatshirt **das Sweatshirt**

to sweep **fegen**
sweet **süß**
sweetener **der Süßstoff**
sweets **die Süßigkeiten**
swelling **die Schwellung**
to swim **schwimmen**
swimming **das Schwimmen**
swimming pool **das Schwimmbad**
swimming trunks **die Badehose**
swimsuit **der Badeanzug**
switch **der Schalter**
to switch off **ausschalten**
to switch on **einschalten**
swollen **geschwollen**
symptom **das Symptom**
synagogue **die Synagoge**
synthetic **synthetisch**
system **das System**

T

table **der Tisch**
tablet **die Tablette**
table tennis **der Tischtennis**
tailor **der Schneider**
to take **nehmen**
  (*photo, exam*) **machen**
  (*time*) **dauern**
taken (*seat*) **besetzt**
to take off (*clothes*) **sich ausziehen**
  (*plane*) **abfliegen**
talcum powder **der Körperpuder**
to talk **sprechen**
tall **groß**
tampons **die Tampons**
tap **der Hahn**
tape (*adhesive*) **das Klebeband**
  (*cassette*) **die Kassette**

tape measure **das Bandmaß**
tape recorder **das Tonbandgerät**
taste **der Geschmack**
to taste **schmecken**
  it tastes good **es schmeckt gut**
tax **die Steuer**
taxi **das Taxi**
taxi rank **der Taxistand**
tea **der Tee**
teabag **der Teebeutel**
to teach **unterrichten**
teacher **der Lehrer/die Lehrerin**
team **das Team**
teapot **die Teekanne**
tear (*rip*) **der Riß**
teaspoon **der Teelöffel**
teat (*for baby's bottle*) **der Sauger**
tea-towel **das Geschirrtuch**
technical **technisch**
technology **die Technologie**
teenager **der Teenager**
telegram **das Telegramm**
telephone **das Telefon**
telephone card **die Telefonkarte**
telephone directory **das Telefonbuch**
telephone kiosk **die Telefonzelle**
to telephone **anrufen**
television **das Fernsehen**
telex **das Telex**
to tell **erzählen**
temperature **die Temperatur**
  to have a temperature **Fieber haben**
temporary **provisorisch**
tender **zart**
tennis **das Tennis**
tennis court **der Tennisplatz**
tennis shoes/trainers **die Turnschuhe**
tent **das Zelt**
tent peg **der Hering**

tent pole **die Zeltstange**
terminal (*airport*) **der Terminal**
terminus **die Endstation**
terrace **die Terrasse**
terrible **schrecklich**
terrorist **der Terrorist/die Terroristin**
thank you **danke**
  thank you very much **vielen Dank**
that (one) **das (da)**
the **der, die, das**
theatre **das Theater**
their **ihr**
theirs **ihre/r/s**
them **sie**
  (to) them **ihnen**
then **dann**
there **dort, da**
  there is/are **es gibt**
therefore **deshalb**
thermometer **das Thermometer**
these **diese**
they **sie**
thick **dick**
thief **der Dieb**
thin **dünn**
thing **die Sache, das Ding**
to think **denken**
  (*believe*) **glauben**
  I (don't) think so **ich glaube (nicht)**
third **dritte/r/s**
thirsty **durstig**
this (one) **das (hier)**
those **jene**
thread **der Faden**
throat lozenges/pastilles **die Halspastillen**
through **durch + acc.** (*see grammar, p. 182*)
to throw **werfen**

to throw away **wegwerfen**
thumb **der Daumen**
thunder **der Donner**
ticket (*travel*) **die Fahrkarte**
  (*theatre etc.*) **die Eintrittskarte**
ticket office **der Fahrkartenschalter**
tide (*high/low*) **das Hochwasser/ das Niedrigwasser**
tidy **ordentlich**
tie **der Schlips**
to tie **befestigen**
tight (*clothes*) **eng**
tights **die Strumpfhose**
till (*until*) **bis**
time **die Zeit**
  (*once etc.*) **das Mal**
  (*on clock, see p. 193*) **die Uhr**
timetable (*trains*) **der Fahrplan**
tin **die Dose**
tin foil **die Alufolie**
tinned **Dosen-**
  tinned milk **die Dosenmilch**
tin opener **der Dosenöffner**
tip (*in restaurant etc.*) **das Trinkgeld**
tired **müde**
tissues **die Papiertaschentücher**
to **zu + dat.** (*see grammar, p. 182*)
  (*with named places*) **nach + dat.** (*see grammar, p. 182*)
toast **der Toast**
tobacco **der Tabak**
tobacconist's **der Tabakladen**
toboggan **der Schlitten**
today **heute**
toiletries **die Toilettenartikel**
toilets **die Toiletten**
toilet paper **das Toilettenpapier**
toilet water **das Eau de Toilette**
toll **die Maut**

tomato die Tomate
tomorrow morgen
tongue die Zunge
tonic water das Tonic
tonight heute abend
too zu
  (as well) auch
tool das Werkzeug
tooth der Zahn
toothache die Zahnschmerzen
toothbrush die Zahnbürste
toothpaste die Zahnpasta
toothpick der Zahnstocher
top (mountain) der Gipfel
  on top of oben auf + acc.
  or dat. (see grammar, p. 182)
torch die Taschenlampe
torn zerrissen
total die Endsumme
totally total
to touch berühren
tough (meat) zäh
tour die Fahrt
to tour eine Reise machen
tourism der Tourismus
tourist der Tourist
tourist office das
  Fremdenverkehrsbüro
to tow abschleppen
towards nach + dat. (see
  grammar, p. 182)
towel das Handtuch
tower der Turm
town die Stadt
  town centre das
    Stadtzentrum
  town hall das Rathaus
  town plan der Stadtplan
tow rope das Abschleppseil
toy das Spielzeug
track die Bahn

tracksuit der Trainingsanzug
trade union die Gewerkschaft
traditional traditionell
traffic der Verkehr
traffic jam der Verkehrsstau
traffic lights die Verkehrsampel
trailer der Anhänger
train der Zug
  by train mit dem Zug
training shoes (trainers) die
  Trainingschuhe
tram die Straßenbahn
tranquilliser das
  Beruhigungsmittel
to translate übersetzen
translation die Übersetzung
to travel reisen
travel agency das Reisebüro
traveller's cheques die
  Reiseschecks
travel sickness reisekrank
tray die Tablett
treatment die Behandlung
tree der Baum
trip der Ausflug
trousers die Hose
trout die Forelle
true wahr
  that's true das stimmt/das
    ist wahr
to try (attempt) versuchen
to try on anprobieren
T-shirt das T-Shirt
tube (pipe) das Rohr
  (underground) die U-Bahn
tuna der Thunfisch
tunnel der Tunnel
turn: it's my turn ich bin daran
to turn drehen
to turn off abbiegen
turning (side road) die Abfahrt

twice **zweimal**
twin beds **zwei Einzelbetten**
twins **die Zwillinge**
twisted (*ankle*) **verrenkt**
type (*sort*) **der Typ**
to type **tippen**
typewriter **die Schreibmaschine**
typical **typisch**

U

ugly **häßlich**
ulcer **das Geschwür**
umbrella **der Regenschirm**
uncle **der Onkel**
uncomfortable **unbequem**
under **unter + acc. or dat.** (*see grammar, p. 182*)
underground (*tube*) **die U-Bahn**
underpants **die Unterhose**
underpass **die Unterführung**
to understand **verstehen**
underwater **Unterwasser-**
underwear **die Unterwäsche**
to undress **sich ausziehen**
unemployed **arbeitslos**
unfortunately **leider**
unhappy **unglücklich**
uniform **die Uniform**
university **die Universität**
unleaded petrol **das bleifreie Benzin**
unless **es sei denn**
    unless they arrive **es sei denn, sie kommen an**
unpack **auspacken**
unpleasant **unangenehm**
to unscrew **aufschrauben**
until **bis**
unusual **ungewöhnlich**

unwell **unwohl**
up **auf**
    up the hill **bergauf**
    up the road **die Straße hoch**
upper **obere/r/s**
upstairs **oben**
urgent **dringend**
urine **der Urin**
us **uns**
to use **benutzen**
useful **nützlich**
useless **nutzlos**
usually **gewöhnlich**

V

vacant **frei**
vacuum cleaner **der Staubsauger**
vacuum flask **die Thermosflasche**
valid **gültig**
valley **das Tal**
valuable **wertvoll**
valuables **die Wertsachen**
van **der Lieferwagen**
vanilla **die Vanille**
vase **die Vase**
VAT **die Mehrwertsteuer**
veal **das Kalbfleisch**
vegan **der Vegetarier/die Vegetarierin**
vegetables **das Gemüse**
vegetarian **der Vegetarier/die Vegetarierin**
    (*adj.*) **vegetarisch**
vehicle **das Fahrzeug**
vermouth **der Wermut**
very **sehr**
vest **das Unterhemd**
vet **der Tierarzt/die Tierärztin**

via über
video das Video
view die Aussicht
villa die Villa
village das Dorf
vinegar der Essig
vineyard der Weinberg
virgin die Jungfrau
  Virgin Mary die Jungfrau
  Maria
visa das Visum
visit der Besuch
to visit besuchen
  (*tourist sites*) besichtigen
visitor der Besucher/die
  Besucherin
vitamin das Vitamin
vodka der Wodka
voice die Stimme
volleyball der Volleyball
voltage das Volt

to vote wählen

W

wage der Lohn
waist die Taille
waistcoat die Weste
to wait (*for*) warten (auf) + acc.
waiter der Ober
waiting room der Warteraum
waitress die Kellnerin
Wales Wales
walk der Spaziergang
to walk, go for a walk einen
  Spaziergang machen
walking stick der
  Spazierstock
wall (*inside*) die Wand
  (*outside*) die Mauer
wallet die Brieftasche

walnut die Walnuß
to want wollen
  would like möchte
war der Krieg
warm warm
to wash waschen
washable waschbar
wash-basin das
  Waschbecken
washing die Wäsche
washing machine die
  Waschmaschine
washing powder das
  Waschpulver
washing-up der Abwasch
washing-up liquid das
  Spülmittel
wastepaper basket der
  Papierkorb
watch (*clock*) die
  Armbanduhr
to watch zuschauen
  to watch TV fernsehen
watchstrap das Uhrarmband
water das Wasser
water heater der
  Warmwasserbereiter
water melon die
  Wassermelone
waterfall der Wasserfall
waterproof wasserdicht
water-skiing das
  Wasserskilaufen
water-skis die Wasserskis
wave die Welle
way (*path*) der Weg
  that way in der Richtung
  this way in dieser
    Richtung
way in der Eingang
way out der Ausgang

wax das Wachs
we wir
weather das Wetter
  what's the weather like? wie ist das Wetter?
weather forecast die Wettervorhersage
wedding die Hochzeit
week die Woche
weekday der Werktag
weekend das Wochenende
weekly wöchentlich
to weigh wiegen
weight das Gewicht
well gut
  as well auch
well done (steak) durch
Welsh walisisch
west der Westen
western westlich
  (film) der Western
wet naß
wetsuit der Taucheranzug
what was, das
  what? was?
  what is . . . ? was ist . . . ?
wheel das Rad
wheelchair der Rollstuhl
when (whenever) wenn
  (with past tense) als
  when? wann?
where wo
  where? wo?
  where is/are . . . ?
  wo ist . . . ?/wo sind . . . ?
which welche/r/s
  which? welche?
while während + gen.
whisky der Whisky
  on the rocks mit Eis
  neat pur

white weiß
  (with milk) mit Milch
who (relative) der, die, das
  who? wer?
  who is it? wer ist das?
whole vollständig
wholemeal bread das Vollkornbrot
why warum, weshalb
  why? warum?
  why not? warum nicht?
wide breit
widow die Witwe
widower der Witwer
wife die Frau
wild wild
to win gewinnen
  who won? wer hat gewonnen?
wind der Wind
windmill die Windmühle
window das Fenster
  (shop) das Schaufenster
to windsurf windsurfen
windy: it's windy es ist windig
wine der Wein
wine merchant/shop die Weinhandlung
wing der Flügel
winter der Winter
with mit + dat. (see grammar, p. 182)
without ohne + acc. (see grammar, p. 182)
woman die Frau
wonderful wunderbar
wood das Holz
wool die Wolle
word das Wort
work die Arbeit
to work (job) arbeiten
  (function) funktionieren

world (*noun*) **die Welt**
  (*adj.*) **Welt-**
    World War One **der erste**
    Weltkrieg
    World War Two **der zweite**
    Weltkrieg
worried **besorgt**
worse **schlimmer**
worth: it's worth . . . **es ist . . .**
  wert
  it's not worth it **es lohnt sich**
  nicht
would like (*see 'to want'*)
  möchte
wound **die Wunde**
to wrap (*up*) **verpacken**
wrong (*incorrect*) **falsch**
to write **schreiben**
  writer **der Schriftsteller/die**
  Schriftstellerin
writing pad **der Notizblock**
writing paper **das Briefpapier**

284

X

X-ray **die Röntgenaufnahme**

Y

yacht **die Yacht**
to yawn **gähnen**
  year **das Jahr**
    leap year **das Schaltjahr**
  yellow **gelb**
  yes **ja**
  yesterday **gestern**
  yet **noch**
  yoghurt **der Joghurt**
  you **Sie** (*formal*)
    du (*informal singular*)
    ihr (*informal plural*)

young **jung**
your **Ihr, dein, euer** (*see grammar, p. 180*)
yours **Ihre/r/s, deine/r/s, eure/r/s**
youth **die Jugend**
youth hostel **die Jugendherberge**

Z

zip **der Reißverschluß**
zoo **der Zoo, der Tiergarten**
zoology **die Zoologie**

EMERGENCIES

You may want to say

See also Problems and complaints, *page 170*; Health, *page 158*)

Phoning the emergency services

(Emergency telephone numbers, *page 289*)

(I need) the police
(Ich brauche) die Polizei
*(ish brow*ke) die politsiy*

(I need) the fire brigade
(Ich brauche) die Feuerwehr
*(ish brow*ke) dee foyervayr*

(I need) an ambulance
(Ich brauche) eine Ambulanz
*(ish brow*ke) iyne amboolants*

I've been attacked (mugged)
Ich bin überfallen worden
ish bin ewberfallen vorden

I've been raped
Ich bin vergewaltigt worden
ish bin fergayvaltigt vorden

There's been an accident
Es ist ein Unfall passiert
es ist iyn oonfall passeert

There's a fire
Es brennt
es brennt

There's someone injured/ill
Jemand ist verletzt/krank
yaymant ist ferletst/krank

It's my husband/son/
boyfriend
**Es ist mein Mann/Sohn/
Freund**
es ist miyn mann/zohn/froynd

It's my wife/daughter/
girlfriend
**Es ist meine Frau/Tochter/
Freundin**
*es ist miyne frow/toshter/
froyndin*

Please come immediately
Kommen Sie sofort
kommen zee zohfort

Come to . . .
Kommen Sie zu . . .
kommen zee tsoo . . .

My name is . . .
Mein Name ist . . .
miyn naame ist . . .

The number of this
telephone is . . .
**Die Telefonnummer hier
ist . . .**
*dee telefohnnoommer heer
ist . . .*

Where is the police station?
Wo ist das Polizeiamt?
voh ist das politsiyamt

Where is the hospital?
Wo ist das Krankenhaus?
voh ist das krankenhows

Can anyone speak English?
**Kann jemand Englisch
sprechen?**
*kan yaymant english
shprecken*

Please call the British
Embassy
**Bitte rufen Sie die britische
Botschaft an**
*bitte roofen zee dee britishe
bohtshaaft an*

I want to see a lawyer
**Ich möchte einen Anwalt
sehen**
ish mershte iynen anvalt zayen

I want to speak to a woman
**Ich möchte eine Frau
sprechen**
ish mershte iyne frow shpreken

You may hear

When you phone the emergency services

Kann ich helfen?
kann ish helfen
Can I help?

Was ist passiert?
vas ist passeert
What's happened?

Wie heißen Sie?
vee hiyssen zee
What is your name?

Was ist Ihre Adresse?
vas ist eere adresse
What is your address?

Was ist passiert?
vas ist passeert
What happened?

Wo ist es passiert?
voh ist es passeert
Where did it happen?

Wann ist es passiert?
van ist es passeert
When did it happen?

Können Sie beschreiben . . . ?
kernnen zee beshriyben
Can you describe . . . ?

The police

Kommen Sie mit zur Polizei
kommen zee mit tsoor politsiy
Come with me/us to the
  police station

Sie sind verhaftet
zee zint ferhaftet
You are under arrest

The doctor

Sie müssen ins Krankenhaus
zee mewssen ins krankenhows
You have to go to hospital

Er/Sie muß ins Krankenhaus
er/zee moos ins krankenhows
He/She has to go to hospital

Wo tut es weh
voh toot es vay
Where does it hurt?

Tut das weh?
toot das vay
Does that hurt?

**Wie lange haben Sie das
  schon?**
vee lange haaben zee das shon
How long have you been
  like this?

**Wie lange hat er/sie das
  schon?**
vee lange hat er/zee das shon
How long has he/she been
  like this?

You may want to say

Quickly!	**Schnell!**
	schnell
Call the police	**Rufen Sie die Polizei**
	roofen zee dee politsiy
Call the fire brigade	**Rufen Sie die Feuerwehr**
	roofen zee dee foyervayr
Call an ambulance	**Rufen Sie eine Ambulanz**
	roofen zee iyne amboolants
Get a doctor	**Rufen Sie einen Arzt**
	roofen zee iynen artst
Help	**Hilfe!**
	hilfe
Police!	**Polizei!**
	politsiy
Stop!	**Halt!**
	halt
Stop thief!	**Haltet den Dieb!**
	haltet dayn deep
Fire!	**Feuer!**
	foyer
Look out!	**Paß auf!**
	pass owf
Be careful!	**Vorsicht!**
	forzisht
Danger! Gas!	**Gefahr! Gas!**
	gayfaar gas
Get help quickly	**Wir brauchen schnell Hilfe**
	veer browken shnell hilfe
It's very urgent	**Es ist sehr dringend**
	*es ist zayr **dringent***
It's an emergency	**Es ist ein Notfall**
	*es ist iyn **nohtfall***

POLICE	**110**
FIRE	**112**
AMBULANCE	**112**